Educational
Public
Relations

Educational
Public
Relations

Philip T. West

SAGE PUBLICATIONS Beverly Hills London New Delhi

L B2847
W47
1985

For information address:

SAGE Publications, Inc.
275 South Beverly Drive
Beverly Hills, California 90212

SAGE Publications India Pvt. Ltd.
M-32 Market
Greater Kailash I
New Delhi 110 048 India

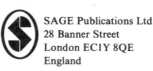

SAGE Publications Ltd
28 Banner Street
London EC1Y 8QE
England

Printed in the United States of America

Library of Congress Cataloging in Publication Data

West, Philip T.
    Educational public relations.

    1. Public relations--United States--Schools.
2. School management and organization--United States.
I. Title.
LB2847.W47   1985   371.2'07   84-24848
ISBN   0-8039-2038-5

FIRST PRINTING

Contents

Introduction

Educational public relations has an interesting past, a provocative present, and an awe-inspiring future. Its past sparks interest because over the years it has played a much larger role in public school support efforts than is often realized or for which it is credited. Throughout this century the value of educational public relations has been continuously rediscovered. History indicates that it was a product of the times. It came into being because it was needed. Public relations practices were accomplishing wonders in fields such as business, industry, and government, and was gradually becoming a discipline of study in its own right. Public relations was becoming increasingly synonymous with the public's right to know and be heard; and public schools, already belonging to the public, were to be the least exempt from carrying out this sacred trust. What is more, educators, recognizing what a concerted public relations effort could achieve for public schools, were virtually enticed aboard the public relations bandwagon. A public made knowledgeable about its schools was likely to support and become involved in them. Educational public relations has not always been in the limelight of public school priorities and educational administration preparatory programs, but neither has it stood in the shadows for very long, despite its frequent association with flimflam, ballyhoo, and the city slicker.

Today educational public relations has achieved both respectability and sophistication within the realm of education. Adeptness in public relations is now typically a skill sought by boards of education seeking new superintendents. Superintendents, in turn, seek in their principals a similar adeptness. Many of these same boards and superintendents employ educational public relations specialists. On the other hand, the public relations-oriented principal is inclined to make some provision for handling building-level public relations. School leaders, in increasing numbers, have come to realize that although public relations skills and programs do not solve all problems, they certainly mitigate them. Educational public relations is the great synergizer. If everyone treats everyone else the way he or she would like to be treated and exhibits trust and honesty in these relationships, common bonds are likely to be forged. Although the ideal way to achieve such a bond would be through one-on-one relationships, this ideal is difficult to attain in a society characterized by complexity, change, mobility, seclusion, and alienation. But it can be attempted within the context of an ongoing, outreaching educational public relations program that sets as its top priority the awareness and meeting of community needs. Thus, school leaders oblivious to the principles and practices of an effective public relations program are at a distinct disadvantage with their communities.

But if the past and present can open eyes to the need for educational public relations, it is the future that raises the eyebrows. The symbol of education in this society has always been the school facility, be it the little red schoolhouse or the ultramodern educational complex. For a time schools sprang up like mushrooms after a heavy rain. Usually the tiniest community could boast its own schoolhouse. Then reorganization and consolidation dissolved some of these treasured fiefdoms, and local control and school spirit took on new and expanded dimensions, much to the dismay of many community members. Presently public schools are bigger and better than ever before. They educate or reeducate practically everyone in society. Yet they still do this, for the most part, within the context of the traditional school setting. The classroom cubicle remains the home of the academic standard, and the teacher is the bearer of that standard. Except for the computer technology that some schools employ in delivering their curricula, public education has not changed much either, particularly in its repeated incursion into the alleged basics.

In the 21st century technology will dictate the shape and location of learning environments, with the home playing an important role in the delivery of instruction. The public school will undergo dramatic change, and so will the nature and form of its public relations efforts. This means that no matter how conscious today's school leaders are of the importance of educational public relations, this awareness will be short-lived if ample provisions are not made at the same time for the communication revolution of the future. Indeed, many would claim that this revolution is already here.

   This text does not pretend to give all the answers for the many public relations problems that may be expected to confront school leaders of today and tomorrow. Neither does it encompass all the opportunities that may be within their grasp. However, it is designed to address both in considerable degree. This text views educational public relations as an integral part of the preparation of school leaders. It also views an educational public relations program as a critical component of any school system. No school that professes an interest in its community can afford to be without one. Nor can even the smallest school system be devoid of someone who is ready and willing to provide public relations leadership. True, not every school system is financially capable of employing a full- or part-time public relations director, but most can free someone of other duties to the extent that basic public relations tasks are handled with relative ease.

   For schools with or without public relations directors, this text offers an array of strategies that should facilitate program initiation, implementation, and evaluation. Within the text principles and practices are interrelated, and case studies and vignettes are used to explore both. While the text examines past, present, and future dimensions of educational public relations, its focus is overwhelmingly on the present. The contention of the text is that schools that successfully synergize their programmatic efforts in public relations will earn and retain the trust, support, and confidence of their communities.

• 1 •

The Historical Setting

PUBLIC RELATIONS

Although the focus of this text is educational public relations, it would seem inappropriate not to say a few words about the broader field of public relations. After all, educational public relations did not spring into existence of its own accord. Rather, it was merely a by-product of the evolving history of public relations, which may well have begun when people first came together to share common interests and progressed with their attempts to influence one another (Steinberg, 1958). Yet if it is true that complexity of human relationships gave rise to public relations (Harlow & Black, 1952), perhaps it is more fitting to assume that public relations really began in the marketplace, where people came not only to barter or buy with the coin of the realm even the simplest of goods and services, but to sell what wares they had and where repeated transactions with the same people signaled the dawning of trade and customer relations.

But public relations had its roots in public opinion; and public opinion, although evident in varying degrees in earlier cultures, did not take on any great importance until the Hellenic and Romanic civilizations. Public opinion was an integral part of the Grecian and Roman way of life. The Greeks cherished democracy, and the Romans had a term, "vox populi," which, when translated, meant "voice of the people." Moreover, during the time of Julius Caesar and right up to the 4th century A.D., Rome even had a daily newspaper, the *Acta Diurna*. After the fall of Rome and throughout the Middle Ages, public opinion was of dwarfed significance, while the Renaissance that followed, along with the Age of Enlightenment, once again saw its rise in importance. In the American colonies public opinion was notably at work in staging the Revolutionary War, with the Constitution and Bill of Rights that ensued guaranteeing democratic freedoms that encouraged individual expression (Bernays, 1952).

Although the first organized public relations activity may well have begun with the efforts of the ancient guilds of medieval Europe to make lawful business privileges that eventually became abuses (Griswold & Griswold, 1948), it took the "public be damned" attitude of business in the late 19th and early 20th centuries, the exposes of the muckrakers, mass media development, and the opinion-molding machinery of World War I to make it a budding profession (Steinberg, 1958).

Although Ivy Lee has been characterized as the earliest genuine public relations counsel (Griswold & Griswold, 1948), as well as the father of "modern public relations," it was not until the middle of the 1920s that he chose to identify himself as a public relations adviser (Hiebert, 1966). By that time Bernays and Fleischman had gone from "publicity direction" (1919) to "public relations counsel" (1922) (Bernays, 1952).

An exjournalist turned publicity person, Lee saw his work as consisting of the adjustment of relationships between clients and public through extensive communication (Hiebert, 1966). Bernays, too, sought harmony between client and public, declaring that the public relations counsel's job was essentially to define, adjust, and interpret, or even discard, goals and policies to gain public understanding and acceptance. The key was to ferret out maladjustments and adjust them, and the role was that of statesman (Bernays, 1952).

One of Ivy Lee's most significant and lasting contributions to the emergent public relations field was an inherent outgrowth of his position that the public be kept informed, expressed in a statement issued to city editors that was contrary to the practices of business of the times and press agentry (Cutlip & Center, 1971). From Lee business learned the merit of keeping the public factually informed (Steinberg, 1958).

Bernays, on the other hand, was not only a leader in laying the cornerstone of public relations and in its subsequent development, but also the scholar whose extensive and penetrating writings aided in acknowledging public relations as a legitimate field of endeavor (Griswold & Griswold, 1948). For example, he was the first to write a book on public relations, *Crystallizing Public Opinion,* 1923 (Cutlip & Center, 1971). The contributions of Bernays (now in his early 90s) as pioneer, practitioner, and scholar today permeate the broad field of public relations, notwithstanding its educational scion.

But both men brought public relations to the policy-making level of business, as did George Creel to government during World War I (Griswold & Griswold, 1948). Creel chaired the Committee on Public Information, which, through a massive information program, sold the aims of a wartime government to the public (Cutlip & Center, 1971).

The development of public relations during the first half of the 20th century was divided into four phases by Bernays, according to Harlow and Black (1952). The first period, pitting the muckrakers against business and involving much business publicity to gloss over its abuses, extended from 1900 to 1914. The second, hinged on governmental efforts during World War I to achieve the public's moral and financial support, was dated 1914-1918. The third, during the years 1919-1929, had business turn to public relations to attract the public and build good will. And the last, 1929 to the beginning of the 1950s, revolved around public relations activities that imparted to business a public responsibility. Cutlip and Center (1971), whose dates and explanations differ only slightly from Bernays' four phases, offer a fifth, dating from 1945 to the present, which is essentially public relations coming of age as a profession.

Given the rapid rise of information systems and widespread economically produced and purchased technology (fixed and portable) to which public relations specialists now have easy access, it might be appropriate to designate still another phase, say from about 1975 to the present, called the electronic phase of public relations. Indeed, with information dissemination and retrieval being the mainstay of their profession, it would be difficult for public relations specialists to avoid using the tools of instant communication on a grandiose scale. Furthermore, the dangers fraught from an overloaded information society represent an ethical challenge to public relations specialists intent on keeping the public informed and client and public together.

Today the public relations function permeates society. There is an array of different kinds of "relations" that owe their existence to what is more definitely described as public relations, among them stockholder relations, customer relations, hotel relations, employee relations, labor relations, governmental relations, and educational public relations. Despite this ambiguity there can be little doubt as to the purpose of the role. And, as will be seen later, this ambiguity carries over into the field of educational public relations when schools attempt to incorporate this role into their organizational structure.

In conclusion, there were many people, practices, and events that contributed to the formation and growth of the public relations profession. The fact that only a selected number were considered here to tell the "public relations story" may be attributed to the constraints of space, rather than to any lack of appreciation on the part of the author.

EDUCATIONAL PUBLIC RELATIONS

To paraphrase a quote from a 1950 American Association of School Administrators (AASA) yearbook, educational public relations is as old and as basic as the first classroom meeting of teacher and student. But, of course, educational public relations is much more complex than that, as its history will show. In the early days of educational public relations (about 1915) periodic publicity and campaigns, much like the promotional efforts that appeared during World War I, were in vogue, with programmatic continuity becoming increasingly evident in the ensuing decade (Moehlman, 1927).

Indeed, prior to 1918 educational public relations efforts were not only sporadic, but were more often associated with individuals than with groups. One such individual was William McAndrew, whose public relations efforts were aimed at linking school with community in the determination of mutual needs. In 1917 McAndrew, having achieved community acceptance and support of the Washington Irving High School program in New York City, published his success in a monograph called *The Public and Its Schools,* which stressed in a subtitle how the school could learn and give the public what it wanted. Immediately after World War I organized educational public relations efforts did surface, but they were mainly pressurized propaganda-laden attempts to fill war-created teacher shortages, to obtain teacher salary increases, and to acquire new school buildings (Moehlman, 1938a).

The intensity and sophistication of educational public relations efforts during this postwar era may be glimpsed in a monograph published by Alexander and Theisen in 1921. The authors, having studied some 70 successful school campaigns in various sized cities across the country, compiled a series of campaign strategies that school leaders could use to obtain support for their schools.

These initial efforts represented phase one in educational public relations; by 1923, the second phase saw the rise and continuity of publicity programs in the public schools; and the third (1919-1925) was embedded in an effort to separate the Detroit public schools from local politics through the formation and use of an adult education program that would keep the public informed. The result was the first unified interpretative concept of educational public relations (Moehlman, 1938a).

During the academic year 1925-1926, the University of Michigan introduced a course called "Public School Relations," in contradistinction to courses conducted at other institutions labeled "Public School Publicity" (Moehlman, 1938a). Today university courses emphasizing educational public relations have become commonplace.

In 1927 Moehlman, indisputably the father of contemporary educational public relations, published his now classic text, *Public School Relations*. In it he drew a careful distinction between information service and publicity, equating the latter with press agentry and propaganda rather than with public relations. To him, public school relations was an information service based on organized facts and provided by school officials to keep the public informed about the school's educational programs. Unlike publicity, the intent of which was said to glorify, the purpose of this service was to inform.

In a 1924 monograph entitled *Publicity and the Public School* (Miller & Charles), however, publicity, for want of a better word, was chosen to describe a school information service aimed at improving the public's understanding of its schools and at improving education in general. Too, in the monograph publicity campaigns were considered tantamount to propaganda and personal aggrandizement was shunned. Nonetheless, the primary thrust of the monograph, unlike the book Moehlman would shortly write, was school-press relations, with interpretation directed at both newspaper reporters and educators to facilitate understanding between the two.

By 1927 23 states had enacted legislation requiring boards of education to report at regular intervals to the public about the conditions and needs of their schools (Moehlman, 1927). Surely this served as an impetus for the need and rise of information programs.

It is interesting to note that, however opposed he was to propaganda, publicity, and press agentry, Moehlman seems to have let the nomenclature of the times slip into his work on at least one occasion. For example, potential educational public relations participants were viewed as "agents" rather than as publics. Divided into three groups, these agents included, in the first, a wide range of school employees; in the second, parents, children, parent-teacher associations, and a variety of clubs; and in the third, those generally excluded in the first two groups: the press, business, public servants, and leading citizens (Moehlman, 1927).

Moehlman (1927) recommended that a full-time public relations specialist be employed in cities with populations of more than 50,000, with a one-half- to three-quarters-time specialist employed in cities of 20,000 to 50,000. Typically, the public relations specialist was to be housed in the child accounting department. But in large school systems there was to be a special division for public relations.

In 1935 the association that would eventually become the National School Public Relations Association (NSPRA) was born in Denver, Colorado at the annual convention of the National Education Association. Then called the National Association for Educational Publicity, the association would, in 1936, be identified as the School Public Relations Association (Wherry, 1982).

In 1938 the concept of social interpretation was described by Moehlman (1938b), in a text bearing the same title as the concept, as embracing both public relations and publicity. Coined by Moehlman in 1936 in the January edition of *Nation's Schools,* social interpretation went beyond educational interpretation. The latter, spawned by the Great Depression and publicized in a 1937 superintendency yearbook, was construed by Moehlman as essentially a one-way communication process (Moehlman, 1938a). Grounded in ethics and shunning propaganda, social interpretation would keep the people in touch with the schools and the schools in touch with the people. Through an adult education program whose aim was an informed public opinion, social interpretation would engender a school-community partnership (Moehlman, 1938b). The attainment of public confidence and support, much as it is today, appeared to be the ultimate goal.

In 1950 problems similar to those that had beset the period immediately following World War I loomed largely again. A shortage of teachers and a lack of school buildings were created by rising school enrollments. A result was an American Association of School Administrators' yearbook devoted to the theme of school public relations. With an accent on two-way communication, the book stressed school-community cooperation and downplayed publicity and interpretation.

In the forefront was the welfare of the child, the meeting of whose needs would be facilitated by a parent-teacher partnership. The key to support was public confidence. The need for a director of public relations in large cities was also addressed in the yearbook. This person would typically be a professional educator and rarely a publicist. "Selling" was not perceived as a virtue in the yearbook; the good school would speak for itself (AASA, 1950). The same year that the yearbook was published the School Public Relations Association changed its name to the National School Public Relations Association, by which it is known today (Wherry, 1982).

In 1952 Harral, too, claimed that school public relations could not be sustained by publicity alone. Emphasizing a community school perspective, he called for a program that was based on an informed public opinion and on strategies that would produce active school support.

In 1955 Stearns wrote that the public acceptance that schools had enjoyed prior to World War II had vanished and that administrators must give heed to community relations to regain this support. Unlike those previously discussed, Stearns's kind of community relations program had a place for showmanship and advertising, provided facts were not distorted. As an example of such showmanship, Stearns called to mind an American Association of School Administrators' pageant that depicted school goals and values for the public.

However low key, the tune of selling played in another text of that year. In it publicity, along with selling, were distinguished from press agentry and propaganda, both taboo, and claimed to be not only respectable for an educational public relations program, but in keeping with the times. In effect, publicity of a continuous nature was the mainstay of a public relations program. Publicity brought good will, understanding, and support (Brownell, Gans, & Maroon, 1955).

Strands of a different kind were also apparent that year. Viewed as an easement to an improved understanding and support of the schools was a proper amount of public participation. Through participation the public also had an opportunity to be involved in educational determination and assessment. This right to participate in public ownership of the schools was evidently basic to sound school-community relationships (Campbell & Ramseyer, 1955).

Two years later, in *School Public Relations*, Moehlman and Van Zwoll (1957) reemphasized the importance of the interpretative process in a school public relations program. Moehlman died before the work was completed, but the book, although updated, is strongly reminiscent of his earlier pioneering position.

Precisely 15 years later interpretation was to take on a more restricted meaning than that attributed to it by either Moehlman or Van Zwoll. For in 1972 Bortner classified interpretation as an intermediate step in educational public relations and claimed that interaction constituted the most effective kind of public relations policy. Actually, interpretation as defined by Moehlman and redefined by Moehlman and Van Zwoll has much in common with Bortner's interaction.

In 1975 Saxe, too, was to stress interaction, as may be evinced by the title of his text, *School-Community Interaction*. With Saxe, however, public relations was to take a back seat to school-community relations, public relations being, rather than a comprehensive program, merely a strategy to influence the opinion of a given community.

The following year Kindred, Bagin, and Gallagher (1976), moving away from the negative connotations often associated with school public relations, also stressed community relations and the overt involvement of citizens in the decision-making process of the schools. But community relations, as depicted by them, is synonymous with what one might expect to find under the rubric of school public relations.

In the past few years there has emerged a renewed interest in selling as an integral part of an educational public relations program. Called marketing, this interest is reflected in a number of ways. One such way is to emulate the Madison Avenue approach to public relations, launching sophisticated campaigns (Ostrow, 1980). Another is to sell schools like products—cars or soap, for example—by advertising their attributes (Ellison, 1980). And a third builds on planning and research with public participation foremost in mind (Banach, 1981). Running concurrent with this new and growing interest that was once frowned upon in educational public relations circles is the perennial need to involve and interact with the school's publics in a variety of person-to-person settings, perhaps ideally exemplified in the community education movement.

The history of educational public relations, although revealing both similar and dissimilar points of view, is nevertheless consistent in one respect. Schools need the understanding and support of their publics in order to succeed, and educational public relations is vital for ensuring that success.

Although definitions abound of the public relations efforts that have been ongoing for more than a half century in public schools, the definition that best reflects the stance of this text is as follows:

Educational public relations is a systematically and continuously planned, executed, and evaluated program of interactive communication and human relations that employs paper, electronic, and people mediums to attain internal as well as external support for an educational institution. Its premise is that support and appreciation are rooted in understanding and involvement. Its intent is to link institution and community in a way that makes goal accomplishment mutually satisfying.

SUMMARY

Public relations began in antiquity, manifesting itself at the marketplace where people came to trade, buy, or sell goods or services. But its formidability, traceable to the grandeur of past civilizations, may be attributed to evolving efforts to keep the public factually and constantly informed. Of the many pioneers in the field of public relations, two stand tallest—Ivy L. Lee and Edward L. Bernays. Lee's stance that the public must be kept informed set the stage for a budding profession and Bernays' scholarly writings established its authenticity as a legitimate field of endeavor.

Educational public relations is one of the many descendents of public relations, among which are included stockholder relations, employee relations, labor relations, and trade relations. Although many have contributed to the growth of educational public relations, Arthur B. Moehlman deserves the most credit for pioneering the field. Through his writings he was able to make educators aware of the importance of educational public relations. Moehlman equated educational public relations with social interpretation, the purpose of which was to bridge the information gap between school and community.

Over the years educational public relations has been characterized by a variety of approaches, ranging from publicity to information and interpretation to involvement and marketing, with brief incursions into showmanship and the hard sell dotting its existence. Today the notion of marketing the schools seems to be gaining supporters in educational circles. But with the rapid rise of computerized information systems and the exponential growth of information, public relations specialists of all kinds are already being challenged to function within a new setting, in which few precedents serve as an easement into the future.

About 50 years ago the National School Public Relations Association (NSPRA) was born. In coming of age its voice has echoed throughout the nation. Educational public relations has become part and parcel of the American educational heritage.

• 2 •

Contemporary Dimensions

Today the schools are in serious competition for the tax dollar, along with many agencies, organizations, and institutions and notwithstanding their own municipal governments. Taxpayer revolts are by now legion, especially in some states. The tremors resulting from Proposition 13 in California and Proposition 2 1/2 in Massachusetts are still being felt in educational circles. Underemployment is high, the jobless are many, and the nation's economy continues to have its ups and downs, with the purchasing power of the dollar severely reduced by inflation.

Meanwhile demands for educational accountability, which began in the early 1970s, have continued to increase, the hue and cry of reform, mainly a return to the basics, increasing as test scores decline. Concomitant with this decline have arisen allegations of teacher incompetence. Adding to the turmoil have been dwindling school enrollments, teaching staff reductions, and a teacher talent drain into business and industry that has created shortages in certain subject matter areas such as trade-oriented subjects, mathematics, and frequently the sciences. Further complications have resulted from teacher strikes, student discipline problems, and desegregation efforts. Then, looming up as threats to the continued survival of the public school, up to now guaranteed by tradition, have been proposed voucher and tax initiative proposals.

Since the late 1970s educators have watched the barometer of public confidence with a careful eye. An often repeated theme at educational conferences has been the regaining of public confidence. This strong concern for the public's confidence in its schools is nothing new, historically speaking. The record shows that in both the 1920s and the 1950s a similar concern was very much evident. What is new, however, is the trend to have the public schools incorporate marketing techniques, much like those used in business and industry, into their public relations programs. The purpose is to sell the schools to the public, to whom many educators, opposed to such tactics, vehemently argue they already belong. The outcome is a client-consumer orientation, with education being packaged and promoted like any other marketable product. Given these circumstances, the educational public relations specialist emerges as press agent, advertising executive, marketing research specialist, or a combination of all three.

Despite its newness, this trend has its roots in both past and present: in the heated to tepid selling penchant of schools of the past; in the competing educational alternatives in schools and curricula of the late 1960s and early 1970s; and in the magnet schools of today.

The justification for the marketing trend may well derive from the feeling that information programs, even those embraced by various modes of interpretation, have proved insubstantial in obtaining either public support or interaction and that marketing will produce the desired results.

Certainly, the argument can be made that marketing will revitalize the public's interest in its schools, making them more appealing not only to their immediate clients (parents, students, and the vast number of adults enrolled in community education programs), but to the general community, particularly business and industry as beneficiaries of the academic talent of schools. Marketing may even generate considerable pride in schools and thereby heighten staff and student morale. On the other hand, sheer puffery or exaggerated claims are likely to do more harm than good for schools; for quality, not advertising, can be the only assurance of a rise in public confidence and support. More important, however, is the level of direct and continuous involvement that marketing might inspire among community members. For if marketing can generate and sustain involvement, it has served its purpose.

Whether the marketing trend is likely to continue depends largely on a widespread reprioritization of education and a resurgence of available school dollars, a realignment or reinterpretation of the basics, or new educational alternatives made possible by advanced technology that drastically reshapes the nature and function of public education.

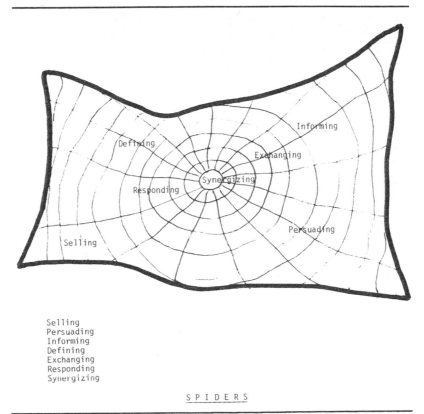

Selling
Persuading
Informing
Defining
Exchanging
Responding
Synergizing

S P I D E R S

Figure 1   The Web of Educational Public Relations

THE WEB OF EDUCATIONAL PUBLIC RELATIONS

The purpose of an educational public relations program may vary from district to district, and at one time or another it may be characterized by any or all of the seven dimensions contained in Figure 1, easily called to mind by the acronymn SPIDERS.

Selling

The first of these dimensions is selling, once a taboo in educational public relations but now coming to the fore as marketing. On its lowest level selling can be seen as flimflam, ballyhoo, or the "hard sell." It has little concern for the "mark" (or purchaser) and is devoid of any ethical obligation, including whether the product works once it leaves the shop. Translated into educational public relations, it means puffery, press agentry, and deceptive advertising.

At its highest level, however, selling may be construed as marketing in which the client's needs and interests are researched and planned for in order to gain his or her approval and support. It is scientific and systematic in its development of a product or territory. Packaging becomes important in marketing because it has the potential of transforming the commonplace into something fresh and exciting, often creating a need where no apparent one exists. Diversified advertising, including themes and campaigns, is essential to promote the product.

In the public school sector this level of selling implies surveys, steering committees, limited citizen involvement, and a network of communicators and communications to publicize the effort and thereby achieve product acceptance. What it does not suggest is any large-scale involvement either in or after the effort. Despite the greater assumption of responsibility for the product that marketing suggests, once needs have been determined as adequately met by that product, subsequent efforts are directed at selling general acceptance rather than merely informing; and communicating is principally one-way.

Persuading

At its lowest level persuading may be identified with propaganda and attempts to distort or deceive. It is reporting good news but concealing bad and preaching by word but not by deed.

At its highest level it is akin to educating in the most palatable manner in order to motivate people to act in their best interests. It is skillfully organizing a message to get a much needed point across. It is the reliance on experts to achieve credibility and trust. Although this level of persuasion may come across as the "good ole boy" approach or as a sophisticated emotive appeal, its purpose is essentially the same. It seeks compliance, conformity, and consensus of action. Participation at this level is viewed as a mode of influence instead of as a forum for differing and dissenting ideas. Although truth may be the goal of the persuader, this truth, no matter how well intentioned, is narrowly constricted to the persuader's perspective. An example of this kind of persuasion is the public school professional persuading a school community that he or she, because of training and experience, always knows what is best for it. Yet, however sincere the motive and logical the rationale, this persuasive truth is often in dispute. Stressing acceptance and eschewing feedback, save favorable overt action, persuasion is one-way communicating.

Informing

At its lowest level informing is meagerly conceived, limited, and sporadic. Misdirection may also arise, with the right information being improperly channeled and difficult to locate. Inadvertent inaccuracies often flourish at this level. The goal is to fill up a publicity scrapbook rather than to inform, and column inches or story count constitutes the mark of a successful educational public relations program. There generally is no intent to deceive at this level. Conduct is determined largely by omission rather than commission, although "whitewashing" can and does sometimes occur. Occasionally, as a gesture of good will, power, or loyalty, some effort is made to edify a particular individual, usually one's superior.

At the highest level information is systematically and comprehensively planned and organized and is disseminated continuously and promptly. It is also directed at appropriate audiences. Through receipt of such information one is able to get an accurate picture of the school. Its communication mode is one-way.

Defining

Defining at its lowest level is partial and obscured. Its selectivity tends to include some groups but leave out others and to express particular preferences by its choice of words. It interprets some but not all parts of a school program. It glosses over issues that might, if probed, cause school officials to experience embarrassment or exasperation.

Defining at its highest level means structuring messages for different audiences and eliminating the educational jargon that staves off understanding. The view from this level is that both internal and external groups are potential interpreters through which the school story can be told and retold. Every effort is therefore made to organize these groups into functional communicator networks. At this level staff inservice becomes exceedingly important. But after all is said and done, defining is still one-way communicating because the initiative to communicate still rests with the school.

Exchanging

Exchanging at its lowest level means a limited exchange of information as a result of personal preferences. It suggests the acceptance of some ideas as well as the denial of others. It is participation at the token level. In this sense one might encourage the input of an advisory group but redirect it to conform to some previously determined notion or policy. Exchanging can be continuous but devoid of purpose. It can represent ideas culled from surveys, panels, and forums that will have no effect on school policy, or letters or phone calls that miss the aggrieved point completely. As such it is the "incongruity" of communication that prevails, with both sides listening more to themselves than to each other and consequently hearing nothing to reshape or sharpen their perspectives.

At its highest level exchanging is the recognition of the importance of feedback. It is an open door policy, or the manifestation of an administrative team at work, or a properly functioning advisory committee that can expect the results of its work to be given full consideration by school leaders. Although exchanging does not promise action, it implies a free flow of information that will facilitate action. Entertaining student, staff, and community needs with intention to fulfill them characterizes this level of exchanging. Exchanging also ushers in the process of two-way communicating.

Responding

Responding at the lowest level is marked by ambiguity and defensiveness. Attempts to pursue a meaningful dialogue between groups are first patronized and then tactfully or boisterously dismissed as irrelevant. Erudition and wit frequently transform the rational into the arcane or the laughable, and circumlocutions become the amusement of the day. Argumentation and an unwillingness to budge on a certain issue frequently typify what transpires during a given meeting, in which every issue becomes a veritable challenge. Because information is viewed as power, information necessary to produce intelligent bilateral decisions is withheld to give one group dominance over the other, as is often the case during crises forms of administrative-teacher collective bargaining.

At its highest level responding is characterized by receptivity, cooperation, and consideration. Information is shared for the mutual benefit of both parties, divergent points of view are seen as necessary and important, and aims are altered and consolidated to achieve realistic and desirable progress. Responding of this caliber is democracy at work, heralding responsible and responsive change. An educational public relations program that embraces this level of responsiveness should fully enjoy the benefits and support that participation portends. In the classroom, in faculty and citizen advisory committees, in administrative teams, and at the bargaining table this level of responding produces an intelligent, integrative problem-solving approach in which all can share and take pride. Two-way communication is clearly evident here.

Synergizing

Synergizing is the optimal representation and interaction of the seven dimensions of communicating within an educational public relations program. Synergizing, however, goes beyond mere addition; for, as these dimensions ideally interlock, they add up to a whole much greater than the sum of its parts. This new dynamism results in an educational public relations program that is strong, durable, and sensitive to the needs of all concerned, the immediate and extended school family and the community at large.

In summary, the strength of each dimension lies not in the solitary metaphorical strand that goes into the weaving of the web of educational public relations nor in the haphazard or purposeful accumulation of these strands, however operationally interlaced they may appear at first sight. Tensile strength is in the totality of the web itself, at which point synergy becomes functional and the beauty of nature is complete.

DUAL PRIMARY ELEMENTS

Interestingly enough, educational public relations, when reduced to its primary elements, is no more than an amalgam of human relations and communication. A knowledge of human relations is essential for understanding and working with individuals and groups. A public relations-oriented person must exemplify and epitomize behavior that makes the professional aspects of organization as personal as possible. However great a program, people relate to people first and program second.

On the other hand, no matter how personable an individual, if lines of communication are repeatedly impeded or obstructed, rapport between leader and follower is soon to be lost. Good communication is two-way; structured and executed to maximize information sharing, feedback, and the meeting of community needs.

Devoid of either of these elements—human relations or communication—or scantily representing them, an educational public relations program cannot be expected to achieve any appreciable or lasting success. When both elements are absent, an educational public relations program simply does not exist.

Human Relations

People have a penchant for seeking models. They tend to gravitate toward those whom they can admire, those who not only embody and reflect their interests but who are interested in them. They want to count among their valued friends those who are knowledgeably informed and unflagging in their commitments. The human relations role of the public relations-oriented person is described in the following statements:

Radiate Confidence. No one takes pleasure in associating with failures or those who preach failure, no matter how amiable they are, usually not even for a little while. A nagging and persistent fear seems to linger in people's minds that failure may be contractible. Success, however, is typically construed as symptomatic of further and still greater success. Thus, those who appear successful, whether or not they are, have no difficulty in attracting a following; for if success is contagious, most people would surely like to be incubated with it. Equally important is that a good self-image is a prerequisite to feeling good about others.

Evince Expertise and Honesty. People, in their desire to learn the truth, seek the opinions of experts. By being well-versed in the business of education, one invites questions. Answered knowledgeably and truthfully, these questions pave the way for further dialogue between school and community while fostering credibility, trust, and understanding, all of which lend themselves to needed support for schools.

Demonstrate Product Conviction. Not to believe emphatically in the importance of schooling and in the overall proficiency and competency of one's own school system is to be a poor spokesperson, indeed, for that school system. Laudatory performances are contingent upon not only product knowledge but product conviction. Without product knowledge a speaker transmits to a listener hesitancy, confusion, and suspicion, with the latter soon changing to obvious mistrust. Similarly, product conviction is essential if others are to be convinced that a product has merit.

Dress with Decorum. How one dresses is frequently interpreted as a measure of success or success potential. The seedily dressed person seems to wear the stamp of misfortune and need, if not abject poverty, regardless of the wealth the wearer may actually possess. Thus, although appearances may be deceptive or false, they tend to govern people relationships to a large extent. For example, it is unlikely that someone wanting to sell an expensive home at a sizeable profit would be lured into placing it with a real estate salesperson who drove a 10-year-old car and dressed in threadbare clothing or in a fashion designed for a bygone era. The salespotential of such a person would be highly dubious. Likewise, a shabbily attired or poorly groomed principal greeting a parent new to the community is apt to raise a curious parental eyebrow and bring about an immediate loss of confidence.

Moreover, styles that are outdated suggest ideas of the same ilk from their wearers. Dressing with decorum also implies matching color with occasion. Much like body language, which can spark defensiveness or receptivity, colors have signals that can repel or attract. Using them to one's advantage is, therefore, important.

Walk, Talk, and Listen with Purpose and Care. While a vigorous and measured pace transmits to an observer purpose, busyness, and concern, an amble may convey the impression of aimlessness and free time and a promenade, pomposity and haughtiness. Again, whereas talking too fast may reflect the insecurity or indifference of speaker to audience, talking too slowly may convey a sluggishness of thought. Talking too much or too little is also laden with dangers. Selected and fitted like an expensive wardrobe, words should be worn with comfort and confidence and displayed with ease and taste.

Practiced listeners are a virtual rarity, and even those who labor to listen often succumb to distractions. When listener eye contact is reduced and shifts of attention range from notable to blatant, the speaker becomes discomfitted and communication is substantially impeded. Much of the same is true of the speaker who is unable to sustain eye contact. Here a lack of eye contact may be interpreted as distaste, disinterest, or deception. If right and lasting impressions are to be created, the eye-to-eye approach must be meticulously adhered to by every speaker and listener.

Be Affirmative and Mannerly. Unlimited horizons await those who can find opportunities in problems. Like its antithesis, pessimism, optimism can be contagious. It has an alluring quality that invites sharing. In the midst of simple adversity a smile, because of the reciprocity it induces in a recipient, can precipitate an exchange of amiability that mitigates pain. A hand outstretched in friendship accompanied by a pleasant greeting, particularly by name, is uplifting to the recipient, who, cast in the limelight, is suddenly made to feel important. And even important people like to be reminded of their importance. The individual who treats others attentively and respectfully quickly earns their esteem.

Consider Students as Clients. Be they young or old, students should be viewed as clients. By subscribing to the notion that customer satisfaction is critical to the success of any enterprise, one becomes acutely aware of differences that may exist between current educational services and growing community needs. Although the stance that a client is always right may reflect only a portion of a larger response, it is certainly a part that, if entertained, lends itself to continued dealings.

Display Interest in Others. When people display an interest in others, these same others are likely to become interested in them. Accoutered with respect and concern, interest prompts a rebounding effect, with the boon greatest for the original giver. Kindness has its own rewards. Good or bad, the tendency is for most people to be immersed in themselves. By realizing this and acting on the knowledge that honest and caring expressions of interest lead to a sharing of ideas and gradual commonality of interests, one can amass many satisfied customers, consumers turned friends who will be prone to render support whenever it is needed.

Avoid Gossip and Rumors. Anyone who speaks disparagingly about others should expect no less. It is time to seek new horizons when a place of employment loses its luster, becoming neither promising nor pleasant. The only gossiping to be done is the kind that one would not mind being aired on a public address system because that is often how the most secret of secrets are treated by those who have sworn to keep them. For maximum effect, any eagerness to criticize should be tempered by a willingness to be criticized. Rumors can be destructive. Partial truths deceive because they invite fabrications to account for information gaps. Worse yet, the originator of a rumor is often its unknowing victim. To paraphrase a World War II saying, many a school has been scuttled by a slippery lip.

Encourage Participation. People who become engrossed in school projects and activities are likely school supporters. When these projects and activities are closely in tune with their needs, interests, abilities, and aspirations, their enthusiasm will become apparent to others, friends, neighbors, and acquaintances, and the school story will gain a wide audience. Acting as a fount of good will for the school, they will lavishly dispense the news that the school is thriving and under competent leadership. On the other hand, when participation is minimal or absent, support is typically found wanting and criticism is notable.

Communication

Simplistically, the function of communication in an educational public relations program is to ascertain that schools and communities are in agreement on their educational goals. Society is moving at an accelerated pace, and educational goals must be continually reviewed and revamped to accommodate change. Leadership postures change, too. What was viewed ample for yesterday's community may be deemed inadequate now. Without ongoing and responsive communication schools and communities will shortly discover that they are operating at cross-purposes. Although a steady flow of communication is no ironclad guarantee that schools will always be on target in meeting community needs, they can, by sharing information, seeking feedback, and promptly acting upon it, significantly improve their chances of hitting a bull's-eye.

But a formalized two-way communication system does not spring into existence on its own. It stems from a well developed board policy that authorizes and fiscally assures the continuity and perpetuity of an educational public relations program. Policy constitutes a school's first organized attempt to communicate with its community and sets the stage for employing a specialist to provide leadership for the educational public relations program.

Communication, as described here, is comprised of three entities: information sharing, feedback, and meeting of community needs. The importance of the first two is gauged by how smoothly and efficiently they accomplish the third.

Information Sharing. The sharing of information, when properly handled, consumes a considerable amount of time. It entails not only working with people, but with publications and electronic mediums; and it requires knowing something about a variety of skill areas, principally speaking, listening, writing, editing, printing, graphics, photography, and computing. Printed types of information are exemplified in press releases, building-level and districtwide publications, board reports, brochures, and annual reports. Nonprint, or electronic, types of information sharing include radio and television public service announcements. Costing a school district only the time and materials to develop them, they serve as an excellent way to extend its communication reach. A merging of print and electronic mediums is best viewed within the context of the computer, in which electronic transactions are already fulfilling the promise of rapid information sharing, now mainly in business and industry, but soon in schools.

People types of information sharing are equally diverse. Here information can be channeled through meetings with administrative, teaching, and special services personnel; student groups; PTAs and PTOs; band and booster clubs; school, neighborhood, and districtwide committees; back-to-school night; education week; telephone trees of influential citizens who disseminate and receive information about the schools; school volunteer organizations; home visitations; kaffeeklatsches; speakers and information bureaus; hot lines and rumor clinics; and board meetings.

Feedback. Obviously, most of the previous methods of sharing information can and should produce feedback. But feedback must be structured to provide optimal effects, assuring both responsiveness and responsibility in terms of receipt, assessment, and return. One of the most effective methods of acquiring feedback is through a districtwide or central public relations advisory committee. Ideally constructed, this committee should include the following: a board member; a central office administrator; a building-level principal; a teacher from an elementary and a secondary school; a building custodian; two secondary school students (probably a ninth and a twelfth grader); two parents; two other community members (preferably a nonparent and a senior citizen); and the educational public relations specialist, who serves as the committee's chair. The makeup of the committee should provide for minority group representation. To make it workable, the committee should ordinarily not exceed a membership of 15.

Complementing the central committee should be similar advisory committees at the building level, with the principal or someone else assigned to this public relations function. A community school director or a teacher with a reduced class load might well be charged with the leadership responsibility for a given committee and asked to perform building-level public relations tasks. These committees, although usually somewhat smaller in size, should be designed to include a cross section of the neighborhood. While the memberships of the two kinds of committees would be expected to meet every month, committee chairs would need to attend an additional monthly meeting. The purpose of this extra meeting would be to pool and sort the flow of feedback generated by the committees before relaying it to the administration and board.

A corollary of this structure would be the creation of another type of feedback: the reporting of individual school activities and events relative to the achievement of districtwide goals. This reporting would be made possible by the building-level public relations representative who collects and forwards all information to the school district's public relations director. A standardized reporting sheet that identifies reporter and school would enable this representative to keep the public relations director informed about activities and events as they occur in classrooms and schools throughout the school district.

Feedback may be secured in other ways, some of which include the following: forums; neighborhood associations; formal and informal opinion leaders; citizens who attend school functions; community education participants; student course evaluations; suggestion boxes; school surveys; letters and phone calls to administration and staff; letters to the editor and editorials appearing in the local paper; and radio and television commentaries.

Meeting Community Needs. Although there are many ways to determine whether community needs are being met by the school, the school survey (or opinionnaire) ranks as one of the most effective, particularly when it is conducted on a personal basis. Still, a sampling of needs should not be restricted to groups external to the school. Students, teachers, special services personnel, and administrators should be asked to give their opinions. Students, for example, are important sources of school information for parents. Moreover, a student unhappy with a teacher or school can quickly produce a set of irate parents. An older student or adult unhappy with a teacher or school may not only drop out of school, he or she might be the first to vote against badly needed school referendums. In effect, when input is severely limited or ignored, all members of the immediate school family experience a decline in morale, which, left unremediated, results in a significant loss of productivity for the system.

An analysis of school issues appearing in daily and weekly newspapers over long periods of time constitutes another method of learning whether community needs are being met. If overlooked or unresolved, issues can result in troublesome and recurrent problems. It is, therefore, important that public relations specialists maintain a record of unsolicited news space with an accuracy and vigor equal to the press release scrapbook they prepare for the school system.

Individual needs culled from course evaluations, when viewed collectively, provide valuable insights, particularly for community educators, whose programmatic success is wholly dependent on the satisfaction of their clients. The nature and extent of community involvement in school functions, regular or community education sponsored, provides other insights. Then, too, written or oral complaints can be translated into levels of satisfaction or dissatisfaction with a school district's aims and activities, some of which may be thought of as neither necessary nor desirable by its clientele.

Considered by many as evidence that a school district is meeting community needs is the repeated passage of budget and building referenda. Ironically, apathy could provide the same results if tax increases were small and well within the budgets of most community members. Although any support is frequently interpreted as a sign of something right happening within the school community, support that can be truly traced to the meeting of community needs is the only kind that can have any permanence. All other kinds create a false sense of security that is quick to dissipate at the first indication of approaching hard times.

SUMMARY

In today's society the public schools are being forced to compete for funding and support. Taxpayer revolts, inflation, unemployment, and underemployment are just a few of the variables causing repercussions in the educational sphere. Meanwhile, accountability demands placed on public school educators have risen awesomely. Again, as traditional educational public relations approaches undergo careful scrutiny in terms of their efficacy, the public school's need for an effective public relations program intensifies.

Educational public relations in action may be likened to the intersecting and interactive strands of a complex web, in which educators find themselves entangled in different ways at different times as they attempt to communicate with their diverse publics, internally and externally. The acronym SPIDERS best describes the various dimensions of this web. Seven in number, they are as follows: selling, persuading, informing, defining, exchanging, responding, and synergizing. Each of the first six dimensions has low and high levels. For example, selling at its lowest level denotes flimflam and ballyhoo, and at its highest level, a sophisticated marketing approach. When all six dimensions are operating effectively, they may be thought of as functioning synergistically.

Viewed from another perspective, educational public relations is a combination of human relations and communication. The first of these elements is concerned not only with the projection of a successful self-image, but with the cultivation of favorable interactions with others. The second focuses on information sharing, feedback, and the meeting of community needs. Optimally implemented and nurtured, these elements engender considerable support for public schools.

• 3 •

Function in an Electronic Age

Educational public relations can be expected to undergo drastic changes during the next few decades. Already many educational public relations specialists are turning to the computer for an instant and ongoing receipt and exchange of information. Moreover, while computer use in public schools intensifies within administrative and classroom contexts, a growing number of personal computers are finding their way into homes, some 200,000 to 300,000 in 1982 and probably about a million in 1983 (Andrews, 1983). Contributing to this deluge are the awards or grant programs of computer companies that loan or donate computers to schools (National Association of Secondary School Principals [NASSP], 1982).

Perhaps the most important reason for the widespread use of computers, aside from the multiplicity of functions they provide, is their declining cost. Daily the economy they offer steadily improves. For a pittance of the cost they commanded a few decades ago, they can now be purchased for business, education, and entertainment by a large segment of society. And bigness has been transformed into smallness, as the compact computer of today busies itself performing the work of its giant ancestors with considerable ease.

Yet as computers grow smaller, television sets increase in size, offering lifelike images on built-in or three tube projection viewing screens that leave little to the imagination of the viewer and producing a cinematic effect in the home. For example, three tube projection sales have been set at 300,000 to 500,000 yearly for 1983–1985 (NASSP,

1981). Increasing the versatility of the television set and expanding its viewing capabilities are video cassette recorders, video disc players, and video cameras; global satellites and satellite dishes; and cable television programming, some of which has been successfully aired to demonstrate interactive opportunities.

The omnipresence of television screens is awesome. They are everywhere: homes, schools, offices, factories, cars, spacecrafts, ships, beaches, and, lately, even on wrists. And in the home of the not-too-distant future, they may be expected to assume wall-sized proportions and be built with a computer circuitry that affords interactive and storage capabilities reminiscent of science fiction fantasies that dazzled earlier generations.

Caught up in this maelstrom of technological innovation, public education is destined to undergo a startling metamorphosis. Education will move from school facility to home, and the school, as it currently exists, will cease to be. Accelerating this transformation will be declining energy resources, the high cost of housing, flextime computer-generated employment in the home, the interactive wall-sized television screen, and lifelong learning. The single family unit, which so typifies the residential style of present-day society, will be largely supplanted by condominiums, octoplexes, and apartment buildings. Here, learning will become an integral part of the home, in which a modular style of abbreviated living space will be electronically controlled and heightened to produce interchangeably the illusion of both proximity and expansiveness. Within these residential complexes will be educational centers called learning studios that will be equipped with the latest in electronic gadgetry to facilitate learning.

Functioning as an information hub to network and mediate the information flow of most institutions, organizations, and agencies within a given community will be today's public school system. Aided by media satellites and computer technology, this information hub will serve as a vast instructional delivery system, charged with the responsibility of carrying out several specific information tasks: policy making; needs assessments' communication; curriculum development; allocation of human, financial, and material resources; and community education networking (early childhood to late adult education, or "cradle to grave" learning).

In the intramediated sphere of the emergent mediated community will be a variety of media learning centers that act as way stations to residential learning studios and living spaces and that in many instances, directly service clusters of single family units. In the intermediated sphere residential networking coordinated by the hub will embrace a variety of information sources: professional preparation centers dealing with specialized training in a variety of fields; universities emphasizing research activity; community colleges that principally provide educational enrichment and paraprofessional skills; parks and recreation centers that focus on leisure time activities; business and industry with an array of educational training programs, including skills updating; and a human resource agency that offers, among other things, information about ecology, family, medicine, law, employment, nutrition, housing, and finance. While information emanating from the hub will be targeted at media learning centers and studios, cross-feeding among all within the network will occur.

In the emergent mediated community traditional administrative roles will be significantly altered. Spearheading information hub activities will be a director of information systems, who either reports directly to the executive charged with administering education throughout the entire community or is that executive. Should the former rather than the latter role prevail, it will probably be designated as a director or superintendent of community education. Also contained within the information hub will be a variety of media support personnel: senior administrators, media content supervisors, technicians, and computer operators. A media learning center's complement will consist of a media administrator and a media staff, the bulk of whom will be traveling teachers. Trained in specific subject matter areas and information technology, these teachers will travel contiguously from center to residentially based learning studio to assist, as needed, media paraprofessionals stationed there.

By the next century it is also expected that the voucher system of education, so bitterly opposed by a preponderance of educators in recent years, will not only have been implemented, but will be on the decline. In any event voucher malls (West, 1974) will have, by then, come into vogue and will be operated by entrepreneurs, presumably experienced educators. These malls will address particular needs or interests of educational consumers; specialize in specific curricular areas, offering remediation or enrichment; and guarantee learning on a refund basis, customer satisfaction governing all transactions. Figure 2 (West, 1981) depicts the emergent mediated community in the 21st century.

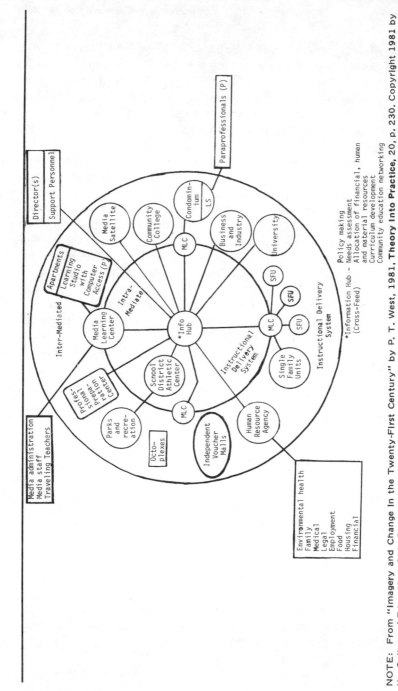

NOTE: From "Imagery and Change in the Twenty-First Century" by P. T. West, 1981, **Theory into Practice**, 20, p. 230. Copyright 1981 by the College of Education, Ohio State University. Adapted by permission.

Figure 2 Emergent Mediated Community in the 21st Century

A SHIFT IN EMPHASIS

Earlier it was pointed out that contemporary educational public relations was essentially a blending of two elements: communications and human relations. In the electronic age of educational public relations technology will modify and expand traditional communication approaches. Information dissemination and exchange will be largely governed by instancy and imagery, rather than by physical movement and personal contact. This shift in emphasis will be engendered by a number of technological factors: market saturation—new communication technology will bombard and envelop society; product permeation—most mechanical products will be computerized; economy—the cost of high tech products will decline as output increases and obsolescence quickens; education—public school students now learning to use high tech products will be both buyers and users in the elctronic age; and ease of communicating—appreciation will come from extended use. This accent on technology will inevitably produce an interest in techno-relations as a means of compensation for the lack of personal contact in traditional communications.

AN ELECTRONIC PR MODEL

In the Gemini PR Model of the 21st century (West, 1981, see Figure 3), educational public relations is shown to consist of two overlapping elements, each of which is based on certain techniques and principles. The first of these futuristic elements is communication and the second, techno-relations.

Communication

Listed in the model are 13 communication techniques, many of which have already enjoyed varying degrees of popularity. Telecommunications and the computer rank departmental status on a growing number of college campuses, with applications of both continuing to crop up in public school systems. Interactive cable television, although largely in the experimental stage, has appeared in some communities, and video conferencing has proven to be a viable and valuable communication technique. Indeed, video interactions now characterize much of the news on television.

While satellites hover over the earth, a satellite dish can be purchased for home consumption for about $2,000 to $4,000 and a micro-

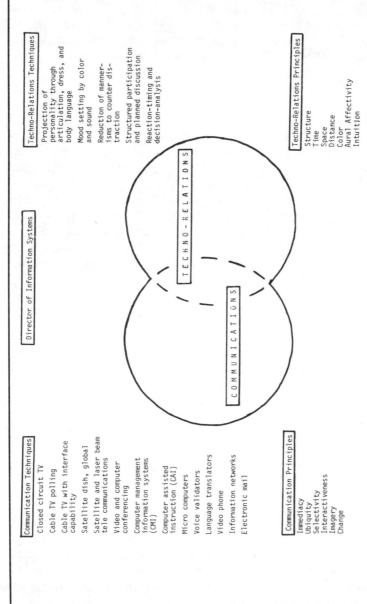

Communication Techniques

Closed circuit TV

Cable TV polling

Cable TV with interface
capability

Satellite dish, global

Satellite and laser beam
tele communications

Video and computer
conferencing

Computer management
information systems
(CMI)

Computer assisted
instruction (CAI)

Micro computers

Voice validators

Language translators

Video phone

Information networks

Electronic mail

Communication Principles

Immediacy
Ubiquity
Selectivity
Interactiveness
Imagery
Change

Director of Information Systems

TECHNO-RELATIONS

COMMUNICATIONS

Techno-Relations Techniques

Projection of
personality through
articulation, dress, and
body language

Mood setting by color
and sound

Reduction of manner-
isms to counter dis-
traction

Structured participation
and planned discussion

Reaction-timing and
decision-analysis

Techno-Relations Principles

Structure
Time
Space
Distance
Color
Aural Affectivity
Intuition

NOTE: From "Imagery and Change in the Twenty-First Century" by P. T. West, 1981, **Theory Into Practice**, 20, p. 231. Copyright 1981 by the College of Education, Ohio State University. Adapted by permission.

Figure 3 The Gemini PR Model

46

computer for much less. Information networks, such as the Source and CompuServ, are already becoming commonplace. In place, too, are computer systems for the management of information and the delivery of instructional materials. Invested with computer interactiveness, teletext may well become the next mass medium (Edwards, 1982), replacing the newspaper before the turn of the century, by which time regular mail will have gone electronic. While the video phone is now possible and voice validators are being used, fairly sophisticated language translators will probably be in existence in another 20 years.

This maze of communication techniques suggests an entirely new set of communication principles. These principles are as follows: immediacy, ubiquity, selectivity, interactiveness, imagery, and change.

Immediacy is wrought by instancy. In the emergent mediated community of the electronic age, message origin is a small consideration. Information flow will be as fast as the button that activates it, with distant and local events imbued with the same freshness. In crises situations instant data will unfetter and improve the ability to act, heightening the responsiveness of public officials to public opinion, the local school superintendent as well as state and national legislators.

Ubiquity is characterized by equality and expansiveness. Everyone everywhere with access to the new technology is capable of receiving the same message at the same time, barring differences in time zones. Once the message is sent, receipt is almost certain; if not directly, then shortly thereafter by alternate forms of transmissions, one of which might even be the result of an over-the-fence chat with a neighbor. With ubiquity there is no place to go or hide to avoid exposure or facing up to the facts, once the information has been sent.

Selectivity has a tendency to impede the first two principles. As reception possibilities are multiplied and magnified, preferences may delay or inhibit the receipt of a given message. On the other hand, the use of the computer or video recorder may substantially increase preferential potential and thereby merely postpone the inevitable. Like immediacy and ubiquity, selectivity has, to some extent, always existed; but with the availability of tying into a variety of computer lines—cable programming that may well exceed 100 channels, regular television programming, and different brands of subscription television as well as video cassettes and discs—preferences become almost endless.

Interactiveness is technologically derived two-way communications. Through technology armchair communicating is not only possible but practical. Using the computer or the interactive wall-sized television, citizens may remain in their homes and participate in a board or PTA meeting, or confer with the teachers of their children on a closed circuit. Similarly, they may become involved in citizen advisory committees or in instructional activities. Interactiveness, although conducive to public support for schools, can also open up new problem areas. In this context there is no limit to participation and largely an absence of control over it, unless some sort of structure dictates its existence and conduct.

Imagery denotes the overall character of the message. Its purpose is to curtail and direct selectivity and to promote change. It may come about from the graphics of the computer screen, alluring holography, or the intimacy of the wall-sized television screen. Imagery is laden with persuasive impacts and competitive in its demand for attention and acceptance. If the message is swiftly acted upon, the image is functioning at an optimal level.

Change, the last of the six communication principles, is contrary to what is expected of conventional educational public relations messages. In the past these messages have been directed primarily toward reinforcing the attitudes held by school supporters and secondarily toward securing the commitment of neutrals. But message design has had little effect in the conversion of opponents. In the electronic age, however, the thrust of educational public relations will be to change public attitudes through the continuous application and direction of the preceding five principles. In other words, messages will be designed to elicit change through imagery that delimits, by calculated appeal, the selection of alternate preferences; and through large scale interactiveness that offers immediate and relevant information to the school's publics.

Techno-Relations

Techno-relations, the intersecting twin of the Gemini PR Model, is a derivative of the communication techniques and principles of an electronic age. Techno-relations constitutes an attempt to cope with electronic realities that are devoid of physical contact. Optimally performed, techno-relations' transactions become palatable substitutes for traditional forms of person to person communicating, however cold or heartless this may sound to human relations purists. For example, the love affair the American public has had over the years with its automobile may be considerably enhanced when the computerized car is suddently endowed with a pleasant set of simulated vocal cords that guide its functioning; and the home computer that converses with its owner or occupant may prove an exceptionally entertaining companion as well as servant. Robots, in fact, may turn into the human's best friend, replacing, as pets, domesticated animals—absurd, perhaps, but definitely plausible. In any event techno-relations evokes, like its communication counterpart, a set of techniques and principles that explain and facilitate both use and effectiveness.

Techno-relations techniques serve to not only approximate but facilitate and enhance human relationships, something that the print medium has never been able to accomplish. Through the aid of the computer, participation can be structured and planned with efficiency and effectiveness. Continuous dialogues lend themselves to massive involvement and intelligent input, in contradistinction to the meeting or conference that inspires no more than token contributions. The computer also makes possible an extensive analysis of the decision-making process. The intimacy engendered by a computer transaction, it may be argued, is far better than the loneliness spawned by an unresponsive crowd. When computers transmit, receive, and record both typed and spoken messages, this new intimacy will be further enhanced. Amateur radio operators, for example, have established strong and continuing friendships by communicating with one another over the years. The educational facility that provides technological opportunities to citizens for an array of such dialogues will, in time, secure and maximize support, and involvement will be the rule rather than the exception.

Visual transactions, via the wall-sized television screen, will give rise to the projection of personality through speech, dress, and body language, with significant efforts made to reduce mannerisms that produce distraction. Mood will be created by color and sound, and interactivity will permit participation in decision-making processes.

Techno-relations principles undergirding and influencing communication interchanges are foreseen as seven in number: structure, time, space, distance, color, aural affectivity, and intuition.

Structure is the drawing together of the disparate but related principles—time, space, distance, color, and aural affectivity—to achieve the illusion of reality and the intimacy of human relationships in message design. Structure makes for credibility and acceptance. Influenced by message contexts, structure influences and encompasses style of transmission and response. Whereas structure is the big picture, intuition, the seventh of the techno-relations principles, is the epiphanic comprehension of that picture. Intuition is a seventh sense—a media sense that in a primitive age might be labeled instinct. Intuition, however, represents the highest order of thinking in an electronic age. It is a highly developed and sophisticated thought process that owes its origin to the advent of an information society, governed by high technology.

Time becomes a composite of both illusion and reality. There is, for example, time spent in actual computer transactions (real time) as opposed to time experienced over extended periods of continuous communicating (computer time). There is the actual staging or production of a televised performance and the experiencing of that performance when it is presented at a later time, once, twice, or on a number of occasions. Adding to this confusion is the video cassette recorder timed to record a performance for playing at a later date and, of course, the actual replay as well as subsequent replays, which could conceivably stretch over years. Time is also bandied about in the replay of this performance by gadgetry that allows for viewing at slow, fast forward, or reverse speeds. Time can even be stopped with a freeze frame control and scrutinized for extended analysis. The computer, too, stores and recalls time segments as well as compresses them.

Space also influences time in the creation of alternative environments on the wall-sized screen. Winter may be simulated in summer and vice versa. the video album of past events may be relived in lifelike dimensions within the confines of a single room. The space a computer occupies, although relatively small, may encircle the globe in the performance of its broad scope functions; and the wall-sized television screen may create and alter space, with the illusion of space further enhanced by three dimensional imagery. In the space of the livingroom or den interactions will occur with groups without any more than their computer or visual presence. Indeed, an entire world may, at one time or another, provide the home with electronic visitors.

Distance will derive its meaning from electronic access rather than actual travel. No place will be too near or too far to visit, and the school will be an integral part of the electronic home. Travel through the computer or wall-sized screen will be as natural as conventional travel, but much more easily done, with the bridging of distance synonymous with the flick of a switch. Attendance at remote meetings will be possible without even leaving the home, and the interaction of distantly located friends and acquaintances may continue indefinitely, with an intimacy and immediacy heretofore unknown.

Color will also play a significant role in techno-relations. This fifth principle, by virture of the mood it creates, will tend to exert a persuasive influence on target audiences. Be it the imagery of a computer or wall-sized television, color will help to impart to technology a human quality. It has long been acknowledged that color produces an emotional effect on the eyes of the beholder. Color adds an element of enjoyment to food; it makes rooms more livable; and, in certain situations, it has the potency of a strong drink (Cheskin, 1947). Colors can be aloof or energetic. For example, blue denotes self-esteem and conservatism; red, activity and inconstancy. Too, colors market products (Bireen, 1945). Categorized under the seasons of a year and matched with the complexion of individuals, colors have been used to guide the selection of wardrobes to convey glamour and beauty (Jackson, 1981). Color of attire can make or break a job interview. In a variety of fields color selection is used to analyze personality (Luscher, 1971). But colors do not appear on a video screen as they do in a personal encounter; one color affects the projection of another, and the set, or background, affects both (Zettl, 1976). Adherence to a second set of color guidelines is, therefore, necessary if color is to be used effectively on the big screen in one- or two-way communications.

Aural affectivity is the sixth techno-relations principle. Based on the use of not only sound but also body language, namely, the science of kinesics, it is intended to achieve intimacy and acceptance in message design. Like certain body movements, sound creates presence. It is as well the bearer of subliminal suggestion. It can be singular or pervasive, isolating or surrounding its audience. It can portend harmony or dissonance, excitement or boredom. Imbued with the proper sound and body movement, a message can motivate an individual to act or react in a predictable fashion. On the big screen images enhanced by well chosen sounds create inviting atmospheres, convincing arguments, and soothing admonitions; and produce auras surrounding individuals, objects, and events that will be long remembered. Computers embellished with human sound, voices of stage and screen idols, close friends, favorite relatives, and the like, can simulate a sense of well-being and amicability in normally cold and impersonal households. Equipped with one's voice, they virtually serve as an alter ego. By matching sound to message, message acceptance will be promoted.

Intuition is the seventh techno-relations principle. The intuitive capability of the information generation will be repeatedly tested, taxed, and sharpened as interactive wall-sized television and computer transactions become commonplace in homes and offices (which, in many cases, will be the same) toward the close of the century. Earlier described as an insight much like an epiphany, this media sense is related to the art and science of anticipatory leadership, which every information or educational public relations specialist will eventually be expected to possess. The art of anticipation will be synonymous with the immediate contextual comprehension of syntactical (spoken or printed) and visual representations, electronically suspended in, or moving through, space and time. Visually the experience will be like looking at a pointillistic painting close up and from a distance. The science of anticipation, on the other hand, will be based on a knowledge of taxonomies, such as color, sound, movement, and spatial design. Thus, viewed from another perspective, this same pointillistic painting expresses a scientific way of applying paint to achieve a particular effect.

EVOLVING PUBLIC RELATIONS

Progression toward the mediated community of the next century will continue to alter extant internal and external modes of communication. For example, replacing the traditional paper pile up of administrative and staff memos, bulletins, board meeting minutes, and district newspapers and newsletters will be closed-circuit computer and television conferencing via cable and satellite dish. Similarly, student activities, field trips, exhibitions, classroom demonstrations, and career days with business and industry participating will be aired in the home on the big screen. Report cards will be computer transmitted directly to the home, and parent-teacher conferences will be conducted on the big screen, electronically connecting school to home. Instruction and administrative record keeping will be the province of the computer.

Members of advisory groups will meet without even leaving their homes, providing input through computer and big screen interactions. Speakers bureaus, forums, panel discussions, and board meetings will be home fare, as will the bulk of instruction emanating from media learning centers. Through global satellites, education will take on an international flavor, with language barriers removed by computerized translators.

Instant referendums will be conducted by computer and interactive wall-sized screens, with voice validators or computer codes to identify votes. A possible precursor of this eventual shift is the recent, experimental use of mail balloting in Oregon referenda, which has already challenged the sanctity of site voting while raising the problem of additional costs (Piele, 1983). Electronig mediums will also assure rapidity in assessing needs and polling opinions. And, most of all, education will move gradually from the school facility to the residential learning studio right into the den or livingroom of the home, where home retrieval systems will maintain accurate records of the education progress of young and old.

THE RISE OF THE TECHNO-BASICS

An educated information society cannot be expected to spring into existence of its own accord. The rampancy and pervasiveness of advanced technology in no way guarantees the development of coping skills. Some people will never learn to live with technology; nor do they want to. But retrenchment in the schools today can prepare youngsters for the electronic age of tomorrow.

There is and will always be dispute about what is basic to a student's education for survival in society. The failure of some children to read is attributed to miseduation about every 10 years. Indeed, the launching of Sputnik in 1957 caused educational critics to look askance at the way science was being taught in the schools and sparked an extensive examination of the K-12 curriculum. One of the results was the new math, which confused a generation of adults and children. Attempts to teach children how to write are more often than not held in disrepute, and reading seems to be a perennial problem, with the hue and cry of "Why Our Children Cannot Read" periodically enjoying top billing on magazine covers. Yet, although a return to the basics is both interminable and currently argued, new basics emerge. Instead of the traditional three Rs—reading, writing, and arithmetic—children are learning computing, perceiving, articulating, auditing, and intuiting (West, 1983).

The roots of society were pictorial. Engraved on the walls of caves were drawings, with which prehistoric people could share or bewilder themselves and others. Pictures came before words. When words followed, each person became a repository of information, with some specializing precisely in that function, namely the balladeer. Ballads were sung while people huddled around campfires, with the epic tales of Ulysses recited again and again, preserving them for posterity. Much later the printing press was invented, and books rendered obsolete the lyre and the balladeer.

Today, although the teaching of reading continues to be a primary concern of educators, electronic mediums—such as television and all its adorning gadgetry, tape recorders, talking book records, and soon the talking computer—portend the decline of the need to read. And as society comes full cycle to its earliest pictorial beginnings with the aid of technology, one might conceivably ask whether reading would have ever come into common use if television, by some technological quirk, had preceded it. Of course, an answer to this question might lie in an examination of the introduction of television in backward cultures. But an answer is unimportant here. For what is truly important is that as schools tool up with renewed vigor to teach students the traditional basics (save computing, which admittedly many schools are now adding to the three R's) the coping basics are rapidly changing.

Computing is a requisite skill of an electronic age. The student, and soon the adult, who cannot operate a computer will find future survival difficult. By the 21st century common household chores, such as shopping and paying bills, will have gone electronic, as will have letter and newspaper writing. Because of the computer the workplace will gradually move into the home, where most household appliances and apparatus will be operated and linked by a master computer. In the household of the future computers will serve as the repository of not only household records, but personal libraries, educational instruction, and games. That same future will reduce arithmetic literacy to the ownership of a pocket-sized computer, which tells as well as totals.

Perceiving will take its place as a basic because the images that inundate the wall-sized screen will demand it. Television, now viewed as predominantly entertainment, will display life-sized productions of classical and contemporary literature, creating sight books that will serve as academic fare. Imbued with the drama of the large screen, history and science, along with other instructional areas, will come alive with a new vigor.

Television will be the source of interactive exchanges for educational, civic, business, and entertainement activities. Meetings and conferences conducted on the television screen will attempt to resolve community problems and update occupational skills. Because television will evolve as an instrument of change, the uninitiated and untrained societal inhabitant of the electronic age will fall prey to propaganda deluges or big brotherism. Thus, perceiving becomes more than just seeing or passive mentation. Akin to reading between pictures rather than lines, it moves in the direction of helping to replace reading as a coping basic. Perceiving is also concerned with the understanding of the psychology of color and the science of kinesics as they mesh with the innuendoes of language. Relating mood and setting to action, it extracts meaning from all three.

Articulating as a coping basic is equally important on the wall-sized screen as, once again, speaking and body movement lend credibility to message transmission and work to produce higher levels of public acceptance. Too, the talking computer will exacerbate the importance of speaking in message transmission. In this sense, articulating will minimize the importance of writing. Endowed with the dual capability to translate oral transmissions into written symbols or to communicate by sound and to store both, computers will make writing unnecessary for most people. What is more, the symbol hunting that formerly traversed the printed page will, in the future, probe pictorial and oral communications. The information critic will be as versed in the skill of articulating as the communicator. And the articulator will often don the guise of a thespian, calling forth the full range of dramatic expression in message design.

Auditing, another techno-basic, derives its importance from listening skills so typically ignored or overlooked in educational settings yet so essential to comprehension, retention, and overt action. Most people hear but few really listen. Listening will be a critically needed skill in an electronic age because it, along with perceiving, will ultimately make obsolete the skill of reading. Already students listen to recordings of books; and adults, in their offices, homes, or on the highway, listen to recordings of speeches or meetings. Even amidst a background of television, radio revivals of dramatic programs of yesteryear repeatedly occur and are accepted with much fanfare. In the future listening, together with seeing, will be taught as routine and accelerated skills. For example, a 2-hour television learning experience may be recorded and played back at a fraction of its original speed. "Fast See" will then become operative as the perceiver tries to comprehend the message or plot of the production in a very short interval of time. "Fast Hear" will also be possible as listening skills are speeded up, with a combination of these two skills resembling traditional speed reading. Training in listening will not only include surface skills but also subliminal detection.

Intuiting, the last of the techno-basics, is coming to grips with electronic realities, anticipating and apprehending as well as discovering the meaning or multiple perspectives in a computed or televised message, together with the apprehension of the conceptual totality it signifies. Intuiting is creative intelligence for an electronic age, to be learned by children and adults and mastered by teachers and administrators, particularly the director of information systems, who will function primarily as tomorrow's change agent.

The techno-basics owe their origin to emerging communication and techno-relations techniques and principles. The fact that they constitute the coping skills for an electronic age makes their acquisition essential. Schools that begin to inculcate these basics into their curricula now will assure for the upcoming century discriminating and interactive educational audiences, capable of quickly assimilating and acting on large quantities of information electronically. In such an age knowing and accessing become virtually the same, but communicating and relating can be entirely different. The overall effectiveness of educational public relations in the 21st century will largely depend on how well people will be able to relate to images rather than to other people. Synergy by air is much different than by land.

SUMMARY

Technology is rapidly changing conventional forms of communication, with the influx of computers, video equipment, cable linkages, and satellite dishes flooding the American scene. As a result of this massive influx the shape of both schools and their curricula, as well as the nature of educational public relations, is likely to undergo a dramatic transformation. In the 21st century learning will move from today's classrooms into residentially based learning studios and into the home itself; and educational public relations efforts, transmitted from a central educational facility called the information hub, will, with ease, pervade an entire community.

This electronic age of educational public relations will require of educational leaders a working knowledge of new techniques and principles, subsumed under the broad headings of communication and techno-relations, which, when coupled, make up what is known as the Gemini PR Model. In this model standard communication understandings are drastically altered, and the human relations element of educational public relations is supplanted by its facsimile techno-relations. Behind the helm of this electronic form of educational public relations stands a director of information systems, who devises and implements electronic public relations strategies and acts as the change agent for tomorrow's schools.

To ensure a discriminating and interactive educational audience for the next century, in which information overlead will be a common occurrence, the public schools must begin to introduce within their curricula the techno-basics. Requisite skills for a technological society, these basics must be learned by children and adults and mastered by teachers and administrators, and especially the person who manages the information hub. Educational public relations transmitted electronically entails a unique synergy, and it is up to the public school to prepare its clientele now to adjust to these evolving and inevitable relationships.

• 4 •

The Role of the Educational Public Relations Specialist

Although most educational public relations specialists have similar responsibilities, and many have similar backgrounds, there is considerable variation in their titles. This same variation exists in their salaries, with the latter particularly evident between males and females (Brannen, 1981).

TITLES AND SALARIES

Among the titles commonly used to describe the role of the educational public relations specialist are Director of Public Relations, Director of Public Information, Director of Information Services, Director of School-Community Relations, Communications Coordinator, Communications Specialist, Public Information Officer, Administrative Assistant, and Media Coordinator (National School Public Relations Association [NSPRA], 1982-1983).

One explanation for this diversity may be attributed to the Madison Avenue image that the term public relations often conjures in the minds of the schools' publics and officials, boards as well as administrators. Intent upon avoiding the suggestion of superficiality or flimflam, so often associated with this image, school officials opt for less connotative titles. Public relations as publicity is generally viewed as a luxury that schools can ill afford to count among their educational trappings. This is especially true when money is tight, unemployment is high, and fiscal accountability is synonymous with a stabilization or reduction of local taxes. Then public relations of any kind becomes suspect as a frill.

School-community relations, but a facsimile of public relations, is euphemistically more acceptable than its counterpart because of the ambiguity it offers. Lacking clarity, the term is currently undergoing an expansion of meaning. It has, in some instances, been used to describe the leadership role of the community educator, out of whose efforts effective school-community relations are believed to evolve naturally through process and program-people linkages. The result is that some specialists with this title are experiencing a significant overlapping of job responsibilities.

The fact that many school officials view the individual who occupies the role of educational public relations specialist as primarily a dispenser of information may help to explain why information and communication enjoy a great deal of popularity in titles. With the widespread use of technology, the awesome respect and concern for the computer, and the frequently heralded information society of the not-too-distant future, information and communication descriptors are easier to justify than the term public relations. In an information society information management and interactive communication assume critical importance.

The title Administrative Assistant, although even more elusive than any of the preceding titles, does portend a movement in educational public relations. It denotes a distinct affiliation with the school management function and mirrors the long and hard efforts of educational public relations specialists to be part of that management. Presumably, intrinsic to the title is membership on an administrative team, council, or cabinet and input into the administrative decision-making process.

The title Media Coordinator, although suggesting print and electronic media direction, appears to be not only a close relative of publicity but also a rather narrow descriptor for contemporary public relations function.

The same variation that may be evinced among the titles of educational public relations specialists exists in the salaries they earn. Brannen (1980), using a $5,000 spread in a six-category, arbitrarily chosen range, noted that there were public relations specialists who earned as little as $10,000 and under (8%); those who earned $10,000 to $14,999 (16.5%); those who earned $14,000 to $19,999 (26.5%);

those who earned $20,000 to $24,999 (17.5%); those who earned $25,000 to $29,999 (20.5%); and those who earned as much as $30,000 and over (11%).

However, far more interesting in Brannen's study was the fact that males earned considerably more than females for doing virtually the same kind of work. A second perusal of her data indicates that, whereas 20% of the males earned $30,000 and above, only 2% of the females earned the same amount. A similar dichotomy was evident at the lowest salary level, at which 3% of the males and 13% of the females earned $10,000 and under. Again, although 47% of the males earned from $24,999 to $29,999, 57% of the females earned from $10,000 to $19,999.

Of course, Brannen's data also reveals that more men than women had advanced degrees, more teaching experience, more time on the job, were more often employed on a full-time basis, and served more often on an administrative team (85% of the males as opposed to 70% of the females). More females than males, however, had public relations experience in fields other than education. Brannen, nevertheless, did not consider these differences important enough to merit the salary disparities between the two groups.

Limited to a sampling of public school public relations directors or their equivalent, males and females who were 1978 NSPRA members, Brannen's study did not extend to a sampling of the entire membership of NSPRA. This membership includes superintendents, principals, agency and association personnel, higher education personnel, and others. Had the study provided this kind of coverage, respondent salaries would probably have been quite different.

In contrast to Brannen's study, however, is a 1983 NSPRA (1984) profile of its membership, which includes, among other things, the salaries of responding members. Presented here, for illustrative purposes, in a somewhat collapsed manner, are some of these salaries. At the high end of the salary range, 1% of those polled reported a salary of $60,000 or more; 5% reported salaries of $50,000 to $59,999; and 15%, salaries of $40,000 to $49,999. At the lower end of the salary range, 17% reported salaries of less than $16,000. The salary category with highest percentage of respondents was $30,000 to $34,999 at 20%. Of those polled, 48% were engaged in public relations activities on a full-time basis.

TRADITIONAL AND CONTEMPORARY ROLES

The traditional role of the educational public relations specialist has been that of a scribe and paper mover, whose purpose typically was to inform but often to publicize. Because writing ability was essential to the role, this person was frequently a teacher of English or journalism who grew into the role of an educational public relations specialist. On the other hand, educational public relations specialists were often recruited, as they are today, from outside the field of education and from the ranks of various media specializations, primarily newspapers. For the most part, the duties of the educational public relations specialist were the preparation of annual reports, staff and community newsletters; the recording and publishing of board meeting minutes; the development of brochures for financial campaigns; and even the supervision of the school newspaper, when the position was half- rather than full-time.

Today, however, the role of the educational public relations specialist is seen as a much broader one. Flatt (1982), in fact, lists 20 roles for the contemporary educational public relations specialist. These leadership roles emphasize a variety of skills: publicizing, advertising, marketing (existing and new products and services), and evaluating; writing, editing, and knowing basic graphic design; conducting budget and building referenda campaigns and public relations inservice for administrators and staff; relating effectively to adults and youth in community problem-solving situations; dealing with oral and written complaints and organizing and administering communication plans for school crises; keeping accurate district public relations records; determining alternative futures; and serving not only as the district's peacemaker and public conscience, but also as one of the superintendent's key advisors, which includes speaking for him or her on occasion.

TRAINING AND EXPERIENCE

West (1980), concerned about the manifold skills and talents that an educational public relations specialist must possess to perform necessary public relations duties, queried public relations specialists about the importance of certain kinds of training and experience to their jobs.

Six categories were addressed in the query: experience as a teacher; training as a teacher; experience as a journalist; training as a journalist;

experience as an administrator; and training as an administrator. Of those polled, 64%, located in 93 school districts in 28 states, responded to the survey question. Of those responding, 67% were full-time directors; 33% had a staff of one; and 59% were employed in districts with a student enrollment of less than 6,000 (26%) or of 6,000–11,999 (33%). About 50% of the respondents had an undergraduate major in either English or journalism, 58% were certified as teachers, and 29% were certified as administrators. At the graduate level the most prominent master's degree was administration, whether educational administration (16%) or secondary school administration (1%). At the doctoral level the same held true, with educational administration having been the major of 5 of the 6 doctoral recipients.

The responses of those polled on the question, "Which of the following do you believe are necessary to carrying out your duties?", are ordered from most to least important.

Experience as a Journalist	65%
Experience as an Administrator	49%
Experience as a Teacher	47%
Training as a Journalist	46%
Training as an Administrator	28%
Training as a Teacher	18%

The conclusions drawn from the study were several. The traditional needs of the educational public relations specialist are apparent in the high ranking that journalistic experience (65%) received, but this need is bound to change shortly, a hint of which may be derived from the much lesser value given to journalistic training (46%). Evidently, needed skills are easier to learn on the job, particularly as traditional journalistic training is not geared to the multiplicity of roles educational public relations specialists play in the schools. Nevertheless, the perceived need for journalistic training is admittedly high when compared to administrative and teacher training needs.

The disparity between administrative experience (49%) and training (28%) is best viewed within the context of contemporary certification requirements. Educational public relations specialists need not be certified as either administrators or teachers to gain public relations employment in school districts or to function as an administrative team member. Administrative certification, coupled with teacher certification, does provide educational public relations specialists access to administrative pay scales and to substantially increased salaries. But the additional, and usually extensive, formal coursework required to secure these certificates, when translated into onerous expenditures of time and money, prohibit many noneducation majors from pursuing this course of action. An alternative is offered by NSPRA, which has instituted an accreditation system for its members. By passing an exam, members can become accredited education public relations specialists. Because of its relatively short existence, the accreditation system has yet to become a pervasive influence in the hiring of public relations specialists by school districts. Barring any national or state educational legislation that would place public relations specialists in a distinct administrative certification category, accreditation seems an appropriate goal for all members, regardless of what kind of certification they hold.

Yet there is clear evidence that of those graduate fields currently sought by educational public relations specialists, educational administration ranks the highest. Of course, the choice of this route is understandable, given the fact that it may be perceived as but an administrative stepping-stone for the large number of educational public relations specialists who have been trained and certified as teachers. There is also some evidence that those whose backgrounds (in this study) included administrative certification (29%) were those who favored administrative training (28%). Finally, that administrative experience should be viewed as important by about half of the respondents signals not only a need for well-designed educational public relations administrative preparatory programs but also the direction in which the educational public relations specialist has begun to travel.

The low ranking given to teacher training (18%) seems to suggest that more than a basic understanding of the teaching process is unneeded in the performance of public relations tasks. The educational public relations specialist must know about teaching to write about it or to relate it to the public relations function, as when providing inservice for teachers or when meeting with advisory or community groups. But formal teacher training has little bearing on typical public relations tasks, such as photography, graphic design, brochure development, and survey construction, and therefore is largely viewed as unnecessary.

Perhaps the most important conclusion to be drawn from the disparities between experience and training is that the educational public relations specialist is able to find too few institutional preparatory programs that contribute to the enhancement of educational public relations task performance and that, in the absence of such programs, experience is an appropriate substitute.

It is, perhaps, appropriate to point out here that the background data reported in the preceding study bears a strong relation to the demographics derived from other recent educational public relations studies, with which the author has been closely associated. For example, 58.5% of the total number of respondents in Brannen's (1980) role comparison study of male and female public relations specialists had an undergraduate major of either English or journalism, with English at 20% for males and 22% for females, and journalism at 35% for males and 22% for females. In Dysinger's (1979) comparative study of critical tasks, public relations specialists reported an undergraduate major of 51% for either English or journalism. However, in Oberg's (1983) evaluation study only 43% of the responding public relations specialists reported an undergraduate major in either English or journalism. This discrepancy, though, is probably attributable to the fact that 6%, or 8, of the respondents reported education as a major, without indicating along with it some kind of subject matter specialization, and another 14%, or 19, did not indicate any major at all.

At the master's degree level educational administration was reported as the most frequent major of public relations specialists at 27% (Dysinger, 1979). Similarly, in Dysinger's study 6 out of 7 respondents, or 86%, had a doctorate in educational administration. In Brannen's (1980) study no comparison can be made. In asking for the specialization of the highest degree of public relations specialists, bachelor's, master's, and doctoral, the questionnaire allowed academic majors to overlap and become indistinguishable. Still, educational administration, which can only be a graduate major, was reported at 25%. In Oberg's study, 21% of the responding public relations specialists reported a master's degree in educational administration, and the figure may be even higher as an additional 3% simply reported administration as a major. In Dysinger's study 63% of the respondents reported teacher certification. In the other two studies this question was not asked.

Again, in Brannen's study 77% of the respondents, 82% of the males and 73% of the females, were employed full-time as public relations specialists. In Dysinger's study 84% of the public relations specialists reported full-time positions. In Dierksen's (1982) study 85% of the respondents reported full-time public relations employment, whereas in Oberg's study only 78% reported full-time positions.

Other pertinent demographic data, such as administrative team membership and school district or community size, are treated in areas that specifically deal with them.

FUTURE ROLES

The evolving interest and growth in the management function in educational public relations has not been unexpected. In fact, when attention is focused on the results of a 1978 Delphi study (Lester & West, 1979), much of the impetus behind this management thrust becomes obvious. Two-thirds of the national leaders engaged in the study (slightly over 20 in number) were forecasting administration as the top priority area for educational public relations specialists to pursue in both the near (0–5 years) and not-too-distant (10–20 years) future.

Administration, as it was then interpreted by these nominated experts, was to include as high or top priority tasks not only the providing of aid and advice in public relations to board and administration (superintendents as well as principals), but the developing of communication strategies that would promote educational credibility and confidence among the schools' publics. Although devising methods of evaluation and making education a national priority were viewed as high priority tasks for the first time period, decision-making assistance to top management through information support was to take precedence during the subsequent time period.

Professionalism, a close runner-up in terms of public relations priorities, added significantly to the administrative concerns of specialists. Under the category of professionalism recognition was sought for public relations as a profession and perceived by leaders as a high priority for time period one. On the other hand, the elevation of the public relations role to top management status was stressed by them as a high priority for time period two. Professionalism also targeted as high priorities for both time periods the building of competence, the development of research skills, and the acquisition of expertise in five distinct areas: social sciences, communications, technology, marketing, and politics.

Perhaps somewhat less directly the category inservice was to aim at bolstering professionalism and the management function. Through inservice the immediate school family would learn the importance of educational public relations and how to practice it successfully. Beyond the typical public relations tasks, community as a high-priority category reflected the management function when it stressed public relations program development to facilitate understanding between the administration and its diverse publics in the matter of school direction. Involvement in the management function could be seen in the category finance, in which communication was directed at both citizens and legislators to procure funding; but task emphasis here and in the categories staff and integration relegated these categories to only a minor role in the total public relations drama.

The foregoing high-priority categories and the tasks that comprised them were derived and collapsed from a list of 133 Delphi leader identified tasks. For time period one, these categories and tasks numbered 7 and 33, respectively. Administration received top billing in the line-up with 9 high-priority tasks. Subsequent categories and tasks in this period were as follows: inservice and professionalism, each with 7 tasks; community with 6 tasks; staff with 2 tasks; and 1 each for integration and finance.

In time period two, administration with 8 tasks once again ranked highest as a category, followed by community, inservice, and professionalism, each with 6 tasks, and finance and staff, each with 2 tasks (Lester, 1979). Spanning both time periods were 28 of these high-priority tasks.

Perhaps one of the most important conclusions that can be drawn from this study is that the role of the educational public relations specialist, admittedly already expansive, is likely to increase in complexity; and as it does, so will its management function.

Although it is conceivable that educational public relations specialists may take on a variety of roles during the next couple of decades, there seems to be ample justification for speculation about the emergence and relevance of five distinct management roles (West, 1982).

Information Management and Techno-Relations

As indicated earlier, technology (essentially the computer and wall-sized television screen supported by a maze of communication devices, which link educational facility with residential learning sites and the living room of the home) may be expected to alter drastically the role of the educational public relations specialist, magnifying, as it were, almost exponentially the information management function. The need for techno-relations and techno-basics, principally computer and visual literacy, will exacerbate this change.

In a recent study conducted by the NSPRA, classroom computers were not only viewed by the vast majority of principals sampled (82.3%) as contributing to the improvement of student learning, they were described in glowing terms when their overall importance in the classroom was addressed (NASSP, 1983). Yet, although the drive for computer literacy is important, so is a parallel push for visual literacy. Today students, by the time they are 18 years old, have spent more time in front of a television set than they have in the classroom (Burke, 1981). As computer and visual literacy achieve prominence in education, the high tech/high touch skills of the information manager will be much in demand.

To reap its benefits, people must learn to live with technology. Technology can bring people together in new and exciting ways (West, 1983). It is up to the educational public relations specialist to make possible what many now construe as not only impossible, but in-humane.

Community Relations Manager

In recent years the educational public relations specialist has become increasingly and often directly involved with the school's community, chairing or holding membership on school advisory committees, establishing and implementing school volunteer programs and speakers bureaus, organizing an array of senior citizen activities, responding to and relaying community complaints, and determining through polling techniques community attitudes about and expectations for the schools, as well as the aspirations parents have for their children.

Added to this involvement is the dual role that educational public relations specialists, along with community education directors, are beginning to play under the rubric of school-community relations, or its equivalent, which sometimes merges the responsibilities of both roles. This is quite understandable, however, as these roles have much in common, including the acquisition and practice of traditional public relations skills as they affect paper, electronic, and people communications.

Committee linkages between the two national groups, NSPRA and the National Community Education Association (NCEA), have acquainted many educational public relations specialists with the community education philosophy and prompted their support for the community education movement. Linkages also have been evident in the conference sessions of these associations. In school systems that employ both role incumbents, efforts to foster high levels of community activity often cause the two to work closely together in a central office setting. At the university level professors who teach community education often teach educational public relations as well.

As technology gradually melds the home with the school and workplace, familial and neighborhood activity may be expected to intensify. With this intensification, community education will pervade not only the home, but virtually every aspect of community life that can be labeled educative. This pervasiveness will be manifested in the K-12 curriculum, in traditional community education program offerings for adults and children, and in the manifold processes that promote responsible two-way communication and participation of community members in the institutions, agencies, and organizations that serve them. The net result will be the emergence of a single role that absorbs the function and accoutrements of both educational public relations specialist and community education director and that goes by the title of community relations specialist or manager.

Consumer Relations Manager

According to a recent Gallup poll (Gallup, 1983), 51% of the public were in favor of a voucher system, with an additional 11% currently expressing no opinion. Again, although 41% of the public school parents polled were opposed to the voucher, 48% favored such a system. Thus, despite wholesale and laborious efforts of educators and associations to ward off the voucher, popular opinion is turning the tide in its favor. While the release of the National Commission on Excellence in Education report, A Nation at Risk, may have helped to prompt this upsurge of feeling, the public's perpetual vacillation in regard to the merits of education is by now legendary.

Since the late 1970s educators have been preoccupied with strategies to restore public confidence in education. Educational associations have come to the fore with numerous suggestions. Yet few of them have been so stalwart as the Excellence Commission's indictment (American Association of School Administrators [AASA], 1983) to the public schools to emphasize in their curricula what it refers to as the new basics. But these basics, with the exception of a half year of computer training, actually signify what might be construed as a reemphasis of the traditional basics, namely a college preparatory curriculum. These basics, although admittedly important, might not be as basic as they first appear, given the growth of technology in present day society.

Generally little is said about improving consumer relations, except what may be implied from current marketing approaches heralded by educational public relations specialists. On the other hand, much is said about declining test scores and growing discipline problems that impede classroom learning. The fact that the cultivation of consumer relations strategies is necessary to overcome either of these problems is seldom broached.

The results from the implementation of a modified voucher plan in a California school district revealed that parents enjoy the opportunity to function as educational consumers. To be able to choose specific programs for their children from an array of curricula held a certain appeal for them (West, 1974). Should a full-scale voucher system be established, this range of choice would be broadly expanded and diversified.

Competing for the consumer's educational voucher might precipitate a deluge of quick learning claims by newly established schools and generate a dire need for consumer counseling. Marketing claims would have to be investigated and standards of curricula monitored and published with some regularity. What is more, the need for consumer relations managers would be as appropriate in public school settings as it would be in private. For, surely, the school that failed to meet consumer needs and preferences would be the school that was short-lived.

However, even if the voucher does not materialize in K-12 education, the public's continuing concern about educational accountability, coupled with the element of choice it has experienced in magnet school settings, dictates that the parent and child and any other educational participant be viewed as clients, or customers, whose preferences must be heeded if continuing support for the public schools is to be forthcoming. As marketing appeals to educational consumers increase in effort and sophistication, one of the roles of the educational public relations specialist is likely to be within the sphere of consumer relations management.

Employee Relations Manager

Educational public relations has a natural affinity with the field of personnel administration. Both fields stress communication and human relations principles and strategies. In recruiting, interviewing, and inducting, the effective communication of policies and practices become crucial, be they those of a public school system or an industrial concern. Recruitment calls for the projection of an institutional or company image and often involves the participation of model employees at recruitment sites to attract their counterparts. Educational public relations, as publicity, serves in a similar fashion as it attempts to project the image of an ideal teacher or school.

An integral part of recruitment is the array of employee brochures that describe the merits of an organization to prospective newcomers, much as a speakers bureau brochure developed by an educational public relations specialist is designed to attract an audience and spread institutional good will through community service. But educational public relations specialists are frequently the creators of both kinds of brochures, their tasks overlapping with those of the personnel administrator.

Interviewing, too, requires proficient public relations skills, as annoying personal traits and mannerisms can easily discomfit the interviewee and mar the interviewing process. Successful two-way communication, so essential in the interviewing process, largely depends on the leader's ability to speak and listen effectively, a fact well recognized by both personnel administrators and educational public relations specialists.

Induction and even withdrawal, specifically resignation, also capitalize on effective communications. As school employees come to learn about their jobs, so, too, the community is kept informed about its schools. Similarly, the employee who leaves the school district is, in many respects, like the parent who decides to move out of a school district. In both cases, communication becomes important to determine the cause.

Personnel administration, like educational public relations, uses the media as a communication device, the former to advertise job openings and the latter to highlight the employees who have been selected to fill them. The dial-a-job telephone approach to employment seekers is also a good deal like the telephone hot line that aims to keep community members alerted to changes in school format.

Then there is the technique of surveying, which both fields must utilize to gauge attitudes and satisfactions. Although principally a technique used by educational public relations specialists to gauge community satisfaction with schools, it is sometimes used, as in business and industry, to detect levels of employee satisfaction and morale.

Finally, there is the educational public relations specialist's emergent role in collective negotiations, which, although frequently disputed as to nature and extent, seems to be expanding in importance, making the public relations specialist the information half of a collective bargaining duo with the chief negotiator. This role has encompassed communication planning for strikes as well as information strategies to keep the public informed.

The result of this overlapping of tasks, coupled with the rising prominence of the collective bargaining aspect of educational public relations, makes the educational public relations specialist a prime candidate for the role of employee relations manager. It is noteworthy that in a number of districts the public relations and personnel function are already being performed by a single person.

Governmental Relations Manager

In an age of accountability and tight money, lobbying at state and federal levels for financial support becomes extremely important. Lobbying for public school funds typically takes place through educational associations and organizations, in which strength of numbers helps to influence legislators; but it may also be initiated at the local level and carried to state and national levels.

In the past public school systems have not been put in the tenuous position of competing with other institutions or agencies for funds; however, the tenor of the times, with its shifting emphasis at the federal level from categorical to block grant funding to states, has tended to transform local priorities into statewide discretionary concerns. Competition has been preeminent, therefore, not only among state departments of education and the programs they represent, but also within local school districts in the kinds of curricula and services they can continue to provide.

At the local level public school systems have even been compelled to compete with municipal governments for a piece of the state pie. Competition for funding has often been keen.

Financial crusades to reduce taxes have added significantly to the funding dilemma. Rising school property, and consumer costs, coupled with declining enrollments and "back to basics" outcries, have precipitated a plethora of citizen actions to ward off tax increases and even diminish school spending through reductions in force and curricular cutbacks.

With pressures mounting on all sides, lobbying and grant writing become prerequisites to a sound school financial program, with the ability to communicate and interpret school budgetary needs to a variety of publics an absolute must. The result is that an educational public relations specialist, whose background includes a knowledge of school finance and the political sciences, will have an opportunity to direct his or her writing and speaking, as well as human relations skills, to the legislative arena. Familiar, also, with a host of legislative funding and private foundation sources, this governmental relations manager (whose facsimile is, in fact, already active in educational associations) will be centered in large metropolitan school districts or serve a consortium of small school districts.

ADMINISTRATIVE TEAM MEMBERSHIP

The management function in educational public relations grows. Over the past few years there has been a steady increase in the number of educational public relations specialists serving on administrative teams. In early 1979 Dysinger reported that 78% of those public relations specialists surveyed in his study were members of administrative teams. Later, Brannen (1980) indicated that about the same number of public relations specialists (77.5%), of whom 85% were males and 70% were females, were serving on administrative teams. In 1982 Dierksen showed 83%, and in 1983 Kazemzadeh, in this case reporting the perceptions of superintendents and not educational public relations specialists, came up with a figure of 86%.

Convinced that administrative team membership made a difference in the role educational public relations specialists played, Dierksen (1982) compared the responsibilities of public relations team and nonteam members. The result was that the two groups differed significantly in their perceptions on 33 out of a possible 45 selected PR responsibilities, 25 of which were labeled as very important and 8 as important. The greatest difference between the two groups was in the responsibility of attending administrative team meetings, which public relations team members, far more than public relations nonteam members, saw as an integral part of their job. Following this item were 3 other closely related team responsibilities, namely, providing general (all topics) and specific (public relations) information to other administrative team members at team meetings and voting on issues that arose during these meetings.

Several other important responsibilities of public relations team members centered on the specific relationships they had with their superintendents. Directed at the facilitation of superintendent-media relations, but extending into the realm of general communications, they consisted of having the public relations team member not only prepare the superintendent for oral and written contact with the media, but also prepare his or her speeches. In turn, the superintendent kept the public relations team member informed about proposed press releases and policy changes. Similarly, charged with the leadership responsibility of working with the media, the public relations team member served as the chief spokesperson for the district.

The comparison also indicated that relations between board and public relations specialist were much more profound at the team member level, at which opportunities to participate in agenda preparation, public relations policy development, and board meeting discussions were greater for public relations team members than for public relations nonteam members. Additional, though disparate responsibilities, included communication during negotiations or strikes with staff and community members, interpreting the school district budget and varied legislation to the community, conducting public opinion polls and programs for new residents, and evaluating the overall public relations program.

Responsibilities that reflected only important differences involved, among other things, inservice for new program presentations for school district personnel, chairing citizen-school advisory committees, authorization to use school files, and board meeting attendance. Other important differences characterizing the team role of the public relations specialist were a job description that denoted team membership, membership on a team that met regularly, and direct access to the superintendent.

For the most part, the responsibilities of public relations team members remained unchanged when compared by various categories of school district size (40 out of 45). However, when the possession of administrative certification was considered as a factor in determining the responsibility differences among public relations team members, the outcome became somewhat more pronounced, with 12 out of 45 tasks. These differences were judged by Dierksen to be important enough to state that certification does pave the way for additional management responsibilities.

In a subsequent study Kazemzadeh (1983) compared the perceptions of superintendents with and without public relations specialists on administrative teams, using the same 45 responsibilities that Dierksen had used. The result was that the two groups of superintendents differed significantly in their perceptions 32 out of 45 times, with higher values given to the responsibilities by superintendents with public relations specialists holding membership on administrative teams.

These differences suggested that public relations specialists holding administrative team membership were much more involved in the decision-making processes of their school systems than were those who held no such membership. The working relationships of public relations team members with board, superintendent, and administrative team colleagues were significantly stronger than the relationships that public relations nonteam members enjoyed working with these same groups. Aside from the heightened responsibilities of team members that directly gave rise to these strengthened relationships were a number of other important responsibilities. Included among them were consulting with central office personnel on public relations matters; providing public relations inservice for teachers; keeping internal and external publics informed about new programs; offering direction to citizen-school advisory committees; polling public opinion; leading the district's public relations advisory committee; preparing communication plans during negotiations and strikes; and coordinating financial campaigns.

Size of school district and educational preparation and experience of superintendents having public relations specialists on administrative teams did not affect the way they perceived this team member's role. Moreover, team members were substantially in agreement with these superintendents. However, whereas superintendents with team members emphasized tasks that involved people relations, public relations team members tended to stress management function tasks.

According to superintendents, the major contribution of public relations team members to administrative teams was in explaining how administrative decisions might affect the school's public relations. That part of the public relations team member's role that superintendents would most like to see strengthened was in improving administrative-board relations.

SUMMARY

Although educational public relations specialists go by a variety of titles and are paid appreciably different salaries, they share, to a considerable extent, responsibilities and backgrounds. Most serve on the superintendent's administrative team, cabinet, or council. Those who do not have somewhat different responsibilities. Those who are administratively certified also seem to have differing responsibilities. Moreover, educational public relations specialists who are certified as public school administrators typically earn higher salaries than their counterparts. Too, administrative certification paves the way for promotion up the school management hierarchy.

Once viewed largely as scribes and paper movers, educational public relations specialists are becoming strongly identified with the school management function, and this trend is likely to grow. What is needed, though, is an increase in the number of higher educational institutions that offer programs tailored to the diversified needs of educational public relations specialists. Educational administration appears to be the most sought after graduate program by these specialists; but even this program, as it is generally constructed, does not provide a satisfactory response to their expanding role. Programs that are in tune with the management role of educational public relations specialists would have to focus on five basic areas: information management and techno-relations, community relations, consumer relations, employee relations, and governmental relations.

In the late 1970s a Delphi forecast indicated that administration and professionalism were high priorities of educational public relations specialists. With its management stress and its accreditation program, NSPRA has taken a significant step toward achieving the image desired by its membership. State departments of education and universities should follow in step to this drumbeat, the first by designing a unique set of requirements for educational public relations specialists; the second by offering a curricula that meets not only these immediate requirements for educational public relations specialists, but also those that the future portends.

• 5 •

Purpose

The educational public relations process, as defined herein, consists of four parts: purpose, plan, participants, and politics. This chapter deals only with purpose.

Purpose may be implicit or directly expressed. If implicit, purpose is likely to evoke only limited action, changing, as it were, as the issue that spawned it is either mitigated or intensified. An implicit purpose has an illusive history, good only so long as it is remembered by the leaders whose conjurations or actions gave it meaning. If directly expressed, purpose becomes etched in policy, has a sense of history and continuity, and serves as a formal guide to all action.

Written and adopted as policy, purpose results in a plan. Effectively developed, implemented, and assessed, this plan becomes synonymous with purpose. The success of a plan depends on many factors: the integrity and rationality that it reflects; the amount of time and money spent on making it work; the technology and facilities to accommodate it; the strategies to ensure its smooth operation; and the efforts of participants, individuals and groups, whose needs, interests, and aspirations it embodies and serves.

If appropriately motivated, organized, and activated, participation assures that purpose will be fulfilled. But participation, along with purpose and plan, can be drastically affected by the political milieu in any community. Community groups intentionally or inadvertently exert pressures on the school. Some of these pressures stem from conflicts of purpose; others spring up because of limited or irrelevant participation.

While the educational public relations process recognizes the importance of differing viewpoints and the inevitability of conflict, it makes
every effort to keep this conflict at a minimal and manageable level.
Pluralistic thought and action is compatible with a democratic society,
but unrelenting and unremediated conflict makes an institution or
organization dysfunctional. When each of its parts is optimally interrelated, the educational public relations process is functioning at its best.

Although the purposes of an educational public relations program
may range from selling to synergizing in a given school district, the
overriding purpose of such a program at the national level has been in
recent years the building or regaining of the public's confidence in its
schools. A strong concern of NSPRA at its annual seminar in Houston in
1977, rebuilding public confidence became the theme of the association's seminar the following year in Portland, Oregon. *Building Public
Confidence in Your Schools* was, in fact, published by the association in
that same year.

The concern of NSPRA was shared by other associations as well,
among them the American Association of School Administrators
(AASA), which had two presidential messages focus on the theme of
public confidence in 1979. Whereas the first highlighted public confidence improvement (AASA, 1979b), the second stressed public confidence building. Indeed, a symposium was conducted by AASA in 1979
on restoring public confidence. Included in its goals were two of
particular importance here: a good communication program and a
policy that clearly underwrites it (AASA, 1979a).

One good indication of public confidence has been the alphabetical
rating (A through F), given by a sampling of the schools' publics in the
annual Gallup polls printed in the *Phi Delta Kappan.* Thus, in 1981
there was some reassurance in the leadership ranks of education that the
decline in the public's confidence in its schools was at a standstill.
Although a rise was not evident, neither was further erosion (Gallup,
1981).

In 1983, however, there was an indication that public confidence
had resumed its erosive path. For example, combined ratings of As and
Bs assigned to the public schools by the public declined from 36% in
1982 to 31% in 1983, with C grades also showing a slight decline of 2%
and combined D and F grades at 20% for both years. In 1974, 48% of
the public graded its schools with either an A or a B, a difference of 15%

over 1983. IN 1974, 11% of the public gave the public schools either a D or an F; in 1983, the combined percentage for these grades rose to 20%. In 1974, also, 64% of parents with children in the public schools gave their schools an A or B rating, whereas in 1983, only 42% did so. Ratings were even lower when they came from individuals who were familiar with the National Commission on Excellence in Education report. Of this informed group, only 12% gave the public schools an A or B rating, and 30% gave them a rating of D or F (Gallup, 1983).

It would be presumptuous to maintain that an effectively planned, administered, and evaluated educational public relations program is the panacea for resolving the public confidence dilemma. However, an educational public relations program does promise a free flow of information between school and community and assures respect for and recognition of the public's right to know. Information is, after all, a determining factor in the shaping of public attitudes. Conversely, people who are deprived of information or kept poorly informed about the institutions that are meant to serve them harbor a mistrust for these same institutions and withhold support when it is badly needed.

An educational public relations program is built on credibility and trust. With integrity and dispatch it initiates school to community communications through print and nonprint mediums, keeping the public knowledgeable about its schools. It also creates a multiplicity of structures that are conducive to person-to-person involvement in the schools. In effect, a fundamental purpose of an educational public relations program is to keep the public fully apprised about its schools and wholly involved in them.

Thus, the determination of purpose is not a matter to be taken lightly by public school leaders; for what is ultimately decided is far reaching in effect. Schools no longer exist in a vacuum. The agrarian school facilaty of yesteryear has been largely displaced by a vast network of educational complexes that have access to a surprising amount of information about one another. What one school system does well, others soon learn abouat and often emulate. If enough do it and they do it in concordance, their actions are imbued with force and meaning.

Nonetheless, the virtues of the little red schoolhouses must never be forgotten. The building of public confidence begins at the local level. Purpose directed toward the fulfillment of local goals compounded will inevitably address and allay national concerns. In this sense, members of both the immediate and extended school family must partake in the development of purpose. Then, and only then, can the purpose of an educational public relations plan begin to inspire confidence.

SUMMARY

Purpose is an integral part of the educational public relations process, along with plan, participants, and politics. Without purpose there is no educational public relations plan. Without a written plan, or policy, purpose is transitory. While participation shapes purpose, the political milieu of a community often dictates who will participate in the determination of purpose and what this purpose will be. At the national level purpose has been directed toward the restoration of the public's vacillating confidence in its schools. At the local level purpose is meant to reflect, through extensive participation, grassroots' goals. As goals are repeatedly met and purposes realized, the likelihood of a rise in public confidence across the nation is substantially increased.

• 6 •

Plan

Educational public relations programs do not come into existence of their own accord. Somebody has to provide the necessary leadership to transform purpose into policy and policy into a set of activities that can be evaluated. That individual is the superintendent of schools. The superintendent must convince the board of education not only that a school system needs effective public relations to gain or maintain the approval and support of its public, but also that a well-planned public relations program will meet this need. This may take a little or a lot of convincing on the part of the superintendent.

Charged with the important trust of administering public funds, boards feel obliged to exercise considerable prudence and to weigh frugally benefit against cost in their policy deliberations. For example, in an Indiana study that had secondary school principals assess public relations efforts in their school districts, 80% indicated that although their boards were interested in effective educational public relations, only 25% of these boards had earmarked funds for this purpose (Caress, 1979).

Nevertheless, although it is often difficult to specify and enumerate precisely what a public relations dollar will buy, it is relatively easy to point to a plethora of problem areas that a modicum of internal or external public relations might help to alleviate. These problem areas may range from poor student and faculty morale to general community dissatisfaction, frequently precipitated by a lack of information or misinformation and manifested most clearly in people problems and in repeated failures at the polls in the passage of budget or bond referenda.

In the performance of their myriad duties, board members need all the assistance they can get. An effective districtwide public relations program can provide much of this assistance, but the recognition and acceptance of this fact must be brought home by the superintendent. Understandably so, boards, like many other segments of society, have a tendency to consider an educational public relations program to be more frill than necessity.

The simplest way to create public relations awareness among board members is to describe the nature, purpose, and extent of an educational public relations program, along with the benefits that may be derived from its implementation. This explanation should be accompanied by district produced or purchased audio-visual materials. The best source of these materials is NSPRA.

A second way is to sample by mail, phone, or personal interview the opinions of internal and external publics to determine satisfaction and dissatisfaction with various aspects of the school. Once problem areas have been identified, strategies can be formulated that display the efficacy of an educational public relations program.

A third way is through case study simulations that tax the ingenuity of board members in solving public relations problems. The assumption is that application elicits insights into the intricate web of educational public relations, and that these brief but intensive glimpses will induce boards to develop an appreciation for planned public relations. Cases that present public relations problems common to most school districts are frequently the fare of seminars, workshops, and association meetings, which board members should be encouraged to attend.

A fourth way to create awareness is through interschool visitations that enable board members to observe model public relations programs. As each school is at the same time similar to and uniquely different from any other school, it is not recommended that programs be adopted in their entirety. Rather, only those components that seem relevant to the district contemplating an educational public relations program should be transplanted.

Still another way of achieving awareness is the use of a needs assessment committee. Functioning as a data-gathering body, this committee can provide board members with the information necessary to determine not only programmatic need, but also areas in which concerted public relations efforts should be made. This committee may provide, as well, the impetus for the development of districtwide and building-level public relations advisory committees.

Finally, consultants may be used to engender board awareness. Professors in educational administration departments who teach educational public relations or its equivalent can amply provide both justification and direction for starting a program. Private consultants specializing in educational public relations can do the same. Also, NSPRA offers a talent pool that can be tapped for this purpose. Institutions of higher education that offer specific training in educational public relations can be of especial assistance to boards, as they are capable of providing lists of employed public relations graduates that can render a similar service.

POLICY DEVELOPMENT

Educational public relations programs unsustained by written policies tend to vary widely in purpose and are of short duration. Although the fact that a policy is written does not guarantee programmatic effectiveness, a written policy does offer direction, continuity, support, and even a legal defense (Bortner, 1972). A written policy also makes clear to board, administration, and staff their communications responsibilities (McCloskey, 1967). Just as important is that a written public relations policy may be viewed as a pledge of financial support for the total educational public relations program (Mayer, 1974).

Participants

There are six aspects of educational public relations policy development. The first is participants, comprised primarily of the who's and how's of policy development. For example, will the board alone determine what a public relations policy is to be like, or will an educational public relations advisory committee make that decision? Again, will the policy be written by the superintendent or by the public relations specialist and merely be approved by the board? Will it be districtwide or individually determined in schools by building-level administrators? Then, too, will an outside consultant be called in to help determine the essentials of the public relations policy? In any event, who does what and how is an important phase in public relations policy development.

Values

The second aspect of educational public relations policy development is values. They set the stage for goal determination. Some of these values are whether schools are to be sold to the public or whether teaching excellence is the best kind of public relations; whether an informed public is supportive or an informed staff, productive; and whether citizen participation imparts direction and meaning to the school program or whether professional educators need no assistance in running the schools. A school system may hold a multiplicity of values, yet until they are crystallized in policy, they are as fleeting as the content of yesterday's newspaper.

Goals

Goals represent another phase of educational public relations policy development. A commonly stated goal, to establish a two-way communication system between the school and its various publics, has its basis in the value that support is achieved through effective two-way communication systems between school and community. Another common goal is to survey community attitudes and expectations about the schools to guide board and administrative action. It is derived from the value that community attitudes and expectations about the schools are important for boards and administrators to know. Other common goals are to develop a good working relationship with the media, to disseminate information to the school's publics, and to eliminate rumor and misunderstanding. Less common goals are to provide inservice for board members, administrators, and teachers and to interpret the school budget to the school's various publics. Yet the fact that these last goals are less common in no way impinges on their importance. Goals are tailored to the values of a particular school-community and may, therefore, vary from district to district.

Structure

Structure, the next aspect of educational public relations policy development, pertains not only to who has what responsibilities in carrying out the public relations program and whether these responsibilities are defined by policy, but also to how the public relations policy is to be written. Out of these responsibilities several questions arise, among them the following: To whom should the public relations specialist report? Should principals carry out their own public relations programs, or should central office personnel alone be charged with this responsibility? Should the roles of board members, administrators, teachers, and other school personnel, including the public relations specialist, be defined in policy?

Structure raises other questions, too. Should the policy be written in broad policy language, giving the superintendent considerable discretion in determining how it should be interpreted and implemented? Should the policy rigorously spell out plans and procedures, be a series of goal statements, perhaps, written behaviorally or expressed in the form of a legal resolution? Should policy be developed from a study of board meeting minutes or from a study of other school district public relations policies? Structure, in effect, sets the parameters of the educational public relations policy, providing the necessary organization for its functioning.

Strategies

Strategies, the fifth aspect of public relations policy development, is concerned with the initiation and extent of activity specified by policy. On one hand, this policy development aspect focuses on who should determine and develop the various tactics alluded to in a public relations policy: superintendent, principals, public relations specialist, or public relations advisory committee. On the other hand, it addresses the extent to which these tactics should be included or specified within a public relations policy. Strategies, an important guidepost to policy implementation, is often overlooked as a viable aspect of public relations policy development. Fearful that specificity will restrict behavior and limit alternatives, policy makers have a tendency to opt for generalities that invite ambiguity.

Assessment

The sixth aspect of public relations policy development is assessment. Without some provision for assessment within a public relations policy, evaluation is frequently an afterthought rather than a preplanned method of measuring outcomes. The commitment to assessment must, therefore, be an integral part of public relations policy development if goals are to be realized. This need for assessment may be contained in a single statement, which points to an ongoing or annual assessment, or even a periodic review. It may also identify the assessor or assessors, board, superintendent, principals, public relations specialist, public relations advisory committee, or outside consultant. What is most important is that policy clearly indicates that some sort of assessment is to be undertaken. This policy directive will ensure that assessment occurs.

In a public relations policy development study conducted by West (1981), educational public relations specialists employed in public school settings were polled nationwide to determine the ideal ingredients of a public relations policy. In this study the six aspects of public relations policy development previously described were translated into 93 selected *is* and *ought* public relations policy development statements. In responding to the two-sided statements, participants were asked to indicate not only how public relations policy was currently constructed in their school districts, but also how it ought to be constructed in them. Used to measure their responses was a 5-point scale that ranged from always to never.

The study ultimately reflected the opinions of 74 educational public relations specialists in 25 states and the District of Columbia, or about half of those polled. States represented were Arizona, California, Colorado, Florida, Georgia, Kansas, Illinois, Indiana, Maryland, Massachusetts, Michigan, Minnesota, Missouri, Nebraska, New Jersey, New York, Nevada, North Carolina, Ohio, Oregon, Pennsylvania, South Carolina, Texas, Wisconsin, and Wyoming (West, 1982).

In all except three instances there were significant differences between present (or is) and preferred (or ought to be) statements addressing public relations policy development. Two further comparisons were made. The first compared public relations specialists with written public relations policies, without written public relations policies, and with public relations policies being written. The second lumped unwritten and being written public relations policies together and compared them to written policies; the assumption here was that being written was more akin to unwritten than to written, as no indication of extent of completion was given. The results of the three tests produced 41 policy development descriptors. These descriptors provide, in anagram fashion, guidelines for the development of an ideal public relations policy. They are grouped here by the policy development aspect that contained them, with no ranking intended (West, 1981).

Participants

- PR policy is determined by a representative committee of board members, administrators, teachers, parents, students, and the public relations director.
- PR policy is written.
- PR policy is districtwide.

Values

- Support is achieved through effective two-way communication systems between school and community.
- Schools belong to the public.
- The public must have confidence in its schools.
- Community members' attitudes and expectations about their schools are important for boards and administrators to know.
- Excellent teaching is the best kind of PR.
- Schools promote good citizenship.
- The school is an integral part of the community.
- Citizen participation imparts direction and meaning to the school program.
- Keeping the press informed enhances school-community relations.
- Mutual trust between community and school is the foundation of any school PR program.
- An informed staff is productive.
- An open school climate is conducive to effective administrative, staff, student, and parent relationships.
- Open board meetings promote good relations between the system and the news media.

Goals

- To establish a two-way communication system between the school and its various publics.
- To disseminate information to the school's publics.
- To report student achievement.
- To develop a good working relationship with the media.
- To interpret board and administrative action.
- To eliminate rumor and misunderstanding.
- To disseminate information to certificateded and noncertificated personnel.
- To improve communication between parents and teachers.
- To provide PR inservice for teachers.

- To provide PR inservice for board members.
- To provide PR inservice for administrators.
- To interpret the school's curriculum to its publics.
- To interpret the school budget to the school's various publics.

Structure

- The PR director reports directly to the superintendent.
- School principals are responsible for carrying out their own PR programs.
- The school's public relations activities are carried out by both the central office and individual schools.
- PR policy is developed with plans and procedures spelled out, while simultaneously providing the superintendent with sufficient discretion for policy interpretation and implementation.
- The role of the PR director is defined by policy.
- The PR policy is a statement of school philosophy.
- The PR policy is a series of goal statements.
- The PR policy defines PR roles of board members, administrators, teachers, and other school personnel.

Strategy

- PR strategies are developed by the PR director and representative PR committee and approved for implementation by the superintendent.

Assessment

- PR policy specifies procedures for assessment.
- PR policy stipulates ongoing assessment.
- PR policy recommends periodic review.

In a subsequent study Barber (1982) had public school board presidents and superintendents rank these 41 descriptors in terms of their importance in educational public relations policy development. The 5-point scale used to gauge importance ranged from very important to unimportant. The result was that superintendents ranked 30 of these descriptors as important and 10 as moderately important to important. Board presidents, however, ranked only 23 of the descriptors as important to very important, 15 as moderately important to important, and 3 as almost moderately important. These 3 borderline descriptors involved the use of a public relations advisory committee, definition of the public relations roles of various members of the immediate school family, and specificity in assessment procedures. Although the superintendents ranked the importance of the descriptors higher than boards in all three instances, the two groups were in close agreement on slightly better than two-thirds (or 68%) of their rankings.

It is interesting to note that while a public relations advisory committee to determine public relations policy was of modest importance to both groups in Barber's study, the same committee was viewed as making a relatively important contribution to the development of public relations strategies. Similarly, board presidents saw a slightly greater need for public relations inservice for administrators than they did for themselves, and superintendents did likewise, only to a lesser degree. While some disagreement was noted between the rankings of board presidents and superintendents in various sized school districts, with various educational attainments, and with various years of experience in their role, this disagreement was relatively minor in all categories, as it was in the previous study (West, 1983) that measured by size of school district the policy perceptions of educational public relations specialists.

When asked to provide other descriptors they deemed relevant to public relations policy development, superintendents focused on public relations as a total system effort with all personnel having a public relations responsibility and involved in inservice and with good external public relations; on the elimination of rumors and the cultivation of school-community understanding; and on the student as a public relations medium. When asked the same question, board presidents stressed the role of the public relations person in relation to the superintendent and board, with the board providing primary direction; the importance of public trust and confidence; survey research to determine public opinion; administrative and fiscal support for the public relations program; the dissemination of information to publics who no longer have children in schools; the reporting of acts without interpreting them; working with PTAs and other parent groups; the advertising of school benefits; the elimination of apathy; public relations policies that are broad and flexible rather than specific; and a oneness of philosophy (Barber, 1982). Overall, the comments of both groups were more reactive and repetitive than proactive and novel.

Of the superintendents and board presidents included in Barber's study, 59% of the former and 56% of the latter indicated that their school district had a written public relations policy. These figures were only slightly less than the 62% reported by educational public relations specialists in West's (1981) study, which were, in turn, just a little less than the 65% reported in Oberg's (1983) study.

Of greater importance is what serves as public relations policy in many school districts. In West's policy study public relations specialists were asked to submit a copy of their district's public relations policy. In compliance 44 of them offered an array of materials that guided their public relations efforts: almost all of them policies of one kind or another, but some of them no more than job descriptions.

Most of the policies were short and vague, allowing considerable latitude in their implementation. Most made no mention of a public relations specialist, while a few included a job description. Some specified a set of procedures, a couple were behavioral oriented, and one was expressed in the form of a legal resolution. In five instances a job description appeared to serve as a public relations policy. In another instance justification for a public relations program was achieved by a statement in a superintendent's job description. In two other instances a board-approved communications guide and a fact sheet were offered as policy equivalents. In still other instances the existence of a public relations policy had to be subsumed from the submission of a corollary document displaying concept or strategy.

A few of the public relations policies were restricted to publications or to public information. Others, lacking in both value and goal specificity, reflected a similar lack of comprehensiveness. The notion of evaluation was absent in all but a couple of policies. Absent, too, in most policies was any reference to the role or responsibility of district personnel, boards, administrators, teachers, and the like, in the public relations program. A few addressed community relations and citizen involvement, but most were drawn up to be broadly interpreted. The overall result was meager direction for anyone charged with the responsibility of carrying out a public relations program.

It can be argued that vagueness allows for initiative or innovation as the need arises. However, vagueness cannot be expected either to offer program continuity and stability or to lend itself to the routine handling of most public relations activity. On the contrary, vagueness may suggest that little of importance falls within the province of educational public relations, an assumption that is exceedingly erroneous and altogether dangerous.

The 41 descriptors already mentioned provide the basis for the development of an effective educational public relations policy. Although all of these descriptors might not be considered as appropriate for inclusion in a policy befitting the uniqueness of a particular school district, these descriptors are sufficient in number to provide for such flexibility. Therefore, by using the descriptors, it is possible to develop a public relations policy that could be effectively used by most public school districts. This policy is depicted in Figure 4.

Although it is generally acknowledged by school leaders that an effective educational public relations program is an outgrowth of a well-developed public relations policy, there is some evidence that administrative certification programs contribute little or nothing to an understanding of the formulation of public relations policy (West, 1980b). For when the perceptions of public relations specialists who were certified were compared to those who were not on the 186 policy development statements (93 is and 93 ought) mentioned earlier, they disagreed only 3 times on how public relations policy is presently constructed. But never did they disagree on how public relations policy ought to be constructed. One explanation for this sameness was that a satisfactory level of expertise in public relations policy development can be attained independently of formal coursework. Evidently acquired by many through practical experience, this expertise is then shared at public relations workshops and seminars. Another explanation was that many certification programs do not include as a requirement coursework in educational public relations; or, when required, such coursework does not stress policy development.

As the importance of public relations policy is so generally acknowledged by public relations specialists and those who employ them, it would seem that institutions that certify potential educational administrators should take heed of this preparation gap. If public relations programs are to be sustained in the face of massive cutbacks and competing interests, it is imperative that all administrators learn both the value of educational public relations and the intracacies of public relations policy development.

To illustrate how the recommended statements might be used by officials in a school district in the development of a PR policy, the following model has been constructed.

The Board of Education of the Oakpark Public School System believes that the public must have confidence in its schools and that mutual trust between community and school is essential. Community attitudes and expectations are, therefore, important for boards and administrators to know, for support is achieved through effective two-way communication systems between school and community. Citizen participation imparts direction and meaning to the school program and keeping the press (media) informed enhances school-community relations, as an informed staff is a productive one. An open school climate is conducive to effective administrative, staff, student and parent relationships, and open board meetings further enhance good school-press (media) relations.

Given these values, the Oakpark Board sets the following goals to be achieved:

1. To establish a two-way communication system between the school and its various publics (a) to interpret board and administrative action, (b) to eliminate rumor and misunderstanding, and (c) to develop a good working relationship with the media;
2. To disseminate information to certificated and noncertificated personnel;
3. To provide inservice in school public relations to teachers, administrators and board members;
4. To interpret the school's curriculum, along with its budget, to the school's publics; and
5. To report student achievement to parents and the public.

To accomplish these goals, the Oakpark School Board authorizes the employment of a full-time school public relations director, whose responsibility is to see that the school district's public relations activities are carried out by both the central office and individual schools, in which school principals are charged with the responsibility of carrying out their own PR activities with the aid of the school public relations director.

To assist the school public relations director, a school public relations committee will be created by the board. This committee will consist of board members, administrators, staff, students and parents. This committee, under the direction of the school public relations director, will develop strategies to attain district-wide school public relations goals and specific procedures for an ongoing assessment of the school district's public relations program. The school public relations director reports directly to the superintendent of schools.

NOTE: From "The Basics of a Written PR Policy" by P. T. West, 1981, **Journal of Educational Communication**, 4, p. 25. Copyright 1981 by the Educational Communication Center, Camp Hill, PA. Reprinted by permission.

Figure 4   A Sample Policy

PROGRAM LEADERSHIP

Once the public relations policy has been adopted by the board, the next step is to identify the person who can provide programmatic leadership. This means that a job description consonant with the six aspects of public relations policy development, as integrated into board policy, must be constructed. Although it is not unlikely that some boards and administrators would have the public relations specialist write his or her own job description, given the special insights into the overall public relations process either possesses, it is far better that school leaders develop a job description before beginning the employment search. A job description meets two important purposes. It expresses a distinct district need and serves as a gauge for measuring individuals against an approved standard rather than against one another. Without a standard those who are least qualified may be chosen to fill a position.

As indicated earlier, the public relations specialist hired should be, at the very least, a composite of journalist, administrator, and teacher and, at the very most, a budding information systems manager with the ability to assume a variety of other roles somewhere in between. Otherwise, the myriad of tasks expected of today's public relations specialist may not be effectively performed.

Typically, the public relations specialist is or should be employed full time. That a large percentage of them are may be directly borne out by demographic data emanating from various studies, among them Dysinger (1979), 84%; Brannen (1980), 77.5%; West (1980c), 67%; Dierksen (1982), 85%; and Oberg (1983), 78%.

Although Kindred, Bagin, and Gallagher (1976) indicated that there is no absolute standard for determining when a district should employ a full-time public relations specialist, they do believe that a student enrollment of more than 5,000 should suffice. Bortner (1972), coming from a slightly different direction, would have a full-time public relations specialist in school communities with a population of 15,000 or better.

In a 1971 NSPRA study about 50.4% of the public relation specialists surveyed (full- and part-time) were in school districts with student enrollments of less than 10,000, of which 30.4% were in districts with less than 3,000 (Kindred et al., 1976). West (1980c), while reporting on the training and experience needs of public relations specialists for task performance, indicated that 59% of those responding were in school districts with student enrollments of less than 12,000, of which 26% were in districts with less than 6,000. In 1982 Dierksen's administrative team study indicated that 51% of responding public relations specialists were in districts with student enrollments of less than 12,000, of which

25% were in districts with less than 6,000. In Oberg's 1983 evaluation study, 52% of responding public relations specialists were in school districts with less than 12,000, of which 27% were in districts of less than 6,000.

Although it is impractical to suggest that even the very small school district should have a public relations specialist, it is certainly not unreasonable that this sized school district have not only a public relations policy but also a program, however limited the latter may be. In the very small or rural school district, superintendents assume the responsibility of defining and meeting their districts' public relations needs. When help is available, it is usually through the efforts of the regional service center.

Unfortunately, superintendents and service center directors do not always see eye to eye on what kind of public relations services a small school requires. For example, Tolson (1982), in a random sample of some 522 Texas public school systems with an average daily attendance of less than 500 and 19 of the 20 service center directors in Texas, indicated that not only did superintendents feel public relations services were more readily available from service centers than they actually were, but also were such services to become available they would use them only irregularly. Superintendents also disagreed with service center directors on the overall importance of the delivery of public relations services to the small school district, with directors much more aware of these needs than superintendents, although generally unable to fill them to the extent they desired.

For example, whereas only 16% of the service centers offered a communication campaign evaluation service, 50% of the superintendents indicated an awareness of such a service. Although 89% of the directors and 76% of the superintendents saw a need for this service, both felt that it would be used only occasionally if offered. Again, although only 42% of the service centers offered a service for public relations staff development, 63% of the superintendents perceived this service as already being offered. Moreover, although 95% of the directors and 86% of the superintendents evinced a need for this service, it, too, would, according to both groups, be used only occasionally. Even more notable is that only 43% of the superintendents, as opposed to 79% of the directors, felt that their center's communication services would be improved if this service were offered. Disagreement was evident in every comparison of this kind. Despite the fact that both groups (95% of the directors and 86% of the superintendents) saw a need for a service that would institute continuous information programs in the small school, only 42% of the centers offered this kind of service. Yet were it to be offered, this service, like the preceding, would be used only occasionally. Here, too, superintendents thought the service more available than it was, with 63% of them indicating an awareness of its existence.

This disparity of perceptions between the two groups Tolson partly assigns to the high mobility of Texas small school superintendents, who average about 3 years in a district before moving on. Apparently impeding the expansion of service center public relations offerings and the growth of public relations programs in small schools was a dearth of financial resources.

PROGRAM STRATEGIES

With the implementation of the educational public relations program comes the development of a series of strategies that target public relations policy goals. Typically, strategy development falls under the province of the educational public relations specialist, who, in consultation with the superintendent, decides on the appropriateness of the strategies to be used. Preferably, strategies are developed by the district-wide public relations advisory committee, chaired by the public relations specialist or on which he or she functions as a resource person. Optimally, strategy development also involves the input of building-level public relations advisory committees. The entire effort is, of course, one that is coordinated by the central office public relations specialist, who, by networking the public relations function, has created a program that capitalizes on the talent of both school and community.

Through the ratings of educational public relations specialists, in response to selected public relations processes, and through their open-ended responses, Oberg (1983) has been able to determine the usefulness of a variety of public relations strategies to these same public relations specialists in carrying out their programs. When Oberg's lists of ranked ratings and open-ended responses are correlated, combined, and categorized, the most useful of these strategies appear to be as follows:

- *Publications and publicity:* (a) school policies, brochures, calenders, phone directories, and newcomer packets; (b) internal and external school newsletters; and (c) special school programs and services publicity.

- *Media relations:* (a) physical accommodations at school board meetings for media personnel; (b) advanced copy of public statements to media personnel; (c) frequent contact with media personnel; (d) diversified use of media personnel; and (e) conference luncheons with press representatives.

- *Community relations:* (a) personal contact with local citizenry; (b) citizenry information networks; (c) citizen hot lines and surveys; (d) speakers bureau; and (e) special recognition and events such as awards, open house, and public school week.

- *Administrative, staff, and student relations:* (a) personal contact with principals and teachers; (b) staff newsletters and suggestion boxes; (c) districtwide public relations inservice; (d) direct communication with superintendent; (e) involvement of administrative team in public relations; and (f) special recognition of faculty, staff, and students.

- *Business relations:* (a) involvement of business in activities and programs of schools.[2]

As might be expected, the categories suggested by Oberg's list of strategies are sufficiently broad to harbor further inclusions. For example, Parker (1978), in discussing fundamentals of effective school public relations, offers several strategies that may be considered germane to these categories. One, which may be appropriately placed under the category of community relations, is a school volunteer program with senior citizens, who simultaneously teach students and learn about the schools. Another is soliciting correspondence from citizens about how they view their schools. Under the category of media relations, inservice for media personnel in the form of planned visitations might well be included. Too, a school column in the local press, provided space can be obtained at no expense to the school, fits nicely under this category. In the same vein, reporting school news in business newsletters would be an appropriate insertion under the category business relations.

Under the category of publications and publicity, school fact sheets or cards, handbooks, annual reports, and newspapers seem to be justifiable additions. Although unspecified under this category, internal and external newsletters should minimally include a board, staff, and community newsletter. Under the media relations category prepared television or radio shows could be included, as could supplying local newspapers with fillers. These short items of facts about the schools, while filling in space between newspapers stories, help to keep education in the public eye. Under the community relations category parent-teacher conferences should rate important consideration. Notes or cards, spotlighting the progress of students and sent to the home, should also be included, along with kaffeeklatsches that bring administrators and teachers directly into the homes of the school's citizenry. Telephone calls to parents by teachers to help them become better acquainted with their students, or to report academic progress, constitute another worthwhile strategy. Too often, teacher telephone calls are reserved for bad news only. Finally, under the business relations category business involvement would chiefly include career days, demonstrations, volunteerism, classroom visitations to businesses, and student participation, as in "manager" for a day, or the like. Although the implementation of some of these strategies cannot be directly controlled by the public relations specialist, it can be greatly influenced during public relations inservice and administrative team meetings.

Beyond these specific strategies, there are the other, more general, strategies to consider offered by Samstag (1955). These include the strategies of *timing:* acting with forethought to create a desired effect; *forbearance:* waiting quietly, patiently, and virtuously for public criticism to pass; *approach:* keeping those who can affect the outcome of an issue constantly informed about its merits; *surprise:* reversing tactics to gain an edge; *participation:* seeking feedback from one's constituency; *association:* using testimonials of prominent people, with whom the public would like to identify, to secure public approval; *disassociation:* attaining objectivity to dispel the appearance of personal interest; *crossroads:* positioning the organization among the groups it serves to exercise control; *personalization:* in education, making schools synonymous with children; *fait accompli:* acting unilaterally without a policy precedent and in light of possible failure or reprimand; *bland withdrawal:* issuing sensational statements and retracting them only when they are contested; *apparent withdrawal:* retreating temporarily from a power position to gain strength in dealing with major issues; *apparent runnerup:* choosing to be number two when the number one spot is unattainable (an application here would be: "Aside from yourself, who is the best teacher in your school?"); *omission:* making awards to some to motivate the performance of others; *reversal:* being the first person to join or quit a group; *mosaic:* eliciting testimonials from a few individuals in a variety of related groups to create a massive impression of unified support; and *understatement:* playing down a product or event to dramatize it. Although ethical judgments may always be made on strategic applications, points out Samstag, strategy itself should be construed as a way of successfully competing with the opposition, whoever they may be.

But strategies do not exist in a vacuum. Each is often complementary to the other, and all are subject to the forces that impel or inhibit a program. They are like the four wheels of a car that carry it forward, provided a sheet of ice on a highway does not exclude the possibility of traction. In the same way a systems approach to planning determines what a public relations program should be like to progress in a given community. The systems approach to educational public relations planning is best exemplified in the Banach-Stech Communication Audit System, which gauges the impact that environmental and community factors have on school district communication and comes up with a total communication planning model that may maximize or minimize such variables as control, openness, formality, and communication output (Banach, 1982).

Finally, strategies are purposeless in any plan if they do not produce results. Thus, strategies must eventually be evaluated for the contribution they make to the accomplishment of the school system's public relations goals, just as these goals must be in concordance with the larger goals of the system.

PROGRAM EVALUATION

As might be concluded from the foregoing, evaluation today, whether practiced or postulated, is a critical component of an educational public relations program. Yet the concern of educators for determining the efficacy of educational public relations programs or activities is not restricted to the contemporary scene. Indeed, Moehlman (1927) included a chapter on evaluation in his now classic school public relations text, and the AASA, in 1950, devoted a chapter to the evaluation of school public relations in its thematic yearbook, *Public Relations for Public Schools.*

Over the years evaluation efforts have been many and varied. For example, as early as 1927 Moehlman was encouraging the use of a somewhat cumbersome weighted rating scale to assess certain aspects of a school public relations program, among them internal and external publications, including the annual report, and the school district's relationship with the parent-teacher association. A much more general and simpler approach to the weighted rating scale method is offered by

Colgate (1970), who uses a list of 33 uncategorized items to evaluate public relations programmatic effectiveness.

Bortner (1979), on the other hand, offers a checklist of 168 categorized items that may be used to assess the effectiveness of an educational public relations program. This checklist also provides a space for comments, should further clarification be necessary. The 7 categories covered by the instrument involve not only staff, students, and parents, but also the community at large. The school's media relations is of principal concern in the category labeled one-way communication, which also includes school publications. The organization and administration of the public relations program heads the instrument, and the school plant, with 4 items, serves as its close.

The most provocative checklist seems to come from a list of 10 questions posed by Fine (1955). Applied to education, these questions translate into whether a public relations program is to create good will for the school district; gain community support; enhance a school district's standing in the community; educate the school's various public to the school's objectives and ways of operating; highlight specific aspects of the school, e.g., services and programs; generate funds for the school district; attract students to the school district; avoid miscomprehension of school policies and practices; create effective internal public relations; and target particular audiences for school communications.

Perhaps best exemplifying another kind of evaluation method, the Yes/No type of response, is the instrument devised by NSPRA in 1972, which contains slightly more than 100 items and relates them to 36 specific public relations standards. Responses are later reviewed on a summary sheet within the context of 8 concordant categories, allowing gains and gaps to be noted easily (Kindred et al, 1976).

Using the data generated from Oberg's (1983) evaluation study, Oberg and West (1983) have constructed a rating scale that attempts to reflect the composite opinions of the responding public relations specialists. Called PROWESS, the rating scale (as depicted in Figure 5) is divided into 7 categories, with each category weighted by the emphasis given to it and the statements that were either elicited or subsumed from the study. The evaluation scale has a total of 100 points, with 88 to 100 points sufficing to indicate maximum agreement, and 62 points or less indicating little or no agreement. However, 75 to 87 points would indicate moderate agreement. The rating scale is not meant to serve as

```
〰〰〰〰〰〰〰〰〰〰〰〰〰〰〰〰〰〰〰〰〰〰〰〰
              P R O W E S S

    Public Relations Oberg West Easy Scoring Sheet
〰〰〰〰〰〰〰〰〰〰〰〰〰〰〰〰〰〰〰〰〰〰〰〰
```

EDUCATIONAL PUBLIC RELATIONS

PROGRAM EVALUATION CRITERIA

    The following scale represents the combined weighted ratings and open ended responses of a national sampling of educational public relations specialists.
    To compare your opinions about evaluation criteria with the opinions of those samples, merely check yes or no to the following statements. Each statement has a point value, and the total possible points that can be accumulated are 100.
    It has been arbitrarily determined that a score of 88 to 100 constitutes close agreement; 75 to 87, moderate agreement; 62 to 74, low agreement; and less than 62, little or no comparative value.

CATEGORY	RESPONSE
I. School Image (10 points)	
•The school system's educational program attracts new students (6)	___ Yes ___ No
•Student daily attendance is high (2)	___ Yes ___ No
•Special programs enjoy a notable enrollment increase (2)	___ Yes ___ No
II. School Financial Referenda (12 points)	
•Bond issues are passed (6)	___ Yes ___ No
•Budgets are passed (6)	___ Yes ___ No
III. School Media Coverage (25 points)	
•School board meetings are covered by the media (5)	___ Yes ___ No
•Special school events, such as PTA and Open House, are covered by the media (5)	___ Yes ___ No
•The media coverage the school receives is both comprehensive and positive in tone (5)	___ Yes ___ No
•The media calls the school to check out rumors (3)	___ Yes ___ No
•All district-media communications are channeled through the PR Director (3)	___ Yes ___ No
•The school has a regular program on the local radio station (1)	___ Yes ___ No
•The school has a regular program on the local TV station (1)	___ Yes ___ No
•The school has a regular column in the local newspaper (1)	___ Yes ___ No
•Filler material submitted by the school is used by the media (1)	___ Yes ___ No
IV. Community Feedback and Involvement (21 points)	
•Comments from citizens about their school system are positive (5)	___ Yes ___ No
•Letters from the citizenry to the local newspaper editor are positive (1)	___ Yes ___ No
•Local businesses are supportive of the school system's program (1)	___ Yes ___ No
•Citizens are supportive of various school groups, such as PTA, Band and Booster clubs (1)	___ Yes ___ No

Figure 5 PROWESS

Category	Response
•The school has an active community education program (1)	___ Yes ___No
•School facilities are regularly used after school hours (1)	___ Yes ___No
•Senior citizens participate in school activities (1)	___ Yes ___No
•The citizenry is actively involved in the school volunteer program (1)	___ Yes ___No
•Citizens often request district PR materials (1)	___ Yes ___No
•Citizens responses to newsletters are positive (1)	___ Yes ___No
•Citizen responses to school originated newspaper stories are positive (1)	___ Yes ___No
•Citizen responses to school originated radio messages are positive (1)	___ Yes ___No
•Citizen responses to school originated TV news stories are positive (1)	___ Yes ___No
•The school system receives regular feedback from its citizen communication network (2)	___ Yes ___No
•The school system receives regular feedback from its PR advisory committee (2)	___ Yes ___No

V. Staff Involvement (11 points)

•Staff members participate in community affairs (2)	___ Yes ___No
•Staff members hold membership in state educational associations (1)	___ Yes ___No
•Staff members hold membership in national educational associations (1)	___ Yes ___No
•The school district is represented by staff at state educational association meetings (1)	___ Yes ___No
•The school district is represented by staff at national educational association meetings (1)	___ Yes ___No
•The staff makes positive comments about the school system's PR program (3)	___ Yes ___No
•The staff requests information from the PR director (1)	___ Yes ___No
•The staff provides tips to the PR director on items to publicize (1)	___ Yes ___No

VI. Administrative Involvement (11 points)

•The administration supports the PR program (3)	___ Yes ___No
•The administration supports the PR director (3)	___ Yes ___No
•The administration is actively involved in state educational associations (1)	___ Yes ___No
•The administration is actively involved in national educational associations (1)	___ Yes ___No
•The administration is represented on the district-wide PR advisory committee (1)	___ Yes ___No
•The administration regularly participates in community affairs (2)	___ Yes ___No

VII. Program Effectiveness (10 points)

•The school system's PR program is recognized at the state level (2)	___ Yes ___No
•The school system's PR program is recognized at the national level (2)	___ Yes ___No
•The results of surveys conducted by the PR director are positive (4)	___ Yes ___No
•Large numbers of citizens respond to school surveys (1)	___ Yes ___No
•School surveys invite quick responses (1)	___ Yes ___No

TOTAL POINTS

NOTE: From **PROWESS** by T. Oberg and P. T. West, unpublished evaluation Instrument. Printed by permission of coauthor.

Figure 5 Continued

any kind of absolute standard; its intent, rather, is to offer some basis for comparison and consensus.

Qualitative judgments about the efficacy of a public relations program are not easy to make. As a result it is common among practitioners to lean toward quantitative assessments to prove their program is alive and well. These counts may be derived from the number and length (column inches) of newspaper articles a school may have had published in the local press; from the number of citizens in attendance at school functions, including community education programs; from the number of accolades or criticisms a school district receives by letter, phone, and personal contact; from the number of times a school bond issue or budget has passed or failed; from the favorable or unfavorable responses received through attitudinal surveys conducted by the school; from the number of times a school district's speakers bureau was used; from the number of citizens participating in a school volunteer or senior citizen program, or for that matter any other program; and from the number of requests for information or publications that a school district's public relations office receives. Actually, just about anything relating to people and communication efforts can be counted, so the list can extend into a rather long one.

According to Muir (NSPRA, 1983), two specific ways to evaluate school publications are through readership surveys and critique panels. Panels do the job of surveys in greater depth.

Less commonly used, but still a viable and valuable evaluation method, is the case study approach. For example, the case study approach could be used to analyze the flow of information up and down the organizational hierarchy and between school and community to determine the effectiveness of dissemination and feedback strategies. Simultaneously, observations could be made of administrative, staff, and student morale and community responsiveness to the school's varied needs and programs, and relationships drawn between these variables and the preceding strategies. Personal interviews would be an integral part of the approach, as would the collection and critiquing of publication exhibits. Included here, as well, would be a detailed description of school and community demographics to provide a contextual framework for testing variables and formulating conclusions.

Committees can also be charged with the responsibility of evaluating a public relations program, but without clear guidelines on what to look for, such assessments turn out to be altogether too subjective and substance free. On the other hand, a public relations advisory committee that is actively involved in melding goal to strategy and strategy to product would be in a good position to make a reliable judgment of the effectiveness of a school district's public relations program. The same committee may have an advantage over an outside consultant, whose objectivity may not compensate for the committee's thorough knowledge of the program's aims and accomplishments.

When all is said and done, it is the effective public relations program that sets up specific goals to achieve and then attains them. For example, if a school district wants to maintain a publication schedule of a specific number of newsletters, part of the overall public relations goal is attained each time a newsletter is prepared, printed, and disseminated. Whether these newsletters will directly influence and produce good internal or external relations is another matter. Until a sufficient number of longitudinal studies can be conducted to prove or disprove the assumption that increased information improves the morale of a school's staff or the attitudinal climate of a community, any action taken must remain grounded in assumption rather than fact.

It has long been heralded that public relations activities can be an instant answer for passing needed school referenda. However, Whisler (1983) found that public relations activities that had been in existence for only 4 years were unlikely to influence voter attitudes at the polls. In other words, these public relations activities did little to muster support for the schools. Hatley and Ritter (1981), on the other hand, claim not only that voters can be influenced in the way they vote, but that a properly designed and continuously conducted school-community relations program, which has at its roots a strong information dispersal plan, is the impetus for shaping this kind of voter behavior. The crux of the matter is that there is uncertainty even among what often passes for absolutes.

It is, therefore, important that boards and administrators not become overly concerned about exactly what a public relations program can do for their school districts. Instead, they should carefully determine what they want it to do and plan their strategies accordingly. Only by establishing an incisive set of goals can they ever hope to accomplish them. If the program does not ultimately meet their expectations, it is probably because they either expected too much or committed too little of the school's resources to ensure its success.

For each school district to exact the most from its public relations program, it must begin devising evaluation activities that extend well beyond traditional approaches. One of these activities might gauge morale before and after a staff newsletter is introduced. Another might follow up on the effects of meticulously planned parent-teacher conferences, relating them, first, to student attendance and attitudes and, later, to community support. Still another could be the determination of the attitudes of citizen volunteers about their schools before and after they perform volunteer services. Coupled with this could be the determination of why some volunteers offer their services to schools for long periods of time and others withdraw them after a short stint. Similarly, vital information about the school could be extracted from exit interviews held with parents who are moving out of the school district or sending their children to a private school. Then, too, the potency of a speakers bureau should not be solely measured by the number of times an administrator or teacher speaks at community group meetings. On the contrary, such activity could be appraised in terms of the community penetration it affords and in the strength of associations it develops between school and community groups. The possibilities are both endless and illuminating as they coalesce into an evaluation research agenda that can be shared by all schools that have organized public relations programs.

SUMMARY

Although the superintendent is the key figure in initiating an educational public relations program, only the board of education, through a written and approved policy, can assure its continued existence. But even written public relations policies do not always provide clear direction. It is, therefore, essential that great care be taken when designing these policies.

There are six aspects of educational public relations policy development. All have an important function in determining the ingredients of a public relations policy. They are participants, values, goals, structure, strategies, and assessment. As a result of a recent national polling of educational public relations specialists, these ingredients were translated into 41 descriptors that could be used to design a public relations policy for schools. In a subsequent study superintendents and boards, reacting to these descriptors, affirmed their importance in policy development.

Not all school districts have the personnel or resources to sustain a full-fledged educational public relations program. Yet even the rural school should be concerned about public relations. In very small school districts the superintendent usually assumes programmatic leadership. In large school districts the educational public relations specialist is responsible for the public relations function. A rule of thumb offered by authorities is that a full-time public relations specialist should be employed in school districts with enrollment of more than 5,000 students and with a community population of about 15,000.

Strategies are vital in an educational public relations program because they are intended to accomplish its goals. Only alluded to in policy, they are later determined and implemented. These strategies may be conveniently grouped under five categories: publication and publicity; media relations; community relations; administrative, staff, and student relations; and business relations.

Ultimately, every educational public relations program must be evaluated. Although a wide range of evaluation techniques may be used to determine the effectiveness of a school district's public relations program, a rapid assessment is offered by an easy scoring instrument called PROWESS. Based on the compiled opinions of a national sample of educational public relations specialists, this instrument is comprised of 7 categories and a list of 49 items, each of which can be answered with yes or no. Although evaluation instruments do provide a barometer for judging effectiveness, the best evaluation is the kind that measures whether a school district's unique goals are being accomplished.

• 7 •

Participants

The Immediate School Family

Everyone in the school or community is a potential contributor to the success of an educational public relations program: a board member who accepts an invitation to observe a special classroom project; an administrator who provides opportunities for teacher creativity; a teacher who sends a happygram to the home applauding a child's academic progress; a student who brags about his or her school; parents who privately or publicly compliment their child's teacher; a senior citizen who serves as a school volunteer; and a local business proprietor who participates in a school system's career day. Conversely, any of these same individuals can hamper a school system's efforts to achieve good public relations: a condescending and self-serving board member; a tyrannical administrator; a disgruntled teacher; a rebellious child; a dissatisfied parent; a tax dissenting senior citizen; and an opinionated proprietor, opposed to anything except the traditional three Rs.

What is more, any one of these individuals may, through attitude or performance, initiate a chain reaction of negative public relations for the school system. For example, a disgruntled teacher can quell a child's interest in learning to the extent that failure is imminent. In turn, the academically unsuccessful child may become a discipline problem, who now, in bitterness, exacerbates the teacher's original unhappy mood. Meanwhile, an irate parent enters the scene, meeting with teacher, or principal, or both to impute the child's failure to the poor attitude of the teacher and the negative classroom climate it has produced. Should the principal agree with the parent and apply pressure on the teacher to modify the alleged disposition, other teachers, taking note of this pressure, soon become insecure, feeling their turns will come next. Having no knowledge of the situation other than hearsay and strongly identifying with their colleague, they view this act of pressure as administratively unjust. Thus poor morale spreads like wildfire. If, of course, enough children fail and the problem is not resolved by the administration, parents and board are likely to clash. Sometime during this unpleasant process, both senior citizens and local proprietors are apt to question the system's overall competence and demand of the board a better financial return for the taxes they pay, which, when translated, calls for a reduction of programs, an elimination of frills, and an emphasis on the so-called basics. The situation may seem somewhat forced or exaggerated; yet it does demonstrate what transpires when bad public relations are at work and how these relations may be sparked by the actions of a single individual. After all, it is not unusual for small, isolated problems to mushroom into major catastrophes, if they go unrecognized or untreated.

The first-line contributors to a school system's educational public relations program are the members of its immediate family; those who make policy, administrate, teach, provide an array of services, and learn. The second line constitutes the parents of the children who attend the system's various schools. Through their participation, patronage, and support, parents can also make a significant public relations contribution. They may be construed as members of the extended school family, as may other groups who can be shown, preferably by their involvement, that they, too, have a vested interest in the school enterprise. Included among these groups are nonparents, parents who no longer have children in school, senior citizens, business and industry, and agencies, institutions, and organizations (West, 1977). But the likelihood of further extending the school family is directly related to the interest, enthusiasm, and performance of the members of its immediate family.

BOARDS

Boards of education, in performing their policy and law-making and evaluative duties, can make or break a school program (Lane, Corwin,

& Monahan, 1967). Acting in disunity, they create havoc throughout a school system. Split boards can cause school employees and community members to take sides on issues affecting the school system, splintering support for needed programs, facilities, salaries, and the like. While disagreement is inevitable at times in the course of making policy (and is, to a degree, healthy), this disagreement should be expressed as orderly, openly, and constructively as possible. Vendettas and vindictiveness have no place in any institution that is to mirror the most sacrosanct tenets of a democratic society. Policy making must be positive in tone, as must the conduct of individual board members when representing the school to the community. While contributions of boards to a system's program may be as diverse as the backgrounds of the individuals who comprise them, there is a distinct contributing role that boards can play in an educational public relations program.

For instance, as already indicated, boards can be positive or negative about the schools they serve. By treating current problem areas as opportunities for change and improvement rather than as the failings of their employees or predecessors, boards increase the likelihood of these problems becoming opportunities. While problems grow into issues and raise grave questions about the competence of school personnel, opportunities generate openness, answers, and internal and external support.

Perhaps a first step toward an effective educational public relations program that boards can take is to comply with what is purported to be their most important responsibility—the employment of a competent superintendent (Lane et al., 1967)—and then to allow that person to do the job, without undue interference. By the same token, boards should prepare a plan that will facilitate communication with their chief executive officer (AASA, 1980). The superintendent they hire should have a strong public relations orientation.

A next step to ensure this effectiveness is to frame and adopt a written public relations policy that will impart a positive and continuous direction for all of the school's internal and external relations. A subsequent step is to hire an educational public relations specialist, or charge someone with sufficient skills in this area to assume the responsibility. Concomitantly, boards must provide the necessary financial and physical resources to accommodate the needs of both program and person.

In the same vein boards would do well to ensure through policy that a districtwide public relations advisory committee is established, and then provide representation on this committee. In small systems the superintendent or some other administrator should be required to provide leadership for this committee. In systems that employ a public relations specialist, this person is a likely candidate for the assumption of this leadership responsibility. It is, of course, possible for boards to establish and operate a standing board public relations committee; yet given the myriads of responsibilities that boards have and the time constraints they impose, it seems that the former option outranks the latter.

In their dealings with the community, boards should maximize open board sessions and minimize executive closed ones (Mayer, 1974). Nevertheless, this openness must not be allowed to occur randomly. Instead, it must be carefully structured to retain the propriety that an officiating educational branch of the state government entails. Suggestion or complaint bureaus instigated by the board may help to mitigate clusters of the local citizenry from dropping in unexpectedly at board meetings (AASA, 1950). If boards have a finger on the pulse of their citizenries, few surprises will be in store for them.

Boards can become aware of community expectations for their schools in other ways as well. Indirectly, they can learn much from their everyday conversations with community members and from the reactions they get to speeches made about the schools at neighborhood or districtwide civic or educational association meetings. Directly, they can extract valuable information from the surveys they initiate, which may range from a simple opinion poll to a comprehensive needs assessment. Directly, too, they can elicit relevant feedback through their representation on districtwide public relations advisory committees.

Boards can keep the community members informed through a regularly scheduled newsletter or newspaper that includes recent board actions, as well as information about the immediate school family and school programs. In this publication news about recent municipal actions that affect the schools (e.g., new parks and recreational facilities and/or municipal library additions: the first complementing a school district's athletic program; the second, its instructional program) may also be included, to place a school district within a total community perspective and to show citizens that their board is knowledgeable and resourceful about most, if not all, of the activities ongoing in the community that impinge upon the school.

Boards, in tune with the changing educational needs of their communities, will institute a community education program and etch it in policy to guarantee funds for its operation. In itself, this board action epitomizes public relations at its best; for in a time of tight money and high accountability, community education promises a significant increase in school facility utilization and an expansion of community participation through needs fulfillment.

Externally and internally boards improve public relations by availing themselves to programmatic or service orientations at board meetings that enlarge their knowledge and understanding of school system operations. Individuals charged with these related responsibilities, in the making of their respective presentations or reports, will be pleased by a board's attention and encouraged to move enthusiastically ahead in their labors. At board meetings formal recognition can be given to both school personnel and students to produce a similar effect. Boards can improve their relations with teachers by taking the time to become acquainted with them and their needs through shared luncheons in the faculty dining area, question and answer sessions at building-level faculty meetings, and prearranged classroom visits. By establishing an internal newsletter and making sure that it contains recent board actions, boards can strengthen their relationship with school personnel at the building level, who are often inadvertently kept in the dark about school matters that directly concern them until they confront them in the local newspaper. It is often said that no news is good news; yet an austerity diet of information has a tendency to produce not only misinformation and rumor, but also insecurity.

Board relations with the media is another important facet of educational public relations. Telling a story as it is and when it happens is the most appropriate route for boards to take, with no comment being the worst of all possible reactions; for it is apt to suggest to the media that there is much more to a story than there actually is and challenge them to make an in-depth probe of a situation or event that could have been elucidated by at least a partial explanation. Media people make their living by reporting news. If this news is withheld, a vigorous effort to secure it can be expected. Truthfulness is important in the performance of any public responsibility. Mistakes can be criticized but in time are accepted or forgotten, mistruths discovered, no matter how small or seemingly insignificant, can cause irreparable damage to the credibility of school officials and tarnish the image of a school system.

The media should be given advance notice of important issues that are to appear on the board agenda, by phone and by receipt of a copy of that agenda; and their attendance at board meetings should be encouraged. These important issues should be addressed early on the agenda on the assumptions that a citizenry well-acquainted with the positive aspects of an issue will support it and that the media, having ample time to make their respective deadlines, will provide adequate and necessary coverage. Often board meetings begin late and end late, some of them lingering into the early hours of the morning. Regular board business may be further extended by a refreshment break, which can conceivably add as much as 30 minutes to a board meeting. Although a cordial diversion, this kind of break is best taken at the conclusion of the meeting.

General accommodations at board meetings are sometimes poor, as if to deter visitors, and specific accommodations for the news media may be not only substandard, but nonexistent. The lack of a place from which the media can operate at board meetings can hardly be expected to produce good board-media relations. The media are a vital means of communicating with the school's citizenry, and every opportunity to strengthen that link within reason and within the board's legal jurisdiction should be taken. While it is important that boards act unilaterally in issuing policy statements to the press, it is also important that major press releases emanating from the superintendent's office are approved by them before they are sent to the media (Mayer, 1974). By keeping themselves and others informed and by listening closely to their employees and citizenries, boards set the direction and pace for an educational public relations program.

ADMINISTRATORS

As might be expected, the potential contributions of administrators, superintendents, and principals to a public relations program are many. While not as formidable as the policy-making contribution of boards, which in an instant can create such a program, they can certainly be more pervasive and persuasive in eliciting both process and product. However, in providing daily leadership at the districtwide or building level, superintendents or principals can either be strong or weak emissaries of educational public relations, depending on the public relations skills they possess. That boards subscribe to the importance of their superintendents having effective public relations skills may be partially evinced in the results of a Kansas study of school boards' superintendency selection criteria (Anderson, 1983). Of the 17 factors that influenced boards in their decision-making processes, 8 (6 of which were rated as very important and 2 as important) dealt in some way with the superintendent's ability to communicate, orally and in writing, with employees, patrons, and boards.

That some superintendents strongly concur with these board perceptions may be seen in another study. When asked to rank in importance experience areas that should be included in a superintendency internship program, Texas superintendents selected experiences that dealt with internal and external communications as their first, second, and fifth internship priorities (Carruthers, 1980). While school-community relations was ranked higher than any other experience by the total group, respondents with more than 10 years of superintendency experience were inclined to select board relations as their top choice. Respondents with less than 10 years, however, chose school-community relations for the same slot. When a further comparison by size was made, school-community relations regained the top ranking by superintendents in large districts; the third spot in medium districts; and first in small districts, along with school board relations and financial matters.

In still another study internal and external communication skills were deemed important, directly or indirectly, by both Georgia administrators and supervisors (Rainey, 1982). Of the 73 performance-oriented statements from which respondents were asked to choose, only 15 were designated as high priority; and of these, 5 were clearly centered on either communication- or information-related activities, with internal, or staff, communications ranking highest and external, or parent and general citizenry, communications ranking third highest. However, when respondents were grouped for comparison, the latter priority was moved to second place by superintendents and secondary and elementary school principals. The importance of internal communications once again surfaced in a study of Arkansas secondary school principals (Vaupel & Sweat, 1982), which revealed that most of their efforts were devoted to this area and relatively few to its counterpart, where significant shortcomings were apparent.

Similarly, the overall responses of principals, elementary and secondary, who were involved in another Texas internship study placed school-community relations third in importance among the rankings of 22 possible internship experiences for the principal (Dennis, 1980). In terms of its contribution to job performance, the entity school-community relations was ranked second by elementary school principals, third by junior high school principals, and fourth by senior high school principals.

Communication has also been seen by elementary school principals as a way of facilitating their involvement in the community (Kline & Tweedy, 1981). Even so, while principals acknowledge the importance of communication in facilitating school community relations, it would appear that their efforts leave much to be desired (Gorton & Strobel, 1981). Moreover, impeding effective school-community relations may be the lack of communication skills that principals display when dealing with parents, whom a recent study indicates sometimes constitute the major source of dissatisfaction for secondary school principals (Nasstrom, 1981). It has also been shown that many principals have neither public relations responsibilities built into their job descriptions nor a written policy to guide their public relations activities; as a consequence program continuity is questionable and financial support largely wanting (Carr & Lows, 1982).

The importance of school-community relations as an experience area in the training of prospective principals and superintendents has also been broached by former Texas interns, who ranked it fourth in a list of 21 experiences that had potential for improving their on-the-job effectiveness as administrators (Wells, 1980). Such training has also been reported as a strong need of community educators occupying a variety of school leadership positions, who view the acquisition of public relations skills as a means of improving community participation in community education programs (Allen, 1982).

Unfortunately, as necessary as school-community relations, public relations, or the like may be to an array of practicing and prospective administrators, skills to ensure this effectiveness are often lacking in administrative internship programs, with the concomitant result that administrators tend to react rather than lead when volatile situations develop (Byrne & Powell, 1976). Seminars, workshops, institutes, textbooks, and further coursework can help to remedy this gap, provided they are available and easily accessible and that administrators wish to partake of them. Closure is unlikely to occur until administrative desire is reconciled with administrative need.

The contributions of superintendents and principals to an educational public relations program vary largely in degree rather than in kind. Thus, while superintendents may influence boards in adopting a public relations policy, so might principals, individually or collectively, suggest to a superintendent the need for a policy. Again, although a superintendent may engage and situate a public relations specialist in the central office to coordinate public relations activities for the entire school system, individual school principals may identify and provide released time for a teacher to handle public relations at the building level. There is a similarity, too, between the efforts of a superintendent to improve administrative, staff, and community relations and the efforts of a principal to relate to building-level personnel and neighborhood groups. A superintendent spearheads a districtwide survey; a principal conducts a neighborhood survey. The superintendent, as district spokesperson, is typically sought after by the media to address system problems and opportunities; in turn, the superintendent seeks to cultivate a good working relationship with them. But neither is the building-level principal, in exercising a leadership role, exempt from media interest or from creating good relations with the media. Also, the personal attributes essential to an effective public relations program must be exhibited by all administrators. To some extent this analogy could be extended to include other administrators as well, principally those with line rather than staff authority, districtwide or building level, such as assistant superintendents of curriculum and assistant principals.

Variations that do exist among the public relations contributions of administrators are typically derived from the specialized tasks they are required to perform and from their overall leadership sphere of influence. For example, one of the public relations contributions of an assistant superintendent of finance, or business manager, would be in interpreting the district budget or emergent bond issue costs to the community. Included among a personnel director's public relations contributions would be the recruitment and selection of personnel whose goals are compatible with the school district's philosophy; the structuring of inservice programs to improve employee performance and morale; the instigation of opportunities and benefits that help to motivate employee performance; and the planning and, possibly, conducting of collective negotiations that minimize employee dissatisfaction and school district disruption. An assistant superintendent or director of curriculum, or curriculum supervisor, would contribute substantially to the district's public relations program by including principals and teachers in the curricular decision-making process; by establishing curricular goals sufficiently flexible to allow for building unit experimentation and creativity; and by recognizing the important instructional leadership role of the principal in curricular implementation and evaluation. The final example pictures the community education director's public relations contribution as linking the entire resources of a community for the benefit of the school district's patrons and as enlisting large numbers of citizens in group efforts to raise the quality of life within a given community.

What follows is a listing of public relations ideas or activities that can be used by most administrators in varying degrees. Although some of the activities are much less appropriate for administrators with special tasks to perform and with fewer direct leadership responsibilities, many can be tailored to meet or support individual role expectations. As public relations suggestions are virtually endless, the list is meant to be a guide and not a cure-all, if such is possible. Again, although many of the ideas and activities have been either alluded to or discussed in earlier parts of the text, they are grouped in seven categories to reemphasize their relevance for administrators.

Practice Good Human Relations. (a) Reflect position integrity and expertise, product knowledge and conviction, and self-confidence; (b) demonstrate a sensitivity to, interest in, and understanding of subordinate and community needs, interests, and aspirations; (c) display courteousness, friendliness, warmth, sincerity, and optimism; (d) treat students as clients and subordinates as coworkers; (e) provide positive and constructive criticism; (f) respect confidentiality; (g) welcome participation; and (h) dress with decorum.

Organize and Reorganize All Public Relations Efforts. (a) Make sure that the school district has a clearly written public relations policy, and adhere to its tenets; (b) develop public relations activities that are consonant with the district's goals and values; (c) assign someone competent to perform the public relations function at the building level and in the central office; (d) form a public relations advisory committee, preferably at both building and districtwide levels; (e) develop a communication network that is comprised of formal and informal community leaders generally perceived by the community as knowledgeable about the school; (f) coordinate all public relations activities with the central office public relations specialist, or with any other person delegated this responsibility; (g) set up school offices to respond promptly, courteously, and proficiently to written, telephone, and personal inquiries; and (h) evaluate regularly to determine and improve program effectiveness.

Multiply Opportunities for Feedback and Cross-Feed. (a) Listen carefully to individuals and groups, and arrange kaffeeklatsches, teas, breakfasts, and luncheons to facilitate information exchanges; (b) seek suggestions, formally and informally, from everyone in the immediate and extended school family and publicize those of greatest frequency and import; (c) conduct rap and gripe sessions with representatives of various groups, allowing problem resolution to emerge from an interplay of their comments; (d) create an open door policy that swings both ways, thereby producing a reciprocal invitation for administrators to visit both classrooms and homes; (e) conduct school, neighborhood, and districtwide surveys to denote internal and external public relations problem areas as well as to gauge overall satisfaction with the school system; (f) establish a telephone hot line to prevent the spread of misinformation and rumors, and answer all calls promptly; (g) respond to complaints in writing and maintain a running file for this correspondence; (h) conduct exit interviews for staff and parents and use this information, as applicable, to improve instructional and activity programs; and (i) seek input from alumni.

Maximize Involvement of Immediate and Extended School Family in School Activities. (a) Allow and encourage intra- and inter-school visitations of faculty; (b) engage students, parents, and other community members in building-level and districtwide curricular projects; (c) seek parental and community assistance in planning cocurricular activities; (d) create a speakers bureau that includes students as well as faculty and administration; (e) invite parents and other community members to visit the schools and their classrooms; (f) inaugurate special days to highlight the roles played by various groups in the school-community: mothers, fathers, grandparents, teachers, doctors, lawyers, bankers, trades people, and so on; (g) invite members of the citizenry, particularly community leaders, to view classroom demonstrations; (h) plan staff sessions to exchange the latest instructional ideas gleaned from recent coursework and attendance at state, regional, and national seminars, conferences, and conventions and encourage continued involvement; (i) arrange school tours and assign students to lead them; (j) encourage administration and staff to become active in community affairs; (k) invite citizenry to follow a student's classroom schedule for a day; (l) organize a senior citizen's program, a school volunteer program, and a community education program; (m) organize and involve citizen advisory committees in systemwide needs-assessment activities; (n) join and work closely with the PTA; and (o) arrange school social functions that bring administrators and faculty members together with community members.

Recognize and Reward Achievement. (a) Recognize the accomplishments of administrators and staff at special building, PTA, or districtwide meetings with congratulatory messages or speeches, accompanied by pins, certificates, promotions, and so on; (b) recognize and reward students at special awards and commencement ceremonies; (c) recognize and reward parents and other community members, publicly preferably but also by personal letter, for their contributions to the school system; (d) initiate efforts to publicize the achievements of administrators, staff, students, and community members in school-related activities, in the local newspaper, on the radio, and on television; (e) encourage calls and notes from teachers to parents that applaud student progress; (f) display student work, drawings, paintings, sculpture, woodwork, metalwork, needlework, and the like in appropriate civic and business sites; (g) arrange opportunities for outstanding students to present their work to teacher groups at meetings or inservice sessions; (h) arrange for outstanding teachers to accompany the recruiting officer on recruiting trips to project a highly professional faculty image and to assist in the interviewing process; and (i) mail out thank you notes for even the smallest school service performed.

Disseminate Information Widely. (a) Publish a staff newsletter; (b) publish a community newsletter or newspaper; (c) develop an information brochure that explains the school program to interested community groups; (d) develop an orientation handbook for parents and an annual report for the general citizenry; (e) devise a school calendar of events for community consumption; (f) publish a handbook for students that acquaints them with school policies; (g) publish the weekly lunch menu in the community newsletter and local newspaper; (h) initiate a welcome wagon to disseminate school information to new residents; (i) fully utilize bulletin boards to enrich curriculum endeavors and to publicize school happenings; (j) use regularly free public service time of local media to publicize school activities and events; and (k) use, as much as possible, store window fronts to publicize school events such as plays, concerts, and PTA or PTO meetings.

Link the School with the Media. (a) Maintain ongoing contacts with media personnel, especially those assigned to provide educational coverage; (b) learn what kinds of news the media prefer and how they would like it prepared for submission, and then give them what they want; (c) invite media personnel into the schools for special tours, to observe outstanding educational activities and special classroom projects and to brief them on school district aims and progress, and on problems that impede further progress; (d) provide the media with a directory of school personnel charged with overseeing various facets of the school program, facilities and services included; (e) learn media deadlines and comply with them; (f) coordinate media requests with the system's public relations specialist; (g) offer to provide the media with a regular educational column or program, and follow through; (h) express appreciation for media coverage; (i) avoid favoritism; (j) provide a media table at board meetings to facilitate media coverage; (k) respond promptly and courteously to media inquiries and avoid "no comment" statements; (l) overlook inadvertent omissions or names misspelled; (m) keep a running record of issues addressed in unsolicited media coverage and compare them periodically with school-initiated releases to determine how well emergent concerns have been addressed by the school; and (n) attempt to understand the media's point of view.

STAFF

There is no pat way of categorizing the different groups of a school district's staff. One way would be to divide staff into two broad categories, certified and noncertified personnel; with the first group consisting primarily of teachers, guidance counselors, librarians, and nurses; and the second, of secretaries and clerks, custodians, cafeteria workers, and bus drivers. A second way would be to dichotomize staff into professional and noncertified employees (Mayer, 1974), and a third would entail a three-way split, such as teaching, nonteaching, and nonprofessional personnel. In the later instance, guidance counselors would be viewed as nonteaching personnel and custodians as nonprofessional personnel, with the teaching personnel category obviously self-explanatory (Bortner, 1972). But secretaries, custodians, transportation employees, and the like have also been labeled as noninstructional personnel (Kindred, Bagin, & Gallagher, 1976) and as classified personnel. In this text, however, the distinction is made between those whose major responsibility is to teach and those who provide various services for the school system.

One reason for this slight deviation is that public school teachers do not fall neatly into the category of full-fledged professional organizations. Teachers, for example, lack professional self-determination; they communicate or apply rather than create knowledge, they hardly ever deal with life and death situations, and they need no more than four years to enter their respective teaching fields (Etzioni, 1964). The fact that teachers in about 30 states have gained a strong entree into the school decision-making process through collective negotiations laws, coupled with the proviso that an increasing number of teachers must complete a fifth year of education to achieve permanent certification, has tended to work toward the advancement of their traditional semi-professional status, but, as yet, has not changed it.

Another reason is that all members of the school staff can be expected to provide some form of instruction to students. Frequently having children follow them around or working for them, custodians can teach, directly or by example, moral behavior to students. Often a problem child will listen to a custodian and no one else, and just as often custodians working in high schools counsel students vocationally (Rafky, 1972). Through their safe driving bus drivers can set an example for students to follow, and secretaries and clerks can teach office procedures to work study students. School nurses are teachers, too. Going well beyond the traditional administering of first aid to youngsters, they are, among other things, involved in the counseling of parents on student health problems; in the conducting of parenthood programs for pregnant young women; in the teaching of teachers about the health needs of certain students; in providing for the health needs of special education students; and in synchronizing the health policies of the school system (Schurr & Houdon, 1977). Functioning in a similar capacity, librarians frequently instruct students on how to use the library, and guidance counselors help students learn how to cope with personal and academic problems.

A third reason is that while teachers, counselors, librarians, and nurses may have taken tests and received licenses and/or certificates, custodians frequently take civil service examinations, have various kinds of licenses to operate complex and expensive equipment, and are responsible for the safety of administrators, students, and other staff members in an entire facility (Rafky, 1972). Although bus drivers, as part-time employees, may undergo less stringent job training than custodians, their responsibility is as prodigious as that of their colleagues. In transporting their young charges safely to and from the school, they must demonstrate excellent driving skills and have a firm grasp of safety procedures, along with an appreciable understanding of children. Obviously, they are licensed for the purpose at hand, and

perhaps they are the recipients of certificates indicative of safety training. Full-time transportation employees would, of course, be expected
to be even more technically skilled.

Finally, before an in-depth examination is conducted of the potential
public relations contributions of the two groups, teachers and special
services personnel, one very important point should be made. Regardless of whatever else they may contribute to a public relations program,
staff members should demonstrate position proficiency. Subsumed
under proficiency is not only knowledge, but also technique or method.

Teachers

Much of the antecedent list of activities offered to administrators to
improve an educational public relations program need not be initiated
by them alone. Teachers should, of their own accord, practice good
human relations with administrators, with one another, with students
and parents, and with the general citizenry. Like administrators, their
behavior should be exemplary when dealing with members of the
immediate or extended school family. Teachers can help to create
numerous opportunities for maximizing the involvement of internal and
external groups. They can seek the assistance of students, parents, and
other community members in the planning of curricular and cocurricular projects. Invitations can be extended by them to members of the
citizenry to view classroom demonstrations and to serve as classroom
guest speakers. Parents can be asked to serve as chaperons on field trips
and at proms and to help out at plays, athletic events, and special days
proceedings. Teachers should also make themselves easily accessible
to parents for conferences; assign meaningful activities to classroom
volunteers; use the phone to introduce themselves at the beginning of a
school year to parents and to learn from them something about their
children (such as nicknames, hobbies, favorite subjects, and career
interests) to ease the strain of new teacher-student relationships and to
pave the way for further communication with the home during the year;
and visit the homes of their students as need and time may dictate.
Then, too, teachers can take the initiative to invite their colleagues into
their classrooms to share an instructional technique they have developed; to share ideas they have gleaned from various sources (such as
universities, association meetings, and school district workshops); and
to solicit their opinions in improving their classroom management or
instructional methods.

Normally, teachers recognize and reward achievement by simply putting a grade on a student's paper or project. But they can recognize and reward student achievement in other ways as well: by sending home success notes or cards; by making success calls to the home; by exhibiting the work of their students at various sites in the school and in the community, on bulletin boards and walls and in display cases and store windows; and by arranging opportunities for students to display and discuss their work with peers and teachers at special school events. However, any display of student writings should be free of blatant errors; for even at the elementary school level, parents, visitors, teachers, and administrators often attribute these errors to poor teaching rather than to a teacher's attempt to motivate students by rewarding their efforts. Teachers can also initiate or participate in events that recognize and reward the performances of their colleagues at teacher association-sponsored breakfasts, luncheons, and dinners.

In the matter of disseminating information, teachers can help in a number of ways. They can contribute articles to internal and external school publications and serve as advisors on student publications that permeate school and home: newspapers, yearbooks, and literary magazines. They can decorate bulletin boards and corridor display cases to preview upcoming instructional units or field trips or to post the results of either of the two. They can serve on welcome wagons or initiate them through their teacher associations. They can dispel rumors by assisting in the operation of telephone hot lines and working with public relations advisory committees and citizen communication networks. They can become actively involved in PTAs and PTOs as officers, committee chairs, or members and act as conduits for transmitting important information about community projects.

In concert with the district's public relations specialist, teachers can be active agents in linking the school with the media by writing articles about school projects and events for publication in the local newspaper and by preparing tape and slide presentations to air on radio and television.

Teaching proficiency in subject matter and methodology cannot be stressed too strongly. Indeed, classroom management problems frequently stem from lackluster or poorly organized lessons, inadequate content, or abstruse content. But adeptness unaccompanied by an obvious enjoyment of teaching and a deep and abiding interest in students is liable to produce few results. Students can sense if teachers enjoy their work, their subject matter, and their students. They can easily distinguish between a rote uninspired presentation and one that is zealously prepared and delivered.

The entertainment aspect of teaching is often criticized, yet successful teachers are those who can dramatize a learning situation. Drama makes learning an inviting and exciting learning experience for students. It fuses teacher personality with subject matter, imbues life and meaning into facts and figures, and forges a bond between teacher and student of understanding and appreciation and of actor and audience. By borrowing freely from the drama, teachers give testament to the notion that teaching is an art as much as it is a science.

Unfortunately, it is difficult to maintain this flair of the drama throughout the day and from day to day. Nonetheless, that teachers make a valiant effort to sustain this emotional vigor is evidence enough to students of their concern for them. Further evidence of this concern is the willingness of teachers to make themselves available to students for extra help on a regular basis. It is vital that teachers raise the expectations of students and then help them fulfill them.

Coupled with these two efforts is the additional concern of teachers to meet and confer with parents to unify school and home in this overall caring process. According to elementary and secondary school teachers surveyed in a Kansas study, parent-teacher conferencing was the best way to improve relations between school and community (Kilgore, 1980). The study also revealed that although teachers believe their contribution to educational public relations is important, only a small number of the schools that employ them have policies addressing this contribution. The teachers considered their most important contribution to be in instigating parental involvement and participation. On the other hand, they felt that the most important contribution of their principals was to sell the school's program to the community.

Another matter that should be of concern to teachers is the manner in which they make homework assignments. Sometimes homework is assigned by teachers, but never read or graded by them. At other times it is assigned by them, not because it enhances conceptual understanding, but because it is assumed to be an expectation of the board and administration. What is more, homework is occasionally unexplained, excessively demanding, and lacking in follow-up. Homework may also be hastily attended to and incorrectly graded. Good teaching, along with good public relations, calls for homework that is relevant, reasonable, and carefully evaluated. If these requirements are unmet, teachers will find themselves at cross purposes with children and parents.

Adding or detracting from the contributions teachers may make to an educational public relations program is the kind of guidance they give to teacher substitutes and interns. Without a plan to follow substitutes generally assume the posture of a babysitter when regular teachers suddenly absent themselves from the classroom. Impromptu planning by phone is a poor replacement for a detailed lesson plan, which not only ensures continuity but also prevents the loss of valuable instructional time. The advantage of having weekly lesson plans on file in the office of the department head or the school's main office is immeasurable in terms of the instructional direction it affords substitute teachers. It is also good public relations internally and externally because it underscores teacher accountability.

The same is true of providing explicit guidance to teacher interns, whose efforts can add much to classroom learning if they are well-organized and sufficiently responsible in nature. Interns can be assets or liabilities, with either contingent upon whether they are permitted to play active or passive roles. Passivity transforms competent interns into wallflowers or clock watchers and frequently earns for them the ridicule rather than the respect of the students with whom they have been assigned to work. Thus, what could have been additional assistance to an already busy teacher becomes instead an onus. The crux of the situation is that if teachers do not treat interns as colleagues and co-workers and do not give them responsible teaching assignments and the authority they imply, students are unlikely to pay any heed to the instruction these interns are capable of providing. By the same token, teachers who assign interns meaningful instructional responsibilities and then supersede their authority or vie with them for class approval similarly inhibit intern effectiveness. Any of these approaches is apt to disrupt the learning process. Relations between school and university may be placed in jeopardy and a potential contribution lost.

Properly managed classrooms make a substantial contribution to an educational public relations program. Teachers who are inflexible in classroom rules, unappreciative of reasons that might satisfactorily account for certain kinds of student behavior, and unable to find the humor necessary to laugh with the students instead of at them typically spend more time on sending students to the principal's office than they do on classroom instruction. If enough teachers repeatedly send large numbers of students to their principal for disciplinary action, the internal relations of a school is on a tenuous footing. And, if enough of these same teachers keep students after school, so that elementary students are kept late and secondary students report late to their jobs, external relations become precarious.

It is, of course, proper that teachers expect respect from their students, but respect, like leadership, is earned rather than endowed. If teachers lead rather than dictate, nag, or demand, if they have ample and understandable content in their lessons, and if their methodology presumes that students will rise to the expectations they have for them, it is not unlikely that students will come to model their own behavior on that of their teacher. Behind every successful student there is a caring teacher, and this caring is at the very core of an effective educational public relations program. In conclusion, teachers, if only by virtue of their large numbers and extended proximity to students, constitute a school's most powerful public relations force. This force can be positive or negative. Wise administrators are, therefore, those who are as supportive of their teachers as they expect these teachers to be supportive of their students.

Special Services

The larger the school system, the greater in number and complexity are its services. With largeness comes a substantial increase in employees and a hierarchy of administrative and supervisory personnel to oversee their activities. Of concern here, however, is not these expanded services, nor the additional superordinate roles and responsibilities they engender, but the support services that have characterized public school operations for many years. Although it is possible to extend the following list, discussion will be limited to seven service areas: counseling, library, health, clerical, food, maintenance, and transportation.

Counseling. The counseling service is an important facet of an effective public relations program. In the daily performance of their duties, counselors contribute to the academic, occupational, and personal growth of students, particularly at the secondary level at which this service is most profuse. Needs, abilities, and aspirations interweave as counselors work with students and parents to help them realize the goals they have jointly set. Using the results of standardized tests they have administered to students, they pave the way for academic remediation and enrichment and the building of requisite learning skills, thereby enhancing the likelihood of goal attainment. They interpret these tests not only to parents for their immediate use in making appropriate educational decisions for their children, but also to school officials for short- and long-range planning purposes. They work closely with teachers, acquainting them with the academic and home backgrounds of students and providing leadership at conferences that bring teachers together with parents to improve student classroom performance.

Students frequently bring to counselors their personal as well as academic problems, and both work together to achieve problem resolution. Sometimes these problems are no more than a facade to gain a friendly listening ear; other times they are quite serious. In any event, the confidences students share with counselors should be treated as sacred trusts and never be bandied about in faculty lounges as idle conversation pieces. Moreover, counselors help to crystallize career choices for students, operate student work study programs, help students acquire scholarships and loans, and strive to place students in colleges most congruent with their needs, interests, and abilities. They also provide leadership in structuring gifted and career education programs, assist in special education programs, and make student referrals to agencies of various kinds to obtain for students any special assistance they may need.

The success of the counseling service is often judged on the number and quality of college placements made and on how many of the school's graduating class have been awarded scholarships. Such information is pap for the community newsletter and local paper. But the efficacy of the counseling service should be judged equally on the guidance it offers the noncollege-bound student. Not all students can be expected to attend college; and of those who do not, many may remain in the community to become pillars of strength for the school, if properly assisted in their occupational pursuits. Often it is the student who fares least well in a classroom setting that later surprises teachers and peers by becoming a highly successful entrepreneur. An able mechanic may not someday just own a garage, but one of three or four automobile dealerships in the school's community. Good public relations is, therefore, intrinsic to a properly administered counseling service.

The concerted activity of counselors within the broader community context is another way of contributing to an effective public relations program. With the educational insights and expertise they possess, counselors make a splendid addition to a speakers bureau. Their informative presentations about the school are greatly welcomed at various community gatherings, such as neighborhood and districtwide educational and civic association meetings. The counseling service provides an ideal bridge between school and community and, more particularly, between teacher and parent, teacher and student, and, sometimes, student and parent. If performed with the utmost of skill and sensitivity, counseling does not merely contribute to a public relations program; it is in and of itself good public relations.

Library. The library service of a school system, which again is most prominent at the secondary school level, makes its strongest contribution to an educational public relations program through its accessibility to the various groups it serves. These groups may include members of the immediate and extended school family. The library that is closed for frequent and extended periods of time to catalogue and inventory its wares may be well-known and even lauded for its organization and administration, but it cannot be praised for its accessibility to its clients. On the other hand, the librarian that skillfully combines organization and administration with service, with a minimum of disruptions or closings, can be said to be operating at a high level of efficiency and effectiveness.

Functioning generally as a staff of one plus student helpers and an occasional teacher or volunteer, school librarians cannot be all things to all people. But most do try and, in doing so, make an appreciable contribution to the school's instructional program and, concomitantly, to its public relations program. For example, the efforts of librarians to maintain a professional library for administrators and staff, no matter how meager the results, are prized by both. Usually, inhibiting this gratuitous gesture is a lack of money more than a lack of time, although time, too, is an important factor in the proferring of a service. Similarly, efforts to provide both groups with a running file of annotations on existing and new acquisitions earn notable praise.

More directly related to the teaching function is the instruction librarians make available to students, or to an entire class upon the request of a teacher, on how to use the library. Ordinarily, librarians assist students in locating needed sources for classroom papers or projects. But when librarians take the initiative to plan with teachers these papers or projects, the benefits derived by students and teachers are multiplied. By making available to teachers lists of free and inexpensive materials, librarians further assist in the instructional process. Lists of library-owned materials, movies, filmstrips, slides, records, and video tapes and discs are of like importance to teachers in their instructional efforts.

Should the school district have a community education program, the library is likely to remain open during the evening to service the academic needs of community participants. In this case, the potential public relations contribution of the school's library service would be considerably expanded. As the doors of the library open to the community, a strengthening of the relationship between the school and its clients would most assuredly occur. To accommodate this need, however, additional staff would be needed, paid or volunteer. But even without a community education program, the library can invite community members to partake of its tomes of wisdom and adventure. Indeed, in the very small community the school library may be the only one available or the best equipped to service the needs of the local citizenry.

Coordination is another important service librarians provide to their clients. If books or materials are not readily accessible in a library, librarians know how and where to procure them with expediency, using networks they have created with other school libraries in and out of the district, with university libraries, with municipal, county, state, and federal libraries, and with private sources, philanthropic organizations and foundations, business, and industry. In the matter of coordination, librarians should provide ample assistance to those charged with library responsibilities in elementary schools, where books may be few in number, but need and interest is rapidly growing. This may be accomplished through periodic visitations and consultations as well as planned workshops that engage faculty throughout the district. A library hot line, as a matter of fact, is an idea worth pursuing.

Along with accessibility and coordination, there is the matter of quality. Best stated in board policy, this action constitutes how books are to be chosen for inclusion in the school libraries. Should no policy exist, the creation and implementation of a library committee comprised of members of the immediate and extended school family is desirable. Often a questionable book can create a community uproar and a charge of well-intentioned citizen groups to scrutinize and ban all kinds of books, including some of the classics, with the net result that librarians feel threatened to make future decisions about library acquisitions. There may even be a trace of insecurity over what has already been added, long after the alleged purge. With the aid of a board policy and a library committee, it is unlikely that such problems will mushroom if they surface.

Last, but not least, there is position expansion. Despite ongoing job responsibility constraints, librarians should take their service directly to the classroom, presenting to students and teachers their priceless wares and skills. They should do the same within the community whenever the opportunity arises, as part of a speakers bureau or through their own efforts. They should write book reviews and send them to the local paper or include them in staff and community newsletters. Whenever possible, they should critique books on radio and television. In every respect they should make the presence of their service and themselves felt by every member of the community. In their own domains librarians can host book fairs and help students to make good choices in their book purchases.

Health. The health service that a school district offers is all pervasive in its outreach. In its concern for the total health, physical and mental, of students, it extends into the classroom, home, and community. Through sight and hearing check-ups and the compilation of student health records, it affords vital information to teachers in meeting the needs of their students. In providing the leadership to optimize this service, the school nurse not only acquaints faculty members with this vital health information but also prepares them for dealing with the health problems of their students when emergencies related to these problems suddenly arise. Because this information is made available to teachers at the outset of a school year, the typically alphabetically arranged seating arrangement can be modified to accommodate students with sight or hearing problems. Providing for health problems early can help to prevent later learning problems.

The health service that the school district affords its students reaches directly into the home, which nurses sometimes phone and visit personally to see that the needs of their many charges are being met. In offering advice to parents about immunization needs, dental care, sight and hearing problems, personal hygiene, and other health concerns, nurses demonstrate most ably the schools' abiding interest in students and their families.

In their referrals to other health agencies, school nurses tap the entire medical resources of a community to serve the needs of students. Their efforts may alert health agencies to possible epidemics and to the need for wholesale immunization.

Finally, in working directly with students, the school nurse is best able to express sympathy, along with expert first aid, when injury or illness strikes. Students often frequent the school nurse's office because of the kind treatment they have received in the past or because they are considering nursing as a career and have chosen the school nurse as their exemplar. Some students have other motives; they simply want to avoid a particular class because of an impending exam. Surrounded so often by students, the school nurse becomes a tremendous source of information about student needs and concerns. Touching so many lives, the school's health service, and more particularly the school nurse, become important allies in generating good public relations for the district.

Clerical. The clerical service offered by a school district also touches the lives of many people, sometimes in unwanted ways and quite dramatically. The superintendent placating, by phone, an irate community member is suddenly disconnected by the switchboard operator who is unable to produce a call back number. A secretary forgets to enter an appointment on a principal's calendar and the principal is out of the building when a parent arrives. A senior citizen who has been invited to make a class presentation, while waiting to be taken to the teacher's classroom, is seated amidst a group of students awaiting disciplinary action from the principal. A secretary cannot find a form requested by a parent because the office files are in disarray. A letter dictated to a secretary and not proofread by the principal ends up in the hands of a local dignitary, who finds several spelling errors in it and reports his findings to a group seeking educational accountability. A group of teachers reporting to work a couple of minutes late is required by the secretary to initial a late sheet. A student delayed at the main office is refused a late slip to class by the secretary. All of these actions indicate not only the range of influence of the clerical staff but also its impact on educational public relations.

The importance of a friendly, attractive, neatly ordered, and efficiently managed office environment should be obvious. But frequently it is not, with the consequence that many who walk through the portals of the school district's various offices are less than satisfied with the services rendered. If a special seating area or room is unavailable for visitors entering school buildings, special attention should at least be devoted to them, with care exercised to avoid unnecessarily long waiting periods.

Disconnected phone calls quickly evoke the ire or embarrassment of callers and tax the patience of listeners. Callers left dangling on the line for long periods of time become irascible. Rudeness, abruptness, or an inability to supply requested information make callers no happier. Yet work study students who know little about the office operation of a school are often assigned the task of answering phones. Notices sent to the home are sometimes laden with errors, as are letters that go out to parents and other members of the community. The school is recognized as a fount of learning; and when errors flourish, its reputation is at stake.

Sometimes the clerical staff is required to provide teachers with limited typing services, particularly in the case of departmental examinations they may jointly construct. Regardless of the nature of the service, work should be completed by clerical staff with dispatch, amiability, and accuracy. Services appropriately rendered will earn for the clerical staff the appreciation and respect of teachers. Cordial and helpful relations with students will produce similar results.

Reminders to return calls, to keep appointments, to respond to written inquiries, and to meet deadlines for various reports are indispensable aids offered by clerical staff to administrators. Other administrative assets include orderly kept records and files that can be located and interpreted with ease. Administrators may expect heightened performances of clerical staff as computerized data banks and word processing equipment become the norm for handling information within school districts, provided adequate and continuous training is made available to clerical staff through periodic inservice. The clerical staff is a vital link in the chain of effective school district public relations. When proficiency, coupled with positive gestures of concern, keynote the clerical service, this link is considerably strengthened.

Food. A school district's food service can contribute much to the physical and mental well-being of members of the immediate school family. For students and teachers the school lunch period signals a respite from the academic rigors of the classroom, with the hot lunch offered by food service staff viewed as a tangible reward for efforts expended. Eating in the school cafeteria gives teachers an opportunity to relate informally with one another and with the administration. It also takes administrators away from busy phones and piles of paperwork, allowing them to get better acquainted with teachers and students.

For some students the lunch they have in the cafeteria will be the only hot meal of the day. For others, those who might ordinarily bring their lunch to school, a hot meal in the cafeteria may be the treat for the week. By the same token, there are always the fast food gourmets who can find nothing to their liking in the daily noon menu. There are, of course, those who criticize the noon meal, usually not because they believe it is of poor quality, but because they think it is their passport to the in group.

Many years ago, while serving as an advisor to a high school newspaper, the author had an opportunity to observe, firsthand, how a little student effort and appreciation could engender almost endless goodwill from the food service staff. Although confronted with a request to write a caustic critique of the school's food service, the author was eventually able to convince his editorial staff that a story featuring the dedicated work of the cafeteria workers would better accomplish their quest for so-called cafeteria reform.

In any event, a feature article entitled "Women in White," highlighted by a photograph of a group of cafeteria workers, was published in the school newspaper. The results were almost miraculous from both sides. The cafeteria workers loved the article and praised the students and their newspaper. The newspaper staff, in turn, overjoyed by the accolades bestowed upon it and the paper, began showing a genuine interest in the menu and had only good words to say about the high school cafeteria. Meanwhile, it seemed that when certain vegetables or desserts were disliked by some of the students, substitutes frequently appeared like magic to replace them; and when other foods found great favor among some of the students, the size of their portions seemed to increase. Had the newspaper staff pursued its original intention, this anecdote would have a far different ending.

Well-prepared, ample, and nutritious meals, cleanliness, and amiability characterize the public relations contributions that food service personnel make daily in the performance of their duties. If the school can be thought of as a second home for students, then the cafeteria is its kitchen.

Maintenance. A school district's maintenance service, like the custodians who provide it, often goes unnoticed until suddenly or desperately needed. A thermostat malfunctions in midwinter, and teacher and students clamor for heat to make a classroom bearable. A pipe bursts in the building, creating a virtual flood, and the principal races around the building to find the custodian to fix it. The front lawn of the school is strewn with an unsightly accumulation of debris from a high wind, and the custodian appears to clear it away. A shelf in a bookroom collapses from the weight of too many books, and the custodian is sought to repair it.

Despite their versatility, talent, and apparent need, custodians may derive only a modicum of respect from teachers, who often irk custodians by calling them janitors or nonacademics (Rafky, 1972). On one hand, teachers presume that custodians do little work and are overpaid; on the other, custodians feel that teachers are always making extra work for them. As a result, custodians and teachers react defensively toward one another.

Caught up in the fervor of their teaching, teachers tend to overlook simple housekeeping monitoring. Desks may be repeatedly written on; papers, allowed to clutter classroom floors; and books, carelessly piled on floors instead of neatly stacked on classroom or bookroom shelves when not being used. When the situation seems to be getting out of control, custodians report offending teachers to their principals. In retaliation teachers look for things to complain about the custodian to their principals. A circle of noncompliance subsequently develops and everyone in the school seems to suffer the consequences.

Maintenance makes the instructional process possible. Custodians see to it that their buildings are not only functional but also presentable. Marked up desks are learning distractions for students and eyesores for visitors. Disheveled classrooms and untidy corridors counter attempts to achieve student self-discipline, without which classroom problems tend to arise. Few in number, perhaps no more than one or two to a building, custodians cannot be expected to respond repeatedly to the elimination of avoidable housekeeping problems. In maintaining the grounds of a school, custodians make a school as presentable and inviting outside as it is inside.

Students generally relate well to custodians, and many may be found visiting with them in their quarters during the school day. Teachers seeking their advice on technical matters or insights into general school practices or problems quickly discover how astute and well-informed custodians are. In sharing their concerns with custodians, teachers impute to them collegial status and pave the way for improved relations. Like other staff members, custodians serve as information conduits within the community. The difference is that in performing their jobs they are endowed with a mobility that brings them together on a one-to-one basis with about as many people as a principal encounters during a given day, if not more. They also have an expanded view of the facility because of this mobility. In light of this difference, they are probably the best source of information about the school for both internal and external groups.

Transportation. The transportation service of a school district may be viewed as relatively unimportant by students and parents until busing is threatened by budget cutbacks or inflationary rises. Then students who might be least likely to applaud a ride on a school bus would direly regret its absence. Parents forced to transport their children to and from school each day would consider it a major inconvenience, having become accustomed to a service that they took for granted.

That the school bus driver has an important responsibility is often overlooked until a serious accident occurs. Then everyone becomes fully aware of the importance of bus maintenance and driver safety in the lives of children. In addition to their ability to drive a bus and their knowledge of safety procedures, bus drivers must have a facility for working with young people. The actions of unruly students can prove harmful to their peers in classroom, cafeteria, or assembly settings; but in a moving vehicle, they can be deadly. Bus drivers must exact obedience from their charges for their own welfare and for the welfare of their classmates. They must, therefore, be skilled in ways of achieving good discipline.

Although bus drivers may not be required to drive their buses in snowstorms or blizzards, they may find it necessary to do so as occasional storms erupt unexpectedly during the school day. In all sorts of inclement weather, provided schools are open, parents can expect the school bus to stop near their homes. Familiar with the students on their respective routes, many bus drivers may linger a bit to ensure their arrival at school, especially when the weather is inclement. Still, any extended delay must be considered by them as an unreasonable inconvenience for those further down the line who are being exposed to the same weather. Buses that are inordinately late in getting to school upset classroom schedules. Consideration, then, must be tempered by promptness.

Bus drivers come in contact with the parents of many elementary school students along their routes; and these contacts, however brief, may leave lasting impressions on parents. Bus drivers perceived by parents as sharing their concern for their children do much to build good educational public relations.

That bus drivers receive, as part of their transportation training, inservice to increase their proficiency is undeniably important. But a school transportation department would do well to prepare slide-tape presentations on bus safety for students and have bus drivers present them at a series of student assemblies at the beginning of a school year. Parents of elementary school students should be invited to this general orientation to solicit their support in ensuring student adherence to bus safety procedures. Simultaneously, copies of school bus routes could be distributed and explained to them. The entire event could be labeled "Safety Day." At the elementary school level one of the activities could be to introduce parents to their child's bus driver.

Usually part-time workers, bus drivers carry their knowledge of the school to an additional work setting, where they are likely to help shape the attitudes of their coworkers about the schools. Then, too, they, like other staff members, influence the attitudes of relatives, neighbors, and personal and business acquaintances. In view of this sphere of influence, bus drivers should be involved in public relations inservice along with other staff members. When this happens, educational public relations can only benefit everyone.

STUDENTS

The student body is, perhaps, the finest public relations medium a school district has in its immediate family. When queried, parents usually point to their children as their best source of information about the schools. For example, in a study that asked parents of seventh grade students to identify their top school information source, 77% picked their children and only 9% the teacher of their children. Administrators, superintendents, and principals provided 2% of this information, and a miscellany another 10% (Dierksen & Oberg, 1981). The notion that students are key communicators is also shared by Dubia (1979), who suggests that not only should students be kept informed about the school but also be asked to comment about the instruction they are receiving.

There are numerous ways to show off a school's student body to a community; the following are but a few: publicizing high test scores, scholarly attainments, scholarship acquisitions, interschool scholastic competition winners (math and spelling clubs); exhibiting student work at community sites and student performances (band and glee club) at civic centers; and succeeding in various athletic events. There are just as many ways to involve students in community activities, such as talent shows; charitable drives (blood, scrap, paper, and clothing) sponsored by a host of civic associations; and service for the aged, impaired, and infirmed in homes, hospitals, rehabilitation centers, and rest homes. More important, though, is for administrators and staff to show off the school to their clients. For public relations to flourish, it is far better that the school adopt a "what we can do for you" rather than a "what you can do for us" attitude; for from the former the latter will naturally evolve.

An academically successful student is much more likely to identify with the aims of a school than one who continuously fails. Failure automatically puts a student outside the group, and repeated failure puts one outside the school, if not physically, certainly mentally, as in passive mentation and rebelliousness. Although teachers cannot insure learning, they can carefully set the stage for it to happen. Amidst a class of 20 or 25, individualization is still possible, as are the use of student tutors and teams to help some students over what seems to them insurmountable hurdles. The main idea is that students be led to believe that they can and will accomplish what they set out to do. To increase their chances of doing so is to have the class function as a cohesive work group. "Lending a hand to all" has long been the motto of community educators, the underlying premise of which is that all can succeed in some capacity.

A student actively involved in the school is apt to believe more emphatically in what the school has to offer than one who walks alone. A comprehensive cocurricular activity program gives each student an opportunity to belong, to be an integral part of the school, and to share in the greater good. It may also keep the student in school. For example, results of migrant student studies conducted in Texas indicate a strong relation between cocurricular involvement and remaining in school (Hinojosa, 1983).

Initiative should be taken by sponsors to inform students about available cocurricular activities and to make it easy and inexpensive for them to participate when motivation is obvious. Students should be polled for their own interests, and sponsors sought when interest is sufficiently large. Most schools have an impressive array of cocurricular activities for students. Some of the more prominent are the Future Farmers of America, Future Teachers of America, Future Homemakers of America, and the 4-H Club. Almost as prominent are newspaper, photography, language, science, math, and drama clubs. There is also the student council or government, plus athletic opportunities, including cheerleading. In other words, there can be something for everyone, provided everyone can be induced to want to become involved in something. And that is the job of sponsors.

The third way to show off the school to students is to demonstrate by word and action a sense of concern for their welfare. Sometimes this can be done with a caring nod or smile; on other occasions with an expression of interest in their accomplishments. To demonstrate caring, principals could periodically invite different students to eat lunch with them in their offices. Teachers might take the time to help a student fill out an application blank or write a letter for a job. A secretary might find the time to type that letter. What is more, the school could set aside a special day for all clubs to meet and share their interests and accomplishments. The result would be a feeling of togetherness, an intimacy not easily attained but definitely possible.

Achievement, involvement, and togetherness may not make every student happy, nor prove to skeptics that the school has good reason to take pride in its program. But the general morale of the student body is apt to be vastly improved by their appearance. If morale is high, communication is going to be positive, be it in the home or in the marketplace. The student who enjoys school, who looks forward to each school day, who likes the school's administration and staff is the biggest support the school can ever have either today or 20 years hence. The child of today is, after all, the parent of tomorrow.

SUMMARY

Everyone in the immediate school family is a potential contributor to the success of an educational public relations program. Understanding what this contribution is and then acting on that knowledge are entirely different matters. While periodic inservice helps to create this vital understanding, only a year-round educational public relations program is likely to produce concordant action. Comprising the immediate school family are boards of education, administrators, staff, and students.

One of the most important contributions that boards can make to an effective public relations program is being positive and open in their relations with one another and with internal and external groups. Another is that they hire a superintendent who is competent and public relations-oriented. Like boards, administrators make important public relations contributions when they practice good human relations skills. Administrators contribute importantly in other ways. Superintendents make a strong contribution by getting boards to adopt a public relations policy. This contribution is enhanced by the hiring of an educational public relations specialist. In implementing board policy, they embellish these contributions by creating a districtwide educational public relations advisory committee. At the building level principals contribute significantly by creating similar but localized advisory committees. Administrators with specialized functions, such as finance or curriculum, make their best contribution by effectively communicating their specializations to school and community.

The public relations contributions of staff stem from two interrelated sources: those whose major responsibility is to teach and those who provide an array of special services for a school system to advance its educational program. Teachers make their best contribution by motivating students to learn. In doing so, they demonstrate artistry and knowledge. Holding high expectations for their students, they exert much effort to bring about this realization. Special services personnel also make valuable contributions. Those involved in counseling tend to establish an appreciable rapport with students as they assist them in resolving personal and academic problems. Under the leadership of the librarian, the library service contributes to public relations through accessibility, coordination, quality, and position expansion. The contribution of the health service is embodied in the efforts of the school nurse, who, in attending to the health needs of students, helps to ensure their academic progress. The clerical service makes its contribution when secretaries and clerks display courtesy and efficiency. Well-prepared, ample, and nutritious meals, cleanliness, and amiability underscore the contribution made by food service personnel. The maintenance service contribution is epitomized in the care custodians give to school buildings. The contribution of the transportation service is best seen in its bus maintenance and bus driver safety programs.

Students also make important public relations contributions. When they are happy and academically successful, they serve as emissaries of good will for the school system. Carried home and into the community is the message that their needs are being effectively met. The result is that the school is viewed by the community as doing a good job.

• 8 •

Participants
The Extended School Family

Parents can be passive or active in demonstrating support for their schools. They can complacently and privately acknowledge the good work of the schools. They can openly attest to their merits, sharing their opinions with friends and acquaintances. They may even vote periodically at the polls to pass a school budget or bond issue and, on a rare occasion, enroll in an evening class. On an open school night each year, they may also make a brief appearance. As this kind of support is on a "hit or miss" basis, it is passive in nature.

When parental support is active, parents assume their roles as second-line contributors to an educational public relations program and function as full-fledged members of the extended school family. Active parents become chaperons for field trips and special events; serve as school volunteers; make classroom presentations; engage in school advisory committees; join band and booster clubs and PTAs or PTOs; and organize and chair campaigns to muster up support for programs, budgets, and buildings. Through this type of involvement parents acquire a feeling of usefulness and importance. The more extensive their involvement, the greater their identity with the school, provided the results of their efforts can be perceived by them as an actual contribution to the school system.

An educational public relations program that maximizes the flow of information from school to parent but minimizes the parental participation it may induce can hardly expect more than passive involvement in school affairs.

PARENT-TEACHER GROUPS

One of the most effective ways of involving parents in schools is through their neighborhood parent-teacher association (PTA) or parent-teacher organization (PTO). The difference between the two is that a school's PTA is part of a national voice that speaks through its parent organization, the National Congress of Parents and Teachers, whereas a PTO is a limited local attempt to bring parents and teachers together. Those who join a neighborhood school PTA are automatically members of the national association, and through their dues structure and special fund-raising events help to support it. For their contributions local PTAs become orchestrated with national efforts to improve education for children.

PTOs, supporting only themselves, operate independently and have a range of influence that extends no further than the schools that contain them. Either can lead to the meaningful participation of parents in the schools, but the PTA, because of its vast network, offers appreciable opportunities to parents and teachers to influence legislation at state and national levels of government in decisions concerning the schools.

Generally, PTA, or PTO activity flourishes at the elementary school, particularly at the first few grade levels. Parents tend to rediscover the schools through their children. When children begin school, they seem so small and helpless that parents cannot bear to part with them. Some drive their children to school even though a school bus stops practically at their doorstep. Others seem riveted to the spot from which their children only a few minutes before were whisked away on a school bus. Still others watch the school bus swallow up their children and then go home to brood about their loss.

Then, as children proceed up the educational ladder, entering junior and then senior high school, they become less dependent on their parents, sometimes to the extent that parents feel shut out of their lives. As teenagers their allegiance shifts to their peers, from whom they seek approval. Although most parents still may be extremely concerned about the grades and report cards of their children, many have begun, by then, to accept the school as "old hat." Noting this decline in enthusiasm, students tend not to notify their parents about upcoming school events. Parents, in turn, suspect that their children would prefer that they absent themselves from such functions, and to some extent, children may feel precisely that way. Parents, by the same token, may have already begun to view attendance at school events as an inconvenience in their own lives. Further dedication may suggest unwarranted deprivation, especially if it is perceived as meddlesome or wanting in additional enlightenment about the schools. The result is that both parties experience a sense of ambiguity; they feel hurt about a passing way of life, their own youth perchance, and guilty over their preference for another.

Many avowed PTA proponents let skeptics dupe them into believing that a high school PTA cannot be as vibrant or as alluring for parents as their initial elementary school encounter. They also tend to believe that secondary students might not welcome the involvement of their parents. The chance of their eliciting the support of teachers at the secondary school level in PTA activities is sometimes viewed as dim. Fortunately, the converse of these beliefs is true.

A narrative serves to illustrate this point. In high school X, teachers were inclined to think of PTA meetings as a waste of time. Because only a handful of parents ever showed up at PTA meetings, teachers derisively referred to their school's PTA as a TTA, in effect, a teacher-teacher association. All teachers were required to attend PTA meetings, and attendance was taken in a rather obvious fashion by the principal and his assistant. Teachers absenting themselves from a meeting were called into the principal's office the next morning to give cause. If cause was lacking, they were admonished. Consequently, about three score teachers sat around grumbling before and after every PTA meeting, criticizing parents and administration.

With a changing of the old guard, a new and optimistic president entered the picture, a teacher whose ideas were unsullied by previous myths about PTA failure in the later school years. In a few days he had met with his PTA officers and whipped into shape a program that he thought would rekindle the interest of parents in PTA activities.

The first program of the year introduced to parents every cocurricular activity in the school, an array of clubs that sought the participation of entering freshmen. Introducing the activities were the sponsors and students of these clubs, who provided demonstrations and explanations.

Advance publicity for this PTA meeting could be found in display windows and on counter tops in stores and businesses throughout the community and in the local weekly paper. Students from the school's art department designed the posters, and scores of others made sure that they were on exhibit everywhere. Although the traditional, student hand-carried notice was used to alert parents to the PTA meeting, its use was thought of as supplementary and secondary to the overall publicity effort.

When the meeting began the new PTA president, who had carefully written a script, introduced the players of the drama with a modicum of levity. Indeed, the whole meeting was treated as a party rather than as business, with a wide assortment of refreshments provided. The PTA president had even baked a cake, as had many PTA officers. Several students in the home economics department did the same under the supervision of their teacher, who was given money from the PTA treasury to buy the ingredients.

At the meeting at least one parent for every student club member was present. In addition, most of the parents of the incoming freshman class were there. They were anxious to see what opportunities awaited their children to enrich their educational experiences. The result was a jammed cafeteria, a host of new PTA members, and a crowd of happy teachers who no longer had to depend solely on one another for company.

Exhilarated by the attendance of parents and the satisfaction of teachers, the new PTA president and his cabinet moved deeper into the interior of the school to generate ways of involving parents. The idea that turned that PTA into a thriving successful association was to have departments compete with one another in putting on the most exciting and informative meeting for parents. Thus, information combined with a good deal of entertainment was the guiding maxim to gain parental interest and involvement.

For the next two years departments put their best foot forward. The athletic department, through its instructors and selected students, demonstrated and described the fundamentals of its program. The industrial education department kept the shops open until 11:00 p.m. for parents to see their youngsters operate the equipment in the shops. They even joined in, much to the pleasure of the students. Essentially, it was a "Dad's Night" and dads came in sizable numbers to participate, as did moms. Meanwhile, projects that students had made in the shop (lamps, cabinets, and tables) were on display in the corridors and were up for sale. The English department, through a meticulously prepared slide presentation, depicted students at work in their classes and exhibited some of its students' writings with an overhead projector. The language department decorated the entire school with posters from every foreign land in which a language was spoken that was taught in the school. The language labs were open and parents were led through them by students who demonstrated their use. The business department, not to be outdone by any of the other departments, brought in about ten of its graduates who were employed in an assortment of business and industrial concerns. The focus of the panel they comprised was on the different kinds of job opportunities that had become available to them upon graduating because they had taken the school's business program. Parents and students came in droves to listen, firsthand, to what they might expect as a consequence of business training, and they asked dozens of questions. After the panel discussion was concluded, an explanatory tour of the office equipment on display in the cafeteria was conducted by the department's business faculty.

The major meeting of the year, which had as its core another entertaining and informative session, brought parents and teachers together to dine on fare that was, to a large extent, donated by individual community members. Phones rang in the homes of parents for a couple of weeks. The calls were made by PTA officers and members to ask parents to contribute one thing or another to the dinner: a loaf of bread, a jar of pickles, a salad, a plate of beans, a cake, and so forth. When deliveries were made, the food functioned as an entree for the donating parent to join the feast. Contributors came and, with a little coaxing, stayed. The meal was a huge success, with parents once again outnumbering teachers, perhaps by as many as 5 to 1. Cakes were raffled off at this meeting, as at all other meetings; prizes were won and collected; new memberships were solicited; and new help organized. Somewhere along the way an interesting development had occurred. Parents now seemed as interested in getting together with one another and with their children's teachers as they were once in simply securing information about the school.

Supplementing the year's four regular PTA meetings were a number of other activities sponsored by the high school PTA: a teachers' breakfast in the school cafeteria cooked and served by parents, along with a dedication of some lasting but inexpensive gift that would adorn the school or its grounds in honor of the teachers, a tree, for example; a night of one-act plays, for which a panel of parents judged best play and best actor and actress and made "Oscar" kinds of awards to participating students and supervising teachers; a communitywide raffle that raised scholarship funds for talented, needy students. The PTA was also instrumental in turning out the vote to pass needed financial referenda and in helping to acquire a new library for the community.

Two years later the no-longer-new PTA president had transformed a once, by necessity, teacher-dominated PTA into a parent-led association with only one of its officers, the treasurer, a teacher. The focus of the new administration moved from entertainment and information to problem-solving activities addressing emergent school issues. The PTA was now in high gear and had a thriving active membership. Parents, once thought to be uninterested in their schools, were present in large numbers to prove the contrary.

All PTA stories may not turn out to be as successful as this one. But just because they do not is no reason that they cannot. The PTA is the school's best friend and every opportunity to embrace it should be taken. Through the PTA passivity is changed to the kind of activity that all schools need to secure lasting and meaningful support.

VOLUNTEERS

One of the public relations contributions of active parents is serving as a school volunteer. According to Tierce (1982), parents (more than any other group), business and industry people, senior citizens, college students, and agency and organizational personnel are involved in secondary school volunteer programs; and these programs, claim their coordinators, make an important contribution to school-community relations. Tierce also points out that although secondary school volunteers spend more time in program involvement than do their elementary school counterparts, they are outnumbered by them, 10 to 1. The contribution volunteers make to the educational public relations programs is, therefore, significantly greater than what the perceptions of the secondary school coordinators would seem to indicate.

Volunteers are extensions of the school family. In performing their roles they become deeply enmeshed in school life. They come to know students and teachers well; they take interest and pride in school accomplishments, having contributed to their realization; they help to defray costs by providing a multiplicity of services that would ordinarily be provided by paraprofessionals or clerical staff, or perhaps not provided at all unless by the teachers themselves; and they serve as student tutors, chaperons, club advisors, and sometimes even make home visitations. In fact, as a Texas Education Agency brochure, *Volunteers in Texas Schools* (VITS), points out, volunteers offer valuable assistance of all kinds. Working in arts and crafts, laboratories, libraries, kindergartens, playgrounds, special education, offices, and varied classrooms, and with teachers, gym instructors, counselors, librarians, and clerical personnel, they not only improve school-community relations and stretch school tax dollars, but also, and more importantly, enhance learning opportunities for students, which is, of course, public relations at its best.

Although it is said that there is an abundance of volunteers available to the schools (National Association of Secondary School Principals [NASSP], 1981), voluntary recruitment remains an important area needing improvement, as do teacher attitudes toward volunteers (Tierce, 1983). Teachers find it difficult to fathom the benefits of volunteer assistance until they have experienced it. Having operated as loners for so long, teachers can easily view classroom assistance as an intrusion into their inner sanctum. Inadvertently or intentionally volunteers may challenge the authority of teachers as they cultivate enduring relationships with students, and teachers may feel threatened. Or teachers may simply associate volunteer initiative or success with a consequent loss of their classroom authority. In either case the result is the same, with rivalry becoming rampant in the classroom. Thus, inservice is critical for both groups so that their respective roles can be thoroughly understood, acknowledged, and respected. Principals, too, have a strong effect on the success of a volunteer program, and for that reason inservice is just as important for them as it is for the other two groups. Competition between teachers and volunteers can quickly lead to a decline in classroom and school morale and the transmission of unfavorable messages into the community by volunteers. But a principal averse to the notion of using volunteers can stalemate a program before it has a chance to prove it has merit.

To start a volunteer program, Mastors (1975) lists 11 steps. These steps begin with awareness, commitment, a management core, and collective participation; run the gamut of goal setting, formalized board approval, fund-raising, and recruitment; and close with evaluation and appreciation for labors expended. The recommended management core includes a board of directors comprised of a limited number of coordinators, especially in large school districts in which membership is determined geographically; a director to organize and supervise the work of school coordinators who, in turn, recruit and train volunteers; a chairperson to raise funds for supporting the program and to oversee the expenditures made by a purchasing officer; and secretarial assistance.

School volunteers can be an indispensable part of an educational public relations program, or they can remain an untapped reservoir of the community. If a program is organized and administered efficiently and effectively, and if appreciation goes hand-in-hand with dedication, the part-time efforts of volunteers will be transformed into full-time public relations efforts.

As already indicated, the school family can be further extended through the volunteer efforts of parents, senior citizens, college students, and individuals working in business, industry, agencies, institutions, and organizations. Some of these groups fall neatly into other categories as well, two of which can be designated as nonparents and parents with grown-up children who have attended either public or private schools.

SENIOR CITIZENS

Senior citizens are often identified by several euphemistic appellations, none of which may have much of an appeal for them. The age range used to classify senior citizens also varies. For example, whereas the so-called gray panther may be aged 50 years or over, the golden ager is probably 65 years or over. Snowbirds is another common expression used to describe senior citizens, as are the words senior citizens themselves. What is of real importance, however, is that the number of citizens 60 years or older in the nation is set at 32 million (NASSP, 1981), and those at 65 plus at 25 million, which taken separately or together constitutes a sizeable political clout (Larkin, 1982). How powerful this clout is can be seen in the leadership role of senior citizens in California's now famed Proposition 13.

To get senior citizens back into the schools, school districts have used an almost endless number of strategies. The talent of senior citizens has been capitalized on in volunteer programs, in school advisory groups, and in school-community communication networks. There have been numerous special days heralding their impoprtance, a Senior Citizens Day and a Grandparents Day, for example. They have been brought into schools en masse on schools buses for tours and hot lunches. They have been issued special activity cards to attend school events without charge. The Grand Prairie Independent School District in Grand Prairie, Texas has, for example, initiated a Gold Card Club for senior citizens. Moreover, the district has developed a *Senior Citizens Handbook* of some 57 pages that explains not only the objectives of their senior citizen program but also its implementation procedures.

Community education programs have also been directed toward eliciting the involvement of senior citizens. These efforts have included, along with numerous others, senior citizens as teachers and participants in community education classes; free admission to classes; special events for senior citizens (dances, for instance); hot lunches in school cafeterias; participation in advisory committees and surveys; and decals, posters, and pins to commemorate Senior Citizens Day.

The population of the nation is graying at an unprecedented rate in its history. In years to come senior citizens will prevail as the largest block of the nation's citizenry. It is easy to overlook senior citizens who have been out of the school's mainstream for many years, but there is no need for this to happen. Education, as it is construed today, is lifelong, and everybody has a role in its making and taking. Senior citizens, many of whom were once intimate members of the school's family, should be welcomed back into the fold with open arms. If the school wishes to retain or regain their support, it must first be sure of what it can and will do for them before it poses the converse.

NONPARENTS

Nonparents, as a group, can also be inducted into the school family, as can parents whose children have graduated from high school or college. Nonparents, be they young marrieds or older childless couples, have a right in helping to determine the school's future, certainly as much any other group. They are taxpayers and have a vested interest in the schools their taxes support. The same is true of parents whose children are now adults. In fact, these two groups, like retirees, may be more available than parents who, in tending to the diverse needs of their preschool children, find themselves virtually homebound. In any event, both groups, through limited or extensive involvement in the schools, can make significant contributions to the school and to its educational public relations program.

The involvement of these two groups can be accomplished in much the same way as already discussed. They can serve as volunteers, advisory committee members, and instructors or participants in community education programs. With little encouragement young marrieds could become especially interested in their school district; for, before not too many years have passed, their children will be an integral part of that district's clientele. But all groups are interested in educational, occupational, and recreational enrichment; and community education can be an ideal source for pursuing these interests. Participation creates support, and support is what an educational public relations program is all about.

BUSINESS AND INDUSTRY

When business and industrial groups are identified and invited to provide assistance to schools, the academic and practical domains of life are in the process of being cemented, and the school family is further extended. Proprietors and executives in both groups, if prevailed upon, will gladly find the time to serve in a variety of school capacities. These proprietors and executives are concerned with the school from two perspectives. First of all, they view involvement as a civic responsibility. Secondly, they are interested in the school because someday they may be employing its graduates. The better educated these graduates are, the greater will be their contribution to the workplace.

The mechanic who cannot read an automobile manual or its equivalent must rely exclusively on wit and dexterity, neither of which may prove useful in many situations. The secretary who cannot spell or type with proficiency, the bank teller who has a math deficiency, and the salesperson whose diction is conspicuously inadequate will be unable to make the organizational contribution demanded of them. This is a strong reason for wanting to aid the schools. It is also a marvelous way of discovering what the school needs to make it better. Perhaps most important is that every time a proprietor or an executive employs a graduate of the school, he or she is displaying confidence in the school's instructional program.

Proprietors and executives can bring valuable specialized knowledge into the school. They can serve as volunteers; assume leadership roles on advisory committees; spearhead fund-raising campaigns; teach in community education programs; and create a communication network that channels information rapidly from school to business and industry and back again. The leadership they offer, their involvement in numerous civic associations, and the image of expertise their positions convey make them vital school assets. Finally, if what they see in the school is good and if what they do helps to make it better, they will be spokespersons that the school can ill afford to be without.

AGENCIES, INSTITUTIONS, AND ORGANIZATIONS

Agencies, institutions, and organizations can be active members of a school's family, if they are called upon to participate. Social service agencies are already tied closely to the school. Food, shelter, employment, and medical care often become joint concerns of agency and school in their attempts to meld healthy minds with healthy bodies. While recreational agencies usually complement a school's physical education program, sometimes they prove to be valid substitutes for certain segments of a school's student body. Legal agencies work with family and school to overcome problems of juvenile delinquency, discrimination, and child abuse. Educational agencies work with schools to develop instructional standards and accreditation requirements for teachers and administrators. Unfortunately, schools occasionally attempt to operate in a vacuum, and relationships that could be cultivated and nourished are allowed to wither.

Standing foremost among institutions eager to develop durable relationships with schools are universities and their faculties. Some of these universitites maintain on-site experimental elementary and secondary schools. These help to prepare student teachers and administrative interns for their educational roles. They also help to develop new teaching methods and instructional materials that can be used by schools in their regions. But more often universities, with the cooperation of schools, establish sites or centers where their prospective teachers and administrators meet their internship responsibilities under the combined direction of school and university personnel.

A school opting for this kind of relationship brings the university into its family with its many faculty and vast resources. Through its participation a school is privy to the latest curricular developments, as these developments, to be judged effective, must be tested in schools. The results of experimentation and the creation of model schools often bring schools into the limelight as collaborative efforts of school and university personnel make the headlines and fill educational journals and popular magazines. Professors and teachers frequently join efforts, too, in gifted, special, and career education programs; in traditional subject matter areas in curriculum development; and in remediation and enrichment efforts. Orientation and scholarship awards for entering students also being schools and universities together in their common endeavors. In other words, all sorts of linkages of schools with universities can and do produce alliances that benefit both. These alliances heighten and improve university-school relations, which, in turn, elevates the importance of education within the larger community.

Community or junior colleges, with their emphasis on academic and vocational preparation, also have objectives and values similar to those held by schools. Thus, articulation, coordination, and cooperation should typify such relationships.

A school's links with foundations can provide needed funds and support for sundry instructional efforts. Foundations, in their philanthropic pursuits, are always interested in schools. Schools are the bacbone of society, and much is expected of them. But through their gifts foundations can help to provide the sustenance to keep them tall and erect, outcomes of which are manifold innovations and model schools.

Then there are the many organizations in the community that can be invited into the school family: civic organizations of all kinds, the Lions, Kiwanis, Knights of Columbus, Rotary, and chamber of commerce, along with a long list of educational organizations, American Association of University Women, Phi Delta Kappa, Kappa Delta Pi, Beta Sigma Phi, plus state and national teacher and administrative organizations. They are all interested in the schools; willing to listen to a school's story; able and ready to replay school successes to community members; wanting to assist in securing scholarships for needy and talented students; and disposed to accept invitations to visit and participate in the schools. When schools take advantage of these kinds of relationships, vital contributions are gained.

The contemporary school family can be as large as school officials are willing to make it. Any efforts to expand the parameters of the school family may require time, planning, and patience; but with the able leadership of the school combined with the many leaders in the community willing to serve, the effort will reap tremendous dividends for all concerned.

SUMMARY

Every school system has the potential for extending its school family. To realize this potential, however, school leaders must initiate ongoing and interactive relationships with a variety of groups. In extending their school family, administrators invite the contributions of parents, PTAs and PTOs, elementary and secondary school volunteers, senior citizens, nonparents, business and industry, and agencies, institutions, and organizations.

Parents can be passive or active in school affairs. When they are active their contributions permeate the school system and their support is virtually assured. Neighborhood PTAs and PTOs are excellent vehicles for involving parents in meaningful activities. Elementary and secondary school volunteer programs provide additional opportunities for parents to become involved. They extend similar opportunities to everyone in the community. Volunteers perform an abundance of meaningful school tasks. While saving the school and community considerable tax dollars, they function, too, as a voice of support for the school.

Existing on seriously limited incomes, senior citizens are prone to offer much resistance to financial referenda. By including them in the extended school family, administrators transform understandable opposition into appreciable support. Meanwhile, through active participation in a school volunteer program, senior citizens are able to make valuable contributions to the education of the community's youth. Nonparents and parents with children no longer in school can also make important contributions. These contributions may even surpass those of parents who have children in school, particularly if they still have youngsters at home. Along with nonparent participation comes educational commitment from a rapidly growing segment of society.

Business and industry have a vested interest in the school. Eventually they employ the school's graduates. By making their talents and resources available, they expand and enrich the education of children. Agencies, institutions, and organizations can make significant contributions as well. Agencies of all kinds (social, recreational, legal, and educational) exist within a community ready and willing to serve the school. Institutions, like the university or community college, offer to the school unique ways to work toward common educational goals; and organizations, civic and educational, stand ready to assist the school when they are invited to play an active role.

• 9 •

Politics

To paraphrase Aristotle, people are by nature political, Americans included, despite their less than mediocre record at the ballot box. Unfortunately, they would rather argue democracy than practice it. A microcosmic view of political struggles in society is offered by Golding (1954) in his classic *Lord of the Flies,* in which he presents preteen English children marooned on an island grappling for power and authority, with a democratic government giving way to a dictatorship. Adding support to this piece of fiction is the manner in which American youth gangs function. They are governed by chieftains and councils. They have territories or turfs to guard, the invasion of which results in war councils, gang wars, and peace parlays.

At a more sophisticated political level teachers form coalitions to produce legislation that will give them the power to bargain bilaterally with boards of education. Then, as associations or unions, they negotiate their demands at the bargaining table. Similarly, university faculties politicize their concerns through unions or senates. In a subtler way educational associations of similar ilk vie for ascendency in the educational arena at state and national levels, thereby inhibiting the formation of strong umbrella networks of teachers or administrators. Contingent upon membership and growth, the latter particularly evident when the power structure is expanding, survival readily embraces the notion of bureaucratic fiefdoms. Too, educational associations are notorious for their political infighting. Threatened by new members espousing change and seeking positions of power, members of the old guard, solidifying their opposition, attempt to coopt, discredit, or ostracize them.

Another example of politics at work is the vying for leadership and control among the various community education delivery systems extant in a particular community, such as local public school district, community college, and parks and recreation department. Frequently impeding efforts to collaborate is the question of turf encroachment.

COMMUNITY POWER STRUCTURES

Every community has a power structure. But who actually controls what or whom is often imperceptible. For example, an organization's old guard may elevate to leadership positions only those whom they can control and replace once they have served their purpose. Thus, those who appear most involved are not necessarily those who hold power. A community's power hierarchy, however, can be determined in a number of ways (Dillehay & Metcalf, 1983). One way is to have community members name those individuals they perceive to be power holders. A second focuses on a determination of the incumbents of major community and business leadership positions. A third comes from an examination of decisions made within the community. And a fourth deals with the identification of status held by individuals in the social sphere, along with the nature of their activities.

A variety of techniques may be employed to elicit the requisite information. For example, the community may be stratified and representatives of each strata asked to identify, through a nominating process much like that used in a Delphi study, individuals they perceive as power holders. Power holders, in this case, emerge from frequency of individual nominations resolved through group consensus. The process may be conducted by personal or phone interviews or by a mail survey. Another technique utilizes media research. Local radio and television open forums may be monitored to determine issues and issue leaders. Program sponsorship and advertisements may be used to identify business leaders. Newspapers may be analyzed for names in the news and the issues, or philanthropic or social activities with which these names are associated. The yellow pages of a phone book or special business directory, if studied over a five-year period, would identify names of business people with some continuity in the community, as well as the proprietors of long-established firms. Information gleaned from the chamber of commerce, Rotary, and the Better Business Bureau would also help to identify business influentials.

Attendance at service organization meetings as a guest may also prove helpful. Those leading or playing prominent roles in charitable drives and in election, issue-oriented, and financial referenda campaigns (municipal and educational) should be identified; as should the progress and success or failure of these activities. A study of the history of the community, as revealed by personal testimonies and library archives, should also be conducted.

But power is not readily shared by those who possess it, and for that reason citizen participation attempts prove threatening to those in power and abortive and unsatisfying to those who desire genuine input into the decision-making process. In describing what frequently occurs when citizens seek involvement in the power hierarchy, Arnstein (1971) constructs an eight-rung ladder of citizen participation that has as its first rung sheer manipulation and as its last direct control; but in which some measure of sharing power does not actually begin until rung six, at which time citizens and power holders form partnerships. Again, although evidence of influence is apparent on rung five, participation is still largely paternalistic in nature; and placation, not input, is the strategy employed. Interestingly enough, rung three has much affinity with the way some school systems operate. They barrage their citizenry with an abundance of information, but disregard the reactions they receive until they mushroom into issues that demand immediate attention. School systems that conduct surveys but ignore responses characterize, through their actions, the consultation that occurs on rung four. Finally, while rung seven involves a delegation of power and the negotiation of differences, rung two, in stressing, therapy, treats dissent as an illness.

ISSUES MANAGEMENT

In recent years political activity and the pressures engendered by it have manifested themselves in various ways in this country. There have been the Civil Rights demonstrations and student Vietnam War protests of the 1960s; the tax reform propositions of the last decade; a preponderant attempt to legislate an Equal Rights Amendment; a questioning of the purpose of social security and advancement of the retirement age; and the current demonstrations against nuclear missiles. More directly related to education have been desegregation snafus and school busing protests; clamors for the implementation of tuition tax initiatives or credits and voucher plans; the push to eliminate sexism in public schools, including sexism in textbooks; a quest for an increase in accountability, particularly in the area of teacher competence; and a return to the basics. Finally, the recent report from the National Commission on Excellence in Education has made education a top contender among issues that may elect political aspirants and unseat political incumbents in upcoming polls. Education has returned to the equivocal days of Sputnik.

Most groups are single-issue-oriented, held together by a few individuals. While group leaders tend to exaggerate their support, public officials tend to underestimate it (Riedel, 1972). Individuals join groups for a variety of reasons, among them the following: similarity of purpose, idealism, personal gratification, status, self-esteem, the expansion of business contacts, and power; and they remain members because of the friendships they develop through cooperative efforts, some of which may eventually be substantially different from their original aim (Lazar, 1971). The point is that single-issue-oriented groups, instead of disbanding when their goal is achieved, raise other issues to keep the group intact (NSPRA, 1983).

Issues management has recently surfaced as another dimension of educational public relations. A forecasting tool, issues management not only anticipates issues that might affect an organization, but also manages them through prioritization, strategy development, implementation, and evaluation (Ferguson, 1983a). To this list should be added communication. As suggested by Ewing (1980), it means communicating to those who have a vested interest in an activity or enterprise. As applied to public schools, it means reporting to the local citizenry. Whereas policy impact analysis is internally directed, concerned, as it were, with the selection of policies to accommodate unanticipated external events, issues management attempts to forecast external events that might change the policies themselves. Again, whereas the former is concerned with functions such as research and development and finance, the latter stresses functions such as public and governmental relations (Renfro & Morrison, 1982).

A recognition of the importance of an issues management program by board and superintendent is essential to its implementation, as are staff and fiscal allocations. Once support is forthcoming, a small task force is formed made up of 6 to 12 people and chaired, for example, by an educational public relations director. Through a workshop comprised of school and community members, a list of issues is compiled, prioritized, and forwarded to the school district's administrative team, which matches issues with individuals best suited to deal with them. These individuals may range from a particular staff specialist to an entire board. Staff reports then travel back to the task force for final action. Following the development of a communication plan to alleviate or resolve an issue, strategies are assessed and made current (Ferguson, 1983b).

Other ways to identify issues include media content analysis, especially the newspaper; public opinion surveys; and dialogues with operations managers and department heads (Campbell, 1983), or principals and central office specialists.

LOBBYING

Regardless of whether or not administrators employ specialized management strategies to deal with emergent issues in their respective communities, they will eventually have to contend with broadly based issues that defy provincialized measures of control. These educational issues may have nothing to do with local concerns. They may, on the contrary, merely reflect the stance of an incumbent administration or a particular legislator (Kaplan, 1982). More likely, they stem from the activities of special interest groups that desire to effect educational change, which, from their points of view, is synonymous with reform.

When issues that affect education become state or national concerns, they move into the legislative arena for resolution. In order to prevent an issue-oriented proposal from becoming law, an educational coalition must be formed to influence legislators to act on its behalf. While this is easier said than done because of the splintered nature of educational groups, a good example of such a coalition was the unity of action achieved by the National Educational Association (NEA) and the American Federation of Teachers (AFT) in thwarting the tuition tax credit proposal of the Reagan administration (Kaplan, 1982).

The area of educational governmental relations is fertile ground for the educational public relations specialist, whose communication expertise makes him or her an ideal candidate for the role of an educational lobbyist. The contemporary lobbyist provides valuable information to legislators, which despite its partiality, would be difficult and time consuming to procure. The lobbyist also provides good will and the suggestion of constituency support (Anderson, Murray, & Farley, 1975). It is interesting to note that legislators are inclined to underestimate the persuasiveness of lobbyists in their personal contacts with them, seeing them more as dependable sources of information rather than opinion shapers; a consequence of which is a misguided assumption that they can easily judge the accuracy of the lobbyist's communication. Simultaneously, they misjudge the persuasive influence of the lobbyist, who considers persuasion, not information-giving, his or her primary role (Pettus & Bland, 1976).

Three categories of activity characterize lobbying (Lewis, 1983). The first and evidently the forte of the lobbyist is face-to-face, or direct, transactions with legislators. The second, indirect in nature, uses local campaigns that signify real or possible votes to induce support. The third is cross-lobbying, or gaining the support of other interest groups on a particular proposal, with the favor to be returned on some other occasion.

Today, with most federal educational funding coming through block grants to states, administrators would do well to delegate the lobbying function to an experienced public relations specialist, preferably someone who is politically informed and adept. This person would function best when serving a coalition of school districts rather than only one. At the same time, funds for the position could be shared by participating school districts.

Essential to the lobbying activity of any school district at the state level is a carefully developed plan aimed at amassing local and neighboring school district support. Successful coalitions are those that endorse proposals that maximize a sharing of benefits among all school districts. Success also depends on a lobbyist's familiarity with state legislators and their positions, with legislative proceedings, with the layout of the state capitol, and with the facts surrounding a given issue, including the position of the opposition. Further enhancing a proposal's success is its sponsorship, as a bill, by a legislative committee; on the other hand, bills requiring individual sponsors should be endorsed by members of both parties, one of whom, a majority member, should be its primary sponsor (Yonally, 1980).

Lobbying is both science and art. It is informative by design but persuasive in purpose. It presumes an understanding of the function of public opinion in a democratic society, as well as a thorough knowledge of political processes; but it thrives on the ebb and flow of interpersonal contact and intuitive insights. It proceeds using carefully formulated objectives and priorities, but is prone to temper them with the rhetoric of compromise. It organizes campaigns and coalitions skillfully and consolidates support into a single voice, but applauds the singular efforts of individuals and groups and shares the limelight with them when success is attained. It tactically seeks alliances, but sacrifices neither credibility nor integrity in the process. It is consistently tenacious in its aims.

CITIZEN PARTICIPATION

Citizen dissatisfaction of one kind or another with the schools need never proceed beyond a rudimentary stage of disquietude if boards and administrators invite realistic and tangible forms of community participation. The growth and subsequent formidability of local issues frequently owe their origin to the indifference of the school's leadership. Earlier it was pointed out that tokenism or rubber stamping is sometimes a motive for using citizen participation. This procedure should be construed as less than effective in staving off problems that may one day bombard the school. Because decision-making opportunities earmarked by this procedure are more illusory than real, the durability of meaningful relations between a school and its community are just as ephemeral. The easing of federal requirements governing citizen participation in Title I programs, wrought by the 1981 Educational Consolidation and Improvement Act, is a good reason that participation should now be extended, extolled, and relevant.

While public school officials appear reluctant to entertain citizen input in the school's decision-making process, citizens tend not only to reflect minimal confidence in the decisions made by boards and school personnel, but also want increased public involvement and decentralized decision making (Lutz & Garnon, 1979). Often citizen participation fails because blame, not remediation, is the course an advisory committee is left to pursue. Through the use of a growth paradigm, problems can be translated into needs, blame into shared responsibility, disagreement into a broadening consensus reinforced by trust, and needs into desirable goal attainment (Azarnoff, 1974).

There is no question that advisory committees can sap the energy and time of administrators, yet anything as important as an advisory committee is worthy of reasonable expenditures of both. A willingness of citizens to participate should never be shrugged off by administrators; for those who are engaged in relevant participation serve as emissaries of good will for the school. Their involvement identifies them as knowledgeable sources of information about the school. To produce effective advisory committees, administrators should ensure that all efforts are directed at specific goals or projects; that advisory groups realize that their purpose is to advise, not dictate policy; and that the life of a committee does not extend beyond designated goal or project completion, save in those instances in which committees are expected to operate on a continuous basis. Although committees should never be allowed to become unwieldy in size, they should be carefully constructed to contain representation from all strata of the community.

For continuing (or standing) committees charters should be drafted bearing, primarily, committee name; objectives; membership number, selection criteria, and terms; attendance and quorum requirements; types and responsibilities of officers; when, where, and how meetings are to be conducted, the latter preferably based on *Robert's Rules of Order* (1978); and an amendment procedure to change by-laws. The function of the committee should be etched in board policy (NSPRA, 1973). As most committees are made up of members with widely different backgrounds, orientation is necessary to bring members closer together in their understanding of the intricacies of school operation, including nature and types of curricular thrust. Some of this knowledge will be derived from the input of school personnel serving on this committee; most, however, should be provided by tours, staff presentations, and exposure to available resources that will facilitate committee progress.

As important as committees are in relating the school story to the community and bringing talent and fresh insights to school leaders, they should not be created just for the sake of involving people. They should always be purposeful in nature, filling a need or a void in a school system. Recommendations of committees should never be tabled for some future consideration; for this is a certain sign that the committee is of little value in the first place. Again, without specific guidelines to follow, committee members may communicate findings to media personnel when approached by them and inadvertently usurp the prerogative of boards. If committee members are not encouraged to do their homework, the report they make may lack substance and credibility. Finally, if a board finds it inappropriate to act on a particular committee recommendation, the reason should be made known to the committee (Goble & Holliday, 1980).

Committees can prove to be valuable resources to school leaders, provided communication channels are kept open and all concerned adopt a positive tone in dealing with one another. The last phase of committee work is a two-way evaluation system that rates the committee on its efficacy in coming up with needed answers and school leaders in their receptivity to act upon committee findings. It goes without saying that committees should be praised for their efforts.

SUMMARY

People are inherently political. When their individual voices cannot be heard, they gather into groups and form associations. To gain strength, they create coalitions. This is as true of educational groups as it is of ecological, nuclear disarmament, or equal rights amendment groups. Issues bring people together; and once they are together, the camaraderie they enjoy keeps them that way. Thus, new issues are sought. When issues are unresolved at the local level, they may advance to state and national levels, where lobbyists gather to elicit support for or against an issue. Within the educational sphere the educational public relations specialist is ideal for the role of lobbyist, provided adequate training and experience in governmental relations has been acquired. Issues may also be raised at the national level that precipitate massive grass-roots involvement and opposition. Issues management has, therefore, emerged as an area of study well worth the time and energy of educational administrators.

At the local level people frequently seek meaningful participation in the school decision-making process. These attempts may be subverted by unseen power holders within a community or diluted by the school's administrative hierarchy. As a result participation becomes sheer tokenism, and participants seek recourse through other channels to address their concerns. In the same vein, the administrative hierarchy may find itself as powerless as token participants in shaping or meeting educational goals.

To optimize their leadership function, educational administrators must take the time to understand the power structures of their communities; identify influentials who will help them achieve desirable educational goals; seek responsive and representative community participation; be aware of and responsive to growing community issues; assess and attend to community needs; and amass the necessary force to abort issues that are incompatible with goals already decided upon by school and community.

The politics of education is nothing new. What is new is that educational leaders are learning how to politicize effectively.

• 10 •

Principles and Practices

Although educational public relations practices often appear countless in number, all are traceable to a relatively few value-laden public relations principles. When public relations policies are fully developed and written, these principles are mirrored in the policy a particular school system endorses, primarily in its choice of values. But written policies are frequently brief, comprised, as it were, of no more than two or three sentences; and discretion is allowed to dictate practice. Finally, in the absence of any policy, discretion dictates public relations activity. In both cases actions serve as the basis for determining the usage of a specific public relations principle. Although no attempt will be made here to relate the full range of public relations practices to the principles that undergird them, a select group of principles will be used to highlight and explore some of the more common public relations practices. In passing, it should be pointed out that many practices have their origin in the same principle.

A-1 *Principle:* Because the public schools belong to the public, it is important for boards and administrators to know what attitudes and expectations the public holds for its schools.

A-2 *Practice:* Determining public attitudes and expectations through the school survey: construction and implementation.

The school survey, or opinionnaire as it is often called, is the method most typically used by schools to determine how satisfied or dissatisfied citizens are with their schools. It is also a means of determining expectations these citizens have for their schools. This does not mean that school leaders are limited to the school survey to detect public attitudes and expectations. On the contrary, opinions can be solicited through forums, panels, school advisory groups, and citizen input at board meetings. But segmented or sketchy input is no substitute for the comprehensiveness of a survey. Neither is it scientific.

The three most commonly used survey methods include the personal, or face-to-face interview, the telephone interview, and the direct mail questionnaire. A further distinction may be made between the questionnaire that is mailed out to respondents and the questionnaire that is hand delivered and subsequently picked up, which is essentially a hybrid of the personal interview and the direct mail-out. On the horizon and, to some extent, already in operation is the computer interview.

Personal

Provided adequate time, money, and supervision are available, the personal interview is the superior of the three methods. But extended periods of time can distort survey results if intervening events are of a magnitude to influence participant responses. For example, parents may view the school as a citadel of serenity one day, and three weeks later, after a virtual riot in the school cafeteria, see it as a place of pandemonium. Yet time can be controlled by increasing the size of the interviewing staff, and staff expansion is possible if a surplus of volunteers or money exists. Even then an abundance of supervision is necessary to train either volunteers or paid interviewers. Through their speech and body language, untrained personnel can transmit clues to participants, who have a certain affinity to act upon these clues, if for no other reason than to please the interviewer with what they construe to be an enlightened response. There is also the matter of distance. Unless interviewers are strategically located in their own neighborhoods, initial and return visits to the homes of participants may require them to do an appreciable amount of traveling. Of course, if money is no problem, neither is distance. Then even volunteers can be compensated for their travel. However, if money is found wanting and interviewers are forced to solicit the opinions of people they know in their own neighborhoods, a certain loss of credibility may be the result. The advantages of the personal interview are several. It is likely to elicit a high rate of return, particularly if questions are of interest to participants. Trained interviewers are keen observers of human nature. They can sort out fact from fiction as they, instead of the respondents, note nuances in speech and behavior. On-site visitations allow interviewers ample time to clarify confusing survey items and to extend lines of questioning. Face-to-face interviews carry with them a sense of importance and humanity that the other methods cannot equal. This last advantage provides the impetus for the block plan survey used by community educators. Here a person living on a block surveys the other residents of the block or neighborhood. Many people are involved in this kind of survey, and survey activity is prized almost as much as the answers it produces. Nevertheless, community education surveys are centered, for the most part, on what people would like to see included in their community education programs and not on how they view the entire school system. In any event, public relations is equated with communication and human relations, and both are derivatives of the personalized survey.

Mail

The least effective method of surveying is the direct mail questionnaire. Mail-out questionnaires traditionally produce a poor return rate, yet the results of these surveys are often used to guide school leaders in their efforts to increase the school's responsiveness to its community. Responses to this kind of survey generally fall into two categories. Essentially extreme points of view, they constitute, on one hand, the opinions of people who are very much in favor with what a school is doing and, on the other, a host of negative attitudes that reflect general dissatisfaction with the school. Mail-out surveys tend to miss the silent majority altogether, people whose opinions would provide school leaders with a more representative description of community attitudes. With its built-in monitoring system, the hand delivered questionnaire promises more information than the direct mail-out, but this procedure is almost as expensive as the personal interview, while offering little assurance that the questionnaire will be completed unless repeated motivational visitations are made.

Telephone

The telephone survey is frequently viewed as the middle-of-the-road survey method, but its ease of administering and high response rate make it by far the most attractive. A canned presentation that regards interviewer textual departures as inappropriate, the telephone interview requires only a minimum of staff training. Emotions are relatively easy to control when reading a script, and a voice is less difficult to deal with than a face. Volunteers are, therefore, better suited for the telephone interview than they are for the face-to-face interview. The cost of using a telephone for a local survey is far less than the cost of using a car to travel the same distance. Even the cost of a local mail-out questionnaire may exceed telephone costs when repeated mailings, coupled with follow-up phone calls, are necessary to secure participant responses. Because travel is unnecessary, the telephone interview may be conducted over a shorter period of time than the personal interview. It is also faster than the mailed questionnaire, which may take several weeks despite specified early deadlines. Moreover, return calls are usually minimal. The telephone interview also promises more reliability than does a mailed questionnaire, with its high response rate and few sampling replacements.

A criticism of the telephone survey is that as everyone does not have a telephone, all individuals do not have an equal chance of being selected. Also, many people have unlisted numbers, and telephone directories, issued each year, do not even include everyone who has a listed number. Thus, bias is introduced into the sample. The fact is, though, that phones are far more commonplace today than they were a few decades ago. And lists (computerized school records, for example) can be found to contain new and unlisted numbers. Finally, should lists of prospective survey populations fail to produce a high percentage of telephone numbers, the telephone interview may be supplemented with the personal interview. All things considered, the telephone interview offers some distinct advantages for school districts with limited budgets.

CONSTRUCTION

One of the easiest and quickest ways to construct a direct mail questionnaire is simply to have respondents rate in quick succession the quality of certain aspects of the school, such as board, administration, and teachers; curricular and cocurricular offerings; counseling, communication, food, health, and transportation services; and buildings and grounds. The greater the detail, the more useful is the response. Quality may be determined through the use of conventional letter grades or a series of adjectives ranging from excellent, or good, to poor. This type of survey requires little effort to construct and few directions to complete.

Surveys that are targeted to address both local and national concerns take considerable planning. A lot of legwork and dialogues with individuals and groups will quickly ferret out what appear to be local concerns. A perusal of national polls, newspapers, magazines, and educational journals will provide insight into widespread concerns.

With regard to personal and telephone questionnaire formats, the basic difference is that the personal interview can be either structured or unstructured, whereas the telephone interview, because of significant time constraints, needs to be tightly structured.

The introduction to a telephone survey is extremely important. It identifies the caller, gives the reason for the call, explains how the prospective participant's name was selected, and asks permission to pursue the interview. An example of such an introduction follows:

> Good morning (afternoon, evening), my name is Harry Plackett and I'm helping the Rainstack Independent School District conduct its annual telephone survey. You may have read about it in your newspaper! (slight pause) This year, I am pleased to say, you have been randomly selected, along with about 400 other parents, to provide your board of education with an opinion that will assist it in its continuing efforts to serve you and your child in the best possible manner. Only a few minutes of your time should be needed to complete this survey. Can I count on you for your assistance?

Once a commitment is obtained, the next step is to explain briefly how questions can be answered. For example, although most may be answered with a yes/no or no opinion, others may require a sentence or two to complete. In order to isolate the information received and to pinpoint areas of concern, it may be necessary to have the respondent think in terms of a single, school-aged child, oldest or youngest. However, if a general impression of the schools is preferred, no distinction should be made. In other words, participants will, in the latter case, answer with all children in mind. Of the two procedures, the former is likely to be more efficacious.

The survey should contain a minimum of open-ended questions. Although such questions provide significant and sometimes serendipitous responses, their compilation is quite time consuming. To facilitate the compilation of open-ended responses, answers to questions are often anticipated and checked when applicable. Unfortunately, however well these answers are anticipated, there are certain to be overlooked possibilities. The questionnaire should be framed by open-ended questions, one near the beginning, upon completion of preliminary inquiries, and one near the end, prior to the gathering of any demographic information. Whereas the former should ask participants to identify school strengths, the latter should ask for suggestions that will lead to further improvement. Thus, while the first may ask participants what they like about their child's school, and thereby begin the questionnaire on a positive note, the second may ask participants what areas of their child's school they would like to see improved or strengthened. The problem of directly asking individuals to identify weaknesses is that they feel obliged to find some even when they may not really perceive them as such.

There should also be an open-ended question located somewhere near the middle of the survey. Strategically placed, the open-ended question tends to revitalize interest and break the monotony of yes/no questions. If the survey is extensive, additional open-ended questions may be used to intensify input and involvement. Four or five open-ended questions are not unreasonable in a questionnaire containing about 40 questions.

The time it takes to respond to 40 questions may range from 15 to 30 minutes, but it is possible to complete a survey of this size in 12 minutes if participants are quick to respond and the interviewer keeps the interview moving at a brisk pace. Survey construction also implies teaming up to brainstorm both questions and possible answers. A well-constructed survey already has some inkling about the expectations of a community for its schools. This information can be obtained by meeting with various groups, among them teacher association leaders, PTA presidents, band and booster clubs, service organizations, school advisory groups, and the chamber of commerce. Dialogues with these groups ensure that the survey will be examining basic community concerns. Some national concerns, as indicated earlier, should also be addressed in the survey.

IMPLEMENTATION

Prior to conducting a pilot study, certain actions may be taken to strengthen the questionnaire's format and content. Individuals or groups can be asked to complete a questionnaire, taking note of readability, item ambiguities and redundancies, problems in syntax, and relevance of questions. A further step may be taken with the personal or telephone interview. A number of face-to-face or phone-to-phone simulations may be conducted. When the initial preparation of the questionnaire has been completed, a pilot study using 5% of the total sample to be surveyed should be conducted. Further questionnaire changes may be necessitated by the pilot study. As soon as these changes have been incorporated into the questionnaire, the survey can begin.

The direct mail questionnaire usually consists of three mailings. In addition, it could include some follow-up phone calls. To avoid a sampling bias, a small percentage of nonrespondents should also be called, simply to determine why they did not complete the questionnaire. The first mailing consists of a letter, a questionnaire, and a self-addressed, postage paid return envelope. The purpose of the letter is to explain the purpose of the survey and to request assistance for completion of the questionnaire. If 80% of the sampled population respond to the first mailing, no further mailings need occur. Because of the low return rate of the mailed questionnaire, a second and third mailing is likely to be necessary. The second mailing, a post card or letter, is a reminder for designated respondents to complete the survey. The third mailing replicates the first in its contents, except that the letter contained in the packet is updated in its request for participation and bears a new deadline date. If a satisfactory response rate is not attained by the end of the third mailing, telephone calls may be made to increase the percentage of returns. The direct mail questionnaire is governed by fixed time lines. The first letter may allow two weeks for the receipt of responses; the second, another two weeks; and the third, still another two weeks. The direct mail questionnaire can produce satisfactory results, if funds and patience exist in modicum amounts.

Quite frequently the direct mail questionnaire is sent to everyone in the community to answer, and no further effort is made to contact prospective respondents. In this case, return postage is probably not included. What is received is what is analyzed. Such a questionnaire may not even require a special mailing. It may appear as a tear out in a school newsletter or newspaper. This method is very economical, but generally unproductive because of its low return rate.

When a population is sampled, and this sample is statistically determined, the number of individuals to be surveyed is considerably smaller than in a comprehensive mailing that includes everyone in a community. This reduction in participants should more than compensate for the extra mailings to selected survey respondents, and survey results should far outweigh the one-shot results of a comprehensive mailing.

The direct mail questionnaire should be numbered so that nonrespondents may be identified for subsequent mailings. To convey respondent anonymity, this number may be written on the return envelope underneath the postage stamp. The use of different colored paper for the questionnaires may serve as a color code to distinguish between categories of respondents.

To ensure the representativeness of the population being surveyed, a sample should be drawn scientifically. Once the sampling error, or chances of being right or wrong, has been estimated and the size of the sample determined, a table of random numbers, found in most statistical textbooks, may be used to select prospective respondents. In a simple random sample, for example, whereas a sample size of 1,000 has a maximum sampling error of 3.2%, a maximum error of 5% would be tantamount to a sample size of 400 (Weisberg & Bowen, 1977). This means that if a group of 400 parents was sampled and 75% of these parents opted for a back-to-basics curricula emphasis, the accuracy of this response for the entire parental population would be plus or minus 5 percentage points of 75%.

A systematic sampling procedure may also be used. Here the names of prospective respondents are drawn at set intervals until a predetermined sample size is obtained, say 200 for a population of 4,000. To decide at what point in a list selection should begin, a number less than the value of an interval should be randomly chosen, preferably from a table of random numbers. If the starting number is 12 and the interval is set at 20, the first person on a list chosen to participate would be number 12; the second, 32; the third, 52; the fourth, 72; and so on until the sample was used up.

A stratified sampling procedure is used to break down a study population into small homogeneous groups, which, when randomly sampled on a particular topic, reflect the opinions of the entire population. Thus, rather than sample all individuals in a community on the pros and cons of an educational issue, the community may be divided into several strata by some common characteristic (occupation, for example), and the results used to reflect the attitudes of the general community. Again, rather than query all teachers in a major metropolitan school system on what they think their public relations role should be, random samples can be drawn from strata representing senior high school, junior high school, elementary school, and preschool teachers to reflect the thinking of all of the school system's teachers.

Cluster sampling occurs when an intensive study of a few areas is made to portray the opinions of an entire community. For example, selected block clusters in various parts of a community could be surveyed to determine whether a school building referendum could be passed, and the elicited opinions from these clusters would be considered representative of the opinions of the entire community.

A systematic sample is frequently easier and less costly to conduct, providing more information and less sampling error, than the simple random sample. The stratified sample offers more homogeneous information than the other two sampling procedures and is characterized by a certain amount of economy because of its administering ease. The cluster sample, in grouping nearby population segments for sampling, is likely to save both time and money because traveling costs are significantly curtailed. Of the four sampling procedures mentioned here, all except the cluster sample requires a list of prospective candidates (Mendenhall, Ott, & Scheaffer, 1971).

Sampling lists can be obtained from school records, tax accounting offices, census reports, voter registrations, telephone and specialized business directories, organization and association membership directories, advertising companies, and so on.

B-1 *Principle:* If the public schools are to continue to exist, the public must have confidence in them.

B-2 *Practice:* Increasing consumer opinions.

In the early 1970s educators seemed to bask in the glory of an educational experiment that was being conducted in the Alum Rock Public Schools in San Jose, California. The experiment was a limited voucher plan that provided parents with an opportunity to exercise educational choice within a single school district. The National Institute of Education (NIE), which provided the leadership for the experiment, sought other takers, but school districts resisted these offers. Despite their growing interest in the voucher, none was willing to follow in the footsteps of Alum Rock. At the time it looked as if New Hampshire might even be willing to consider the implementation of an unregulated voucher (West, 1974); but nothing came of the matter. Eventually,

interest in the voucher waned and the upsurge of educational consumerism was redirected to the magnet school concept.

Interest in the voucher was revitalized toward the close of the 1970s,
and this interest has continued into the 1980s, despite the fact that not
too many years ago Michigan residents turned down a voucher proposal at the ballot box and Californians, for a lack of signatures, failed to get
one there. Meanwhile, a 1983 Gallup poll, already alluded to in this
text, reflected a significant public interest in the voucher.

Essentially, an unregulated voucher plan means that parents of
school children are presented with a chit that is equivalent to the per
pupil expenditure of a given school district and allowed to spend it in
any school they like, public or private, religious or nonsectarian. Some
voucher proponents, however, have looked askance at the sectarian
option, denouncing any violation of the separation of church and state.
If the amount a school district spends on the education of a single child
is, say $2,000, that is the sum or value of the chit. In other than an
approved voucher school, the chit has no redeemable cash value.

Those who tout an unregulated voucher system associate with it an
array of benefits, the most prominent of which is educational consumerism or choice. Choice, in turn, contributes to public responsiveness and
responsibility, increased administrator and teacher accountability,
higher levels of pupil performance and fewer classroom discipline
problems, accelerated innovation and change, a facilitation of desegregation efforts, and ultimately a lessening of educational costs, as the
private sector competes for the educational tax dollar. The assumption
is that schools no longer meeting the needs of the public will either
change or shortly go out of business. The voucher system also promises
greater remunerative rewards for administrators and teachers through
contract management and differentiated staff (West, 1981a).

Those who oppose the voucher system see it as bringing about the
demise of the public schools. One of the purported weaknesses is the
lack of a consistent plan for its implementation. Another is that competition neither assures quality nor choice and that people, instead of
getting what they want, will have to take what they can get. There is also
the danger that educational elitism will impede societal assimilation.
Then, too, schools motivated solely by profit will substitute advertising
for quality. Finally, there are constitutional problems of church and
state, the rise of prejudicial and racist schools, and a discrimination
against the poor, who may have some difficulty in exercising or com-
prehending educational options (Fege, 1982).

Another effort to expand educational consumerism and choice is the tuition tax credit, favored by the current presidential administration. Arguments favoring this tax credit proposal are similar to the arguments favoring the voucher. Arguments against, however, are strongest in substance from the point of view that such a proposal would heavily discriminate against the poor, whose incomes would be insufficient to take advantage of the tax refund benefits associated with the proposal (AASA, 1983b).

In a 1981 battle at the Washington, D. C. polls, a tuition tax credit referendum was soundly defeated at a ratio of slightly better than 8 to 1 votes. The referendum, led by the National Taxpayer's Union (NTU), prompted the formation of a coalition of educational, civic, and religious groups (AASA, 1981). On the other hand, the Educational Voucher Institute (EVI), which began in Michigan and is now located in Washington, D. C., plans to get tax credit initiatives or voucher plans on the ballots of states across the nation (AASA, 1982).

During the mid-1970s, while voucher interest dwindled, the magnet school concept began to grow in popularity. Much like the Alum Rock experiment, which at the time continued to enjoy success, the magnet concept was to offer a rich variety of options for the educational consumer on both elementary and secondary school levels. As to how the public reacted to such alternatives, the author need only recall how many Houstonians camped all night outside a school to register their children in a Montessori magnet school. At the high school level there has been equal enthusiasm, as students have attended, among others, magnets for engineering and the performing arts. Magnet schools have fared well in major metropolitan areas, where choice is enhanced by staff size and specialization, number of buildings, and overall resources. They have also helped desegregation efforts in these large cities (Ishaq, 1984). In effect, the magnet is a transmuted voucher (Premazon & West, 1977).

To combat the voucher and tax credit initiatives, educational associations, such as the AASA (1983a) and NSPRA (1980a), have taken official stands against them, the latter despite the increase of jobs these proposals would proffer for the educational public relations specialist. For in a system devoted to educational consumerism and choice, information, counseling, and marketing skills assume critical proportions.

Educators in various associations have also taken to the telling of good news stories about the schools to increase public confidence, and the news is evidently spreading across the nation and into Canada (NSPRA, 1980b). And articles and monographs discussing the "rightness" of schools are considerably on the rise. Perhaps the lack of confidence expressed by the public in its schools is, as Hodgkinson (1979) suggests, mainly an information problem. The schools are succeeding, but too few efforts are spent on telling the public the good news.

But there is still the element of technology that has been thus far only modestly reckoned with. With the rise of home computers and school-home curricular interaction, choice may move to a new battleground, thereby rendering voucher and tax credit proposals obsolete, along with the public schools themselves, with confidence in schooling largely a matter of self-determination.

C-1 *Principle:* Support is achieved through effective two-way communication systems between school and community.

C-2 *Practice:* Using community education to gain support for the public schools.

Although the leadership privilege in community education may be exercised by sources outside the public school sector (among them universities, community colleges, parks and recreation departments, municipalities, and state educational agencies), the public schools are the primary leaders, coordinators, and dispensers of community education (West, 1977a). Today there are several thousands of community schools in public school systems that stretch across the nation. The community education movement is international in scope.

Both as process and program community education is the quintessence of two-way communication. As a process it symbolizes America's grass-roots heritage and displays the democratic process at work. Through community education hosts of individuals from all strata of a community become involved in planning, implementing, and evaluating activities—some of which concern only the school, others, the community itself. They do this by serving on community school and districtwide advisory committees and neighborhood and citywide councils. From the process come the program, course offerings, services, and even neighborhood or citywide improvements that a community needs and wants. From the process, too, come the coordination of a community's entire resources and the efforts of the agencies, institutions, and organizations that, in delivering them, strive to eliminate their overlap and repetition. While the programmatic facet of community education varies with the dictates of its participants, process, its charismatic counterpart, is imbued with a kind of perpetuity (West & West, 1978).

Involvement, a critical component of educational public relations, is not merely reserved for process. Programs draw people, young and old, in droves into the school to partake of a variety of course offerings that may range from preparing for a high school equivalency examination to spending a week at camp, or from a study of the classics to ceramics or scuba diving. Through these courses individuals update skills wrought by technological change, advance their general education, and engage in recreational and leisure activities. In learning new skills and gaining knowledge, they raise not only their expectations and personal worth, but also their incomes (West, 1977b). When people participate in these programs they are communicating to school leaders their satisfaction with them. When no participation occurs, programs soon vanish.

Community education garners support for the schools because it is persuasive by nature. Its credibility stems from the highly visible forms of participation it offers. This participation is designed to draw upon the expertise of an entire community to resolve problems of school and community concern; to accept challenges that tax the ingenuity of educators everywhere (reducing school vandalism and classroom discipline problems, redefining the basics, combating declining enrollments, to name but a few); and to create opportunities in abundance for the local citizenry. Its attractiveness is inherent in the numerous opportunities and benefits it provides to a school district's patrons. In an age of disintegrating familial relationships and transience, it brings families together to form stable and lasting relationships, providing something for everyone, fathers, mothers, and children. The alliances that it forms through the networking of talents and resources unite diverse groups, including business and industry, into a common cause—the attainment of desirable and community goals. These alliances tap, harness, and redirect massive amounts of community energy and portend significant political clout (West, 1981b).

Community education is a cooperative undertaking with which people can easily identify, providing as it does a forum for addressing individual and group needs, interests, and aspirations to improve the quality of life within a school community. It is financially sound because it expands the school tax dollar, promising full school utilization by keeping school buildings open throughout the year, days and evenings, and sometimes on Saturdays. And participation in courses is inexpensive. Community education also tends to decrease vandalism by instituting in citizens a strong pride of ownership in their schools, which carries over from parent to child (West, 1977b). Community education, in bridging the gap between school and community in unique and sundry ways, creates a natural system of two-way communication, which, in turn, lends itself to increased community support for the public schools.

D-1 *Principle:* An open school climate is conducive to effective teacher performance, the very hub of educational public relations. It also makes for better relationships between and among members of the school family.

D-2 *Practice:* Participatory leadership and shared decision making.

An open school climate is one in which two-way communication flourishes and interpersonal relationships are prized. Openness tends to alleviate or dissipate the traditional individual versus the organization conflict or the parent against the bureaucracy syndrome. Openness dilutes the impersonality of the school bureaucracy and creates an environment in which rules are viewed more as guidelines than as straitjackets. Amenable to change and implementation, it implies a willingness to share ideas and accept responsibility and sets the stage for participatory leadership.

Whether a school has an open or closed climate depends largely on the values administrators hold. If they subscribe to the philosopher king ideology, they act as if they alone were in possession of the truth and they alone were capable of making golden decisions. However benevolent their intentions may be, they provide little latitude for meaningful participation from subordinates. The same is true of administrators who function as social or behavioral engineers. Their primary purpose is to manipulate subordinates into accepting, not making, decisions. With them freedom is merely a state of mind. Administrators who lead existentially, however, invite participation and a sharing of responsibility from subordinates. To them choice leads to personal and professional growth. Negating elitism and sophistry, they model responsible choice and action (West, 1976).

The values of these three types of leaders are reflected in the beliefs undergirding McGregor's (1957) Theory X and Y brands of administration. Administrators who uphold Theory X view their subordinates not only as lazy, naive, and directionless, but also as aversive to change and oblivious to organizational needs. Theory Y administrators, inclined to see subordinates as responsible, self-motivated, and self-directed, are apt to expand opportunities for employees to participate in the formation, as well as accomplishment, of organizational goals and in the evaluation process that assesses their contributions toward these goals. On the assumption that employees are intrinsically motivated to do a good job, Theory Y naturally lends itself to a delegation and decentralization of authority and to individual and organizational growth.

Ouchi's (1982) Theory Z, much like McGregor's Y, emphasizes an individual's capability of wanting and accepting responsibility. Embedded in trust and egalitarianism, it promotes open communication between and among superiors and subordinates, along with a dedication to increased productivity. Here participation becomes the norm, the assumption being that everyone has something to contribute; and in a trusting, secure climate, these contributions will be optimized.

Human beings are motivated by several basic needs, with the satisfaction of one prompting progression to the next. These needs are physiological, such as food, clothing, and shelter; safety, such as job security, medical insurance, and retirement plans; love and belongingness, as in individual and group friendships; esteem derived from self and others; and self-actualization, or self-fulfillment (Maslow, 1970). Unfortunately, when it comes to esteem, individuals are often unable to rise above the childlike attributes that large and impersonal organizations typically assign to them. Conditioned to rely on their superordinates for direction, to feel inferiority and docility, they exhibit organizational withdrawal or rebellion. To deal with this deviant behavior, management then imposes additional restraints and rules upon them, and the problem, instead of being circumvented, repeatedly occurs and worsens. In these organizations lower-level workers take on the characteristics of an assembly line, acting as automatons rather than people (Argyris, 1960).

According to a classic rendition of organizational motivators (Herzberg, 1976), factors that influence job satisfaction in various degrees are recognition, responsibility, achievement, advancement, and growth, along with satisfaction derived from work itself. A composite of 10 studies of 17 populations virtually pairs achievement with recognition and places responsibility next highest in importance. Following responsibility is a tie of work itself and advancement. The bottom-line factor is the possibility of growth, which only infrequently surfaces (Herzberg, 1966).

In an application of Herzberg's theory to teaching, it was discovered that teachers are strongly motivated by recognition and achievement (Sergiovanni & Carver, 1980). Because of its uniformity and narrow use among teachers, responsibility, although important to teachers, was viewed far less as a satisfier than the preceding two factors. Work itself produced only minimal satisfaction, as caretaking or housekeeping duties associated with teaching tended to dull the attractiveness of work. Possibility of growth, as a satisfier, was even lower. Advancement was totally absent as a satisfier as the only way teachers could advance was to leave the classroom.

Recently there has been a tendency to stop viewing teachers as if they were exactly the same. Differentiated staffing, popular as a concept during the late 1960s and early 1970s, and implemented, to some extent, during that period, has resurfaced as a logical way of dispensing rewards, monetarily and prestigiously, to teachers for their varied performances. Here teachers advance up a teaching hierarchy that has rank determine remuneration and responsibility and in which the master teacher is ensconced at the apex of this hierarchy. Rewards implicit in differentiated staffing keep teachers teaching instead of vying for administrative posts. Supply and demand in special teaching, mathematics and science, for example, has also affected the teaching reward structure, as have scant but scattered appearances of merit pay.

These special arrangements, however, are no guarantee that once teachers achieve a discretionary level of income or some gradation in rank and responsibility they will be satisfied with their jobs, particularly if participation in decision-making frameworks is more token than relevant. People become the roles they play and "unbecome" roles they no longer play. If the roles they play are insignificant, the behavior they evoke will be no better. If the roles provide opportunities for self-actualization, they will function as a prophesy of fulfillment (Lane & West, 1972).

Certain kinds of leadership style contribute to openness, participatory decision making, and shared responsibility more than do others. Three kinds of leadership-followership should serve to illustrate this point. They are nomothetic, idiographic, and transactional. The goals of the institution rather than the needs of its employees are emphasized by the nomothetic style, as are rules and regulations. The opposite is true of the idiographic style, in which the fewer the rules, the better. The transactional style, rather than a composite of the two, or a middle ground, moves to and fro on a bipolar continuum, sometimes stressing institutional goals, sometimes individual needs, but always contingent upon a particular situation. The transactional leader tries to merge both goals and needs while realizing that conflict is unavoidable but resolvable (Getzels & Guba, 1957).

In light of its efforts to meld individual to organization in a mutually satisfying way, transactional leadership is compatible with participatory leadership and shared decision making. Because it entertains, not dismisses or glosses over, the possibility of emergent conflicts, it is more realistic and practical than the human relations movement in educational administration. Because it stresses conflict resolution that fully takes into consideration institutional goals and individual needs, it is much more humane than the era of scientific management, which equated people with machines. Transactional leadership, while suggesting that ample provisions are available for group participation, also suggests that leaders have to act on occasion independently of the group. If this were not the case, leadership would be devoid of meaning and administrators unnecessary.

Transactional leadership may even be applied to the classroom. Here teachers, modeling a transactional leadership-learning style, use situational learning strategies (structured to unstructured) to engender the formation of transactional, self-disciplined, and creative children, able to cope successfully in any organizational environment as adults rather than children when they mature (Doan & West, 1976).

In any event, leadership that is characterized by openness and sharing will lend itself to better relationships not only with teachers but also with students and parents. Knowing that the administration believes that they have important roles to play and given the fact that what they say will be heard, appreciated, and acted upon, teachers will rise to the roles expected of them. This respect for responsiveness and personal growth will be taken into the classroom by teachers and eventually carried by satisfied and successful students into the home. It will also permeate the school, generally improving morale and fostering an esprit de corps.

Parents, too, knowing that a climate exists in which administrators and teachers welcome their opinions and share their concerns, will develop a strong affinity with the goals of the school and take appreciable pride in it. This mutuality of purpose will be evidenced in increased parental participation in school activities and school committees. The same leadership that improves communication between administrator and teacher will improve the two-way flow of information between administrator and student and administrator and parent. An open climate prompts the participation of everyone.

The purpose of the school is to prepare children for assuming their leadership roles in tomorrow's world. Quality of instruction is, therefore, critical. Teachers who demonstrate high levels of instructional effectiveness link school to community in a common endeavor. In this sense teacher recognition and participation are inextricably bound.

E-1 *Principle:* When communication skills are deficient, an educational public relations program must be considered less than effective.

E-2 *Practice:* Cultivating writing, speaking, and listening skills.

WRITING

In recent years workshops have cropped up around the country to help educators improve their writing skills. Writing for publication, once the preponderant concern of the professoriate, has been translated by a growing number of educators into an all-pervasive need to write effectively. As of late, educational publications have been increasingly directed at the enhancement of writing skills, and a recurrent theme in K-12 public education has been that students be taught to write clearly and well.

Good writing is a combination of rereading and rewriting, sometimes over and over again until a particular effect is achieved. Good writing is also contingent upon disengagement, or viewing one's work with a sense of objectivity. Time is the factor that activates this critical perspective, time that separates a writer from his or her work, preferably for a few weeks but always for at least a few days. Practiced frequently, disengagement becomes almost automatic. Another aspect of good writing is careful planning. Hurriedly meeting deadlines disrupts the writing process, curtails creativity, impedes the collection of needed facts, and pushes into print passable rather than good writing. Too, good writing has a specific intention. This intention may be to narrate a success story of an innovative curricular project in a particular school district; to describe an honors program for the academically gifted; to explain the need for a tax levy; or to persuade a community to implement a magnet school program. Finally, good writing is designed with a specific readership in mind. Given the overall purpose of writing, namely, that it be read, this last statement is perhaps the easiest to accept or understand.

Although no simple formula exists to transform bad into good writing, the use of certain strategies can prove helpful to educators. Once the intent of a paper has been established, a preliminary topical outline should be constructed. Regardless of content familiarity, the outline should be as detailed as possible. In this way the outline serves as an initial guide for data gathering. Then, as facts and statistics are collected or interviews and observations made, the original outline is revised, its respective elements having been either confirmed or denied as integral to the work at hand. Moreover, if data is gathered on 3 by 5 inch note cards and then lined up with the outline, element to element, the paper will virtually write itself.

Any proposed outline should be divided in the following manner: title, introduction, body, and conclusion. The most useful title is one that clearly targets the intention of the paper. It gives immediate and specific direction to the reader. But the most useful title is not necessarily the title that will capture the attention of a reader. For example, titles of doctoral dissertations, along with the titles of the articles dissertations generate, are usually quite specific but generally uninviting. Articles in popular educational journals often have catchy titles that encourage further reading. The ultimate test is whether the content that proceeds the catchy title is as intriguing. Provided its aim is to attract rather than to mislead, a catchy title is by far the better of the two choices.

Whereas the title may attract, the introduction directs. Contained within it are the ideas, central and supporting, that will be developed in the paper, either deductively (from general to particular) or inductively (from particular to general). In a short paper (2 to 3 pages), ideas that support the central idea, or intention of a paper, may be developed in a few single paragraphs. In a long paper (10 to 15 pages), supportive ideas, in taking on a centrality of their own, may be further divided into subordinate ideas or subtopics. In some introductions the intent of the paper is specifically stated for fear that it will otherwise go undiscovered. However, if an introduction is written correctly, its intention is implicit. This intention will be evident, in fact, throughout the paper. Of course, an introduction can attract too, through the use of a rhetorical question or a few attention-getting sentences.

The body of the paper develops ideas that were alluded to in the introduction. If the intention of the paper is to persuade, the body should present a rational argument that will induce reader acceptance and action. If the intention is to explain, reader comprehension is the goal.

Each paragraph in the body is guided by a topic sentence and supported by a series of sentences. Portions of ideas are carried from one paragraph to another to achieve continuity. Transitional words and phrases also help to achieve continuity within and between paragraphs. Words such as *also, too, likewise, moreover,* and *again,* and phrases such as *what is more, by the same token,* and *on the other hand* are but a few examples.

If a paper's introduction can be likened to a road map and the paragraphs of its body viewed as a succession of conveyances that facilitate travel, then its conclusion is most assuredly its destination. In the conclusion of a paper one of two things occurs: recapitulation or reinforcement. Whereas recapitulation entails merely summing up the gist of the paper, reinforcement, through some eloquent or didactic statement, appeals directly to the reader's emotions to accept the paper's premise.

Just as intent, content, and organization are important in a paper, so is control, which is divided into tone and point of view. The tone of a paper can be lighthearted to hilarious or pompous to grave. Tone can render ideas in one way only to mean another, as in satire. It can downplay facts, as in understatement, or enumerate and embellish them to an unwarranted degree, as in overstatement.

Point of view is essentially the distance between writers and their work and between writers and readers. If the "I/we" approach is used, the point of view of the writer is conveyed to the reader as informal. Carried to the extreme, this informality can deteriorate into the confessional or conspiratorial. If the "you" approach is used, the point of view becomes prescriptive. Lists of do's and don't's fall under the "you" approach. If this approach is excessively applied, it becomes presumptuous and annoying. If the "he/she/they/it" approach is used, writing takes on a formal point of view. Relating always to a third party, this kind of approach avoids the embarrassment of the confessional, the familiarity of the conspiratorial, and the annoyance of the presumptuously prescriptive, without surrendering any of the aims that were to be attained by the use of these approaches. That is to say, much can be imputed to a third party without trampling on the toes of the reader, who may or may not readily identify with this party. While all three points of view are appropriate for specific occasions, the mixing of them in a single paper is not. Yet this is what often happens in the papers of neophyte writers.

Grouped under the broad heading of mechanics are a number of other items that merit at least passing consideration. They are usage, punctuation, spelling, vocabulary, tense, voice, sentence variety, and quotes and paraphrases.

Problems in usage usually revolve around agreement in number between subjects and verbs because of intervening phrases and between pronouns and their antecedents, especially as the distance that separates them increases. Tending to generate agreement problems are indefinite pronouns such as *everybody, none, everyone, either,* and *neither.* Usage problems also occur in the application of certain words: *affect* for *effect, between* for *among, who* for *whom,* and *like* for *as* or *as if.* The most common of these usage problems are addressed in secondary school grammar texts and college introductory composition texts.

The most troublesome aspect of punctuation is inconsistency. For example, in one part of a paper the writer might place a comma before the last item in a series separated by *and,* and in another part of the same paper in a similar construction omit the comma. Again, a writer might lavish a paper with parenthetical expressions but neglect to set them off by commas from adjoining words in a sentence. Introductory dependent clauses such as "While I was walking down the school corridor, I met a teacher who . . . ," although needing a comma are frequently bereft of one. Overpunctuation often occurs, which is just as confusing. Sometimes a comma instead of an end mark is used to separate two main ideas that are not linked by a conjunction such as *and, but,* or *or.* Reading a paper aloud can help to place commas where they belong, but an understanding of a few basic rules is far better than guessing. A common fallacy is that people should write the way they speak. Unfortunately, people with poor speaking skills can hope to do no better on paper.

Spelling problems can be remedied by the frequent use of a dictionary. Unfortunately, people with weak or undeveloped phonetic skills have great difficulty in locating words. The next best course of action is to purchase a textbook that offers a list of commonly misspelled words. For example, Rudolf Flesch's *Look It Up* (1977) offers help to writers with about 20,000 words.

If tailored to the backgrounds of specific readerships, vocabulary, or word choice, need not constitute a problem. This means that although jargon may be appropriate in papers written in specialty areas, it is definitely unsuitable for either a lay or a broadly diversified readership. In lay readership contexts simplicity should govern both word choice and sentence construction. Although a dictionary is quite helpful in word selection, a thesaurus is much more appropriate.

Voice can be active or passive, but the active, or action, voice is the better of the two. Verbs that impart action to a subject are in the active voice. "The superintendent hired a public relations director," for instance, is in the active voice; whereas "A public relations director was hired by the superintendent," which minimizes the action of the subject and stresses what is acted upon, is in the passive voice.

Without sentence variety a paper borders on the monotonous. A series of *he*'s, each beginning a new sentence, when strung together, invokes the ludicrous. With little effort sentences can be rearranged in a number of ways: by adding or subtracting a few words, by altering word order, and by changing tenses. The sentences that follow illustrate this point.

The superintendent selected a public relations director, and the board approved the selection.

> The superintendent's selection of a public relations director was approved by the board.

> The board approved the superintendent's selection of a public relations director.

> Approval for the superintendent's selection of a public relations director came from the board.

> Shortly after the superintendent selected a public relations director, the board approved the selection.

> When the superintendent selected a public relations director, the board approved the selection.

> The public relations director was selected by the superintendent, and the selection was approved by the board.

> The selection of a public relations director was made by the superintendent and approved by the board.

Occasionally, efforts to increase sentence variety produce a misplaced emphasis. For example, "Rushing to make a deadline, the public relations director tripped over a waste paper basket" is quite different from "Rushing to make a deadline, a waste paper basket tripped the public relations director." Again, "While folding a press release, the public relations director cut his or her finger on the edge of the paper" surpasses in clarity "While folding a press release, the edge of the paper cut the public relations director's finger." In these kinds of sentences the subject, or actor, is too far removed from the action and confusion results.

Quotations frequently present a problem because they are merely strung together with no leads provided to understand them. Similarly, quotations used out of context and set against incongruous backgrounds can be misleading. On the other side of the coin, paraphrasing means digesting material and then rendering it in a fashion that reveals that some kind of assimilation has occurred. Care must be taken, however, to retain the gist of the material.

A final point should be made here, namely, that while most of what has been said in the preceding pages applies to all writing, news writing does require a slightly different approach. Modeled on an inverted pyramid, news writing is structurally designed to present facts in descending order of importance, most to least important, in short paragraphs. Thus, when space limitations preclude the printing of an entire article, paragraphs can be deleted without affecting its integrity. News articles are developed to respond to the five Ws—who, what, where, when, why—and how. They are typed on 8 1/2 by 11 inch white paper, one side only, and double or triple spaced, with the text beginning about one-third down the paper. The designation "-30-" concludes an article; "-more-" indicates continuation. For a complete rendition of journalistic style, a number of handbooks may be consulted, among them, *The Associated Press Stylebook and Libel Manual* (French, Powell, & Angione, 1982); *The Washington Post Deskbook on Style* (Webb, 1978); and *The New York Times Manual of Style* (Jordan, 1976). On the other hand, style handbooks that assist a writer in preparing scholarly manuscripts are published by the Modern Language Association, the American Psychological Association, and the University of Chicago Press.

In conclusion, the biggest problem with writing generally presents itself at the beginning of a paper. It is difficult to determine just how to begin, despite the presence of an outline. The best way is to get a few sentences down on paper and worry about how well they fit together after the writing project is under way.

SPEAKING

Speaking is closely allied with writing. A well prepared speech contains the ingredients of a well written paper. What differentiates the two is the extra step that speaking entails. That is to say, where writing ends speaking begins. Writing is like acting on a movie set, where retakes, like rewrites, can be expected to occur with some frequency. Speaking is like acting on a stage; once the play has begun, the only direction to be taken is forward.

On this stage instant feedback takes place. If a speech misses its mark and fails to capture the attention of an audience, some of the listeners may begin to leave. Others remaining seated may just stop listening. Still others may become boisterous and unruly, and in the question and answer period that often follows challenge the speaker's ideas in every conceivable way. In contrast, an approving audience may clap loudly and vigorously or give the speaker a standing ovation.

Writing never produces an instantaneous effect. True, letters to the editor praising or finding fault with an article published in one issue of a journal may be printed in the next. Copies of the article may be requested of the writer. The article may even appear in journals that digest or abstract articles. Because of its uniqueness it may be cited repeatedly in the writings of others. But this is by no means the same as the immediacy that a speech evokes.

It is, therefore, important that a speaker give considerable thought to his or her audience, the occasion at hand, the size and nature of the group, the facility in which the speech will be made, what equipment is both needed and available, the allotted time for the presentation, the time others have taken, individually and totally, to address the audience, and the time of the day or evening.

In writing, the eye travels over the printed page. In speaking, the eye attempts to make contact with the listeners in an audience. If note cards are absent and a relatively unfamiliar speech must be read, eye contact becomes by necessity minimal; and the loss of an audience's attention may be imminent. Indeed, the longer the eyes are fixated on a paper or script, the greater will be the detachment of speaker from audience. Sometimes the original outline of a paper may function as a cuer. At other times a speech may be built around a series of slides or transparencies, a short film, or a demonstration. If the audience and room are small, display cards may suffice. But none of the preceding suggestions should be viewed as a substitute for rehearsal.

Word choice is, perhaps, of even greater importance in speaking than in writing; so, too, are examples. A reader can ponder over a piece of writing for hours and come up with new insights on each reading. But a listener must be able to see at once images or examples that facilitate understanding and appreciation. *Uh*'s, *oh*'s, or *and*'s, if used often enough, can create listener distractions. There has been many a listener who has been bored into counting *uh*'s rather than giving thought to the essentials of a presentation. When time is needed to collect one's thoughts, a slight pause, often confused with purposeful emphasis, is preferable over *uh*'s and the like.

Beyond the presentation itself, a speaker should be groomed for the occasion. At a beach party, at which everyone is dressed in leisurely attire, it would appear strange for a speaker to be dressed in a dark blue, conservative suit. Yet sportswear is inappropriate at a formal dinner party. A speaker should display enthusiasm, confidence, and credibility while attempting to achieve rapport with an audience. A speaker should have good diction and orchestrate word with movement.

A speaker who remains aloof to an audience will usually evoke a reciprocal action. But a speaker who openly warms up to an audience and takes every opportunity to relate to needs, interests, and backgrounds will find that audience taking a special interest in his or her presentation.

LISTENING

Most people would rather talk than listen. In the typical conversation they usually spend more time on figuring out what they are going to say than they do on what is being said. Indeed, what little time they devote to listening is waiting for a pause or cue to interrupt and upstage the other person or persons. The benefits derived from listening often seem dwarfed alongside the instant gratification that comes from an opportunity to share one's ideas and experiences with what appears to be a receptive ear. But the real pay off comes later, when the talker walks away with only the exhilarated moment and the listener departs with an abundance of new information, provided, of course, that listening has actually occurred.

Listening for most people is at the 25% level of efficiency (Samaras, 1980), with this efficiency level becoming notably evident after a 10-minute speech (Carr, 1980). The fact that people talk approximately

3 or 4 times slower than they think (Raudsepp, 1982) would seem to suggest that listening occurs with ease. Unfortunately, listening is often thought of as synonymous to hearing and therefore lacks the deliberateness it demands. Effective listening, unlike hearing, is not only purposeful but planned.

Deliberate listening requires the knowledge and application of a number of guidelines that facilitate a listener's receipt of a speaker's message. In this sense the skill of listening may be viewed as even more important than the skill of speaking; for if no one listens, a speech is of no consequence (Raudsepp, 1982). These guidelines include a listener's willingness to entertain a host of new ideas: some of them out of the ordinary or hard to comprehend, others seemingly incompatible with one's own value system. They also include a display of genuine interest in, together with strict attention to, the speaker's presentation (Samaras, 1980). Equally important as guidelines are inhibiting the mind's propensity to wander, particularly in light of intervening distractions, as well as remaining uninfluenced by the mannerisms, however personally annoying, of a given speaker (Clutterbuck, 1981). Ferreting out important ideas from an array of facts to get the big picture, along with their subsequent clarification from the speaker (Raudsepp, 1982) constitutes still another guideline. Direct eye contact helps too; in serving as a guideline, it establishes a rapport with the speaker, reflecting an attitude of concern for what is being said (Hayes, 1981).

An ongoing summarization of the important points of a speaker's talk is recommended by Samaras (1980); and Vining and Yrle (1980) target the importance of listening for subtle implications in expression in a short listener's self-rating quiz they have devised. These implications may be derived from words and gestures (Raudsepp, 1982). But both of these guidelines have had their validity seriously questioned by Pauk (1981). The gist of Pauk's contention is that any effort either to summarize while the speaker is still talking or to listen for what has been implied but not said will prevent the listener from hearing the rest of what the speaker has to say. Trying to anticipate the speaker's words is, likewise, inappropriate because it may create listener biases.

That listening is important in a variety of ways may be seen in efforts to improve relations between company and customer, superordinate and subordinate, and school and community. The Sperry Rand Company, for example, launched an international training program in listening for employees to make sure that its customers were being heard. While the program began with seminars, it soon became packaged in brochures and cassettes because of its widespread popularity among employees (Clutterbuck, 1981).

Listening to employees is just as important as listening to customers. Dealing with a hostile employee requires patience and time, as well as the full attention of a supervisor, during a meeting of the two. In an environment free of distractions, the supervisor sifts through emotion to find logic and searches for facts and clues that will facilitate both an understanding and a resolution of the employee's problem. Ideas are welcomed and reacted to, and consensus comes about by having the employee play an active role in its attainment (Powell, 1981). The crux of the matter is that the leader who listens can successfully reach a compromise (Palmer, 1982). But effective listening is not only conducive to consensus and compromise; in reducing misunderstandings and mistakes in following instructions, it also improves morale (Harris, 1980).

Listening to a community, perhaps the greatest challenge of all, is what school leaders must do on a year-round basis. They can listen, and generally do, through the polls they conduct to gauge citizens' attitudes about the school. They can listen to the membership of their citizen communication networks. They can listen to parent-teacher groups, band and booster groups, business and industrial leaders, and community education advisory groups and participants. They listen over hot lines, over hot coffee in homes, and in the marketplace. In fact, wherever and whenever people congregate, they can listen and learn.

F-1 *Principle:* The media can assist the schools in keeping the public informed only to the extent that they are kept informed.

F-1 *Practice:* Establishing a close working relationship with the media.

Schools communicate best with their publics, journalists included, through modes of communication that bring these publics directly in contact with school personnel and activities, according to a Tennessee study that polled the opinions of educational public relations specialists and press, radio, and television journalists responsible for school coverage (Hyder & Achilles, 1982). The study also indicated that although most educational public relations specialists viewed their relationships with journalists as effective to highly effective, about a third of the journalists saw the public relations of school systems as ineffective.

The fact that print or broadcast journalists with educational beats favor direct contact with schools, while differing with public relations specialists on the effectiveness of public relations in schools, strongly suggests that school leaders make a significant effort to get journalists into the schools. Schools can accomplish this goal through a variety of quasi inservice strategies. They can conduct guided tours for educational beat journalists that will keep them abreast of the latest educational developments in local schools and nationwide and familiarize them with the terminology spawned by new curricula. They can extend invitations to journalists to observe teachers and students involved in the learning process and thereby help them gain a firsthand insight into its complexities. Similarly, they can be invited to observe special classroom demonstrations or school events that profile the vanguard of school progress.

It would also be beneficial for journalists and schools alike if journalists were to teach an occasional class in their own area of expertise, writing or speaking, or to provide technical and career advice to students enrolled in journalism classes and those who prepare the school newspaper. By taking a turn at teaching, journalists will be able to share teacher and student points of view. Opportunities to meet with teachers during their planning sessions would help journalists understand the instructional problems that daily confront teachers. Helpful, too, would be an administrative open-door policy with journalists. In this way relations during a crisis are not as likely to be strained and inhibiting. Parent-teacher groups could occasionally have journalists as their guest speakers, as could band and booster clubs, future teacher and farmer clubs, and the like, thereby extending and embellishing their reference points. Boards and administrators should extend regular invitations to the media to cover board meetings and accommodate their professional needs when they attend. Some of these meetings should include presentations by school personnel to explain the various programs of the school.

If boards and administrators show a genuine interest in strengthening media relations, media personnel are likely to reflect a similar interest. Barraging the media with press releases and public service announcements may keep the educational public relations specialist busy, but not necessarily productive, particularly when neither public relations specialist nor journalist has taken the time to understand the other's needs and interests. Reciprocity of interest lends itself to mutual appreciation and respect; and working together in cooperative endeavors engenders trust. Such relationships, while promising neither bad nor good press, do mean that the media will have more than a passing acquaintance with what the school is trying to do or has done. Thus, when an incident occurs journalists can, in writing or speaking about it, place it within the perspective of the total school context.

In dispelling 11 myths that make journalists the heavies in the ongoing educational public relations drama, Henry (1979) succinctly points out that the charge of the media is to report education news, not to relate the tales that schools would like them to tell; that is the responsibility of schools and there are ways other than through the media to meet this responsibility. He also points out that the basis of effective school-media relations is truthfulness and frankness. Both lend themselves to credibility, an attribute every school system should possess.

Working closely with the media entails certain responsibilities. If news releases are issued by the schools, they should be sent to all media, none withstanding. All news releases, whether written or on tape, should address the five Ws (who, what, when, where, and why) and how, with facts listed in descending importance. They should be prepared in full consideration of any special requirements any of the media might have. For example, McMullen and Oberg (1982) found that the primary reason that television news directors in a two-station community (one university owned, the other private) did not use the news releases of the two local school districts was improper format. Their next reason for rejection was that submissions were not considered newsworthy.

Bird (1978), in designing a model public relations department for a community college, claims that news releases should have a distinctive air about them and serve as a reminder to editors of previous high-quality content. They should clearly identify not only source, but sender; should further information be required, editors then know whom to contact. News releases should be tailored to comply with expressed media formats and sent only to those media who might print or air them. Once it is evident that print and broadcast news editors are not using some of the releases sent to them, the educational public relations specialist should set up a conference to determine cause of rejection. And regardless of release use, such visits should intermittently occur. Bird also points out that although news releases are basic to a public relations program, feature stories accompanied by photographs are much more likely to attract the public's eye.

A knowledge of media deadlines is critical; otherwise, releases may never be printed or aired. Sometimes conflicts arise when releases seem timed to favor one medium over another or daily over weekly newspapers. Coordination is, therefore, important, especially as weekly papers usually give a school its best coverage. People like to see the accomplishments of their children in print. Should their own names appear alongside the names of their children, so much the better. They exhibit, as well, interest in the accomplishments of the children of relatives and friends. A weekly paper tends to capitalize on these interests. On the other hand, people are inclined to become perturbed when news releases are inaccurate, photographs unidentified or confused, and names misspelled. When papers printing these inaccuracies are assailed with criticism, relations between them and the school are strained.

When a story breaks the media should be contacted as quickly as possible. An extended delay might inadvertently convey the impression of surpressing a story. When the media respond to a call or initiate a story, answers should be devoid of the bogey "no comment," which only arouses the suspicions of journalists and sends them on investigative quests. It is far better to indicate that answers are, for the moment, unknown but will be shortly forthcoming, with follow-up calls assured. "Off the record," another timeworn bogey, can only produce unpleasant results. News that is not publishable can only prove distasteful to one whose profession is to report the news, unless an exclusive story is promised. But this, too, creates difficulties if it upsets other journalists by their exclusion. This is not to say that exclusives cannot be given to journalists who, through their own efforts, have earned them; it merely means that all media should be treated fairly. In responding to a journalist's question, there is also good reason not to speculate beyond what is asked; personal opinions are not facts but they do distort them. Accuracy is always important.

When interviewed by the media, one ordinarily should not request any approval prior to publication; it is considered a breach of etiquette by journalists. Some journalists, those new to the field, may actually prefer that their copy be approved by the interviewee. If the interview is infused with technical jargon, even the experienced journalist may request confirmation. Should errors appear in the interview when it is published, it is best to overlook them unless they are especially important or rampant. A word of thanks is always in order for a story well done.

When dealing specifically with the needs and interests of radio, some thought should be given to the types of programming that characterize radio stations: adult contemporary for ages 25 and over; soul for an indeterminate age group; adult-oriented rock (ACR) for ages 18–25; contemporary hit radio (CHR) for teens, ages 13 years and over; and news. For example, within this group the best way to communicate with parents about the schools might be through a station that caters to teenagers; for chances are that is the type of station that will be aired in a household of adolescents. Again, as the typical radio break is 15 to 20 seconds, an ideal public service announcement would be a 15-second tape recording.

It is possible to call in news releases and have them recorded over the phone, but acceptance is contingent upon station manager preference, a previously made agreement between station manager and public relations specialist, and the quality of the speaker's voice (Bird, 1978). In any event, whatever the announcement is it should be short, have an interesting introduction, and direct requests for further information to the station. If the station is willing to air more than just announcements, a 2-minute tape might feature a student review of a best-selling novel or introduce a teacher new to the community. Or it might offer cooking recipes, gardening advice, and auto care and safety tips, or glimpses into local history, all of which emanate from the school's various departments. Tape recordings of a 15 or 30 minute duration might focus on career education programs that involve school and business leaders or address school issues. Too, a spelling bee might be aired live. What is of primary importance is to match a program with a station's audience.

If the school system has its own radio station, as some do, information possibilities are virtually unlimited. Operated by students and supervised by faculty, a school radio station draws upon the manifold talents of the immediate and extended school family; for it has the potential for involving almost everyone in some way. It also keeps a community interested in and informed about its schools. But its value extends beyond information and involvement; inherently, it is instructional as well. As students plan and develop programming, they improve reading, writing, speaking, listening, and researching skills. On a much broader level, radio, in reporting curricula activities throughout the district, improves communication between and among schools and thereby enhances curricular integration. Through radio administrators can address in a personalized manner parental concerns about certain aspects of a school's curricula. In much the same manner cocurricular activities can be highlighted. Often clubs of all kinds, chorale or folk music, language, drama, debate, and literary, become involved in breathing life into a program. Schools with television stations offer similar possibilities. One is sometimes but a stepping-stone to another.

Local television stations are generally receptive to new and creative educational ideas and are willing to provide on-site coverage, if invited into the schools. Educational television stations located in nearby universities are particularly interested in the schools; unfortunately, school personnel are sometimes reluctant to take advantage of these opportunities. Some public relations inservice at the school system level could easily alleviate this reticence.

Public service announcements for television, as for radio, must also be short, ranging anywhere from 10 to 60 seconds; the shorter they are, the better their chances of acceptance. Indeed, McMullen and Oberg (1982) found that the two television stations in their survey were amenable to using short video tapes as filler. They also indicated the need for involving school administrators in material they wish aired; the prevailing feeling being that school administrators are, in themselves, newsworthy.

Too often a gap exists between the public schools and the media. Schools must breach this gap whenever and however they can. A first step is getting to know the media. A second is to make sure they are kept informed about the schools. And the third, and most important, is to involve them in the schools.

In the not-too-distant future cable television, coupled with two-way computer access, might well make the school its own best information dispenser. But until that time comes, it would behoove school officials to exert every effort to strengthen their ties with the media.

G-1 *Principle:* Citizen participation imparts direction and meaning to the school program and tends to produce commitment and support.

G-2 *Practice:* Enlisting the aid of citizens to conduct financial referenda information campaigns.

People who are involved in the public schools are much more likely to support their financial requests than are those who feel alienated from them, with party identification having little to do with how they vote (ERIC Clearinghouse on Educational Management, 1977). Again, although people whose children attend public schools are inclined to vote more often in favor of financial referenda than are those having no children in these schools (McCain & Wall, 1976), there is reason to believe that the general public may be better public school supporters than parents of public school children, with some exception noted in the case of younger and actively involved parents (ERIC Clearinghouse on Educational Management, 1977). Personal contact during financial campaigns has also influenced voting behavior in a positive way (McCain & Wall, 1976).

Although a continuous educational public relations program plays no small part in getting school referenda passed, the likelihood of passage is largely contingent upon large-scale citizen involvement (Rubin, 1979). Just how important citizen involvement may be to some school administrators can be seen in the following example. Learning that more than 70% of its voters did not have children in its schools, the Columbus, Ohio public school system set a goal for principals to bring 50,000 nonparents into their schools during the 1980-1981 school year. These visits were aimed at correcting any misunderstandings nonparents had about the Columbus schools. The effort was part of a three-year plan to enhance internal and external school support (Gifford, 1982).

Involvement characterizes four of the six steps that Harrison (1972) proffers for bond issue passage. Steps one and two stress early and prolonged information dissemination to create community awareness of impediments confronting a school system in its efforts to provide a quality education for all students and of solutions, local and national, for removing these impediments. Steps three through six deal with the structured involvement of a variety of groups in neighborhood and school settings. These latter steps allow segments of the community, particularly parents and community recognized school information sources, to grapple with educational problems and to share these problems with uninformed peers. They also allow curriculum supervisors, teachers, and students who daily encounter these problems in classroom situations to share their perspectives of them with citizens.

According to Cooperman and Clement (1980), involvement counters apathy, one of the three reasons that alone or together bring about the failure of school financial referenda. The other two reasons are an unacceptable proposal and school dissatisfaction.

Attempts to elicit the support of the opposition through involvement are unlikely to reap any benefits for the school. It would appear that "no" voters tend to feel that financial referenda failures curtail wasteful school expenditures (Gifford, 1982). As little can be done to alter the mind set of potential "no" voters, the best way of handling them is to quench their antagonism. Purportedly, this can be done through the production of cross-pressure (Lutz, 1980). When "no" voters are deluged by positive information about the schools and the economy is relatively stable, they are inclined to stay away from the polls. By the same token, if "yes" voters are barraged by negative information and the cross-pressure produced is harsh, they, too, are unlikely to go to the polls. Still, unless this cross-pressure is very harsh, it will probably not affect the turnout of the hard core of "yes" voters at the polls. Thus, if effectively applied, the strategy builds sufficient cross-pressure on the negative voters while mustering the support of potential "yes" voters.

There are many ways to involve the citizenry of a community in school financial referenda campaigns. They can function as leaders or followers, primary or secondary actors. There are, as well, a number of ways campaigns can be constructed. Most campaign efforts, though, seem to revolve around five distinct areas. These are management, personnel, methods, materials, and assessment.

Management

Campaign management is a product of leadership, organization, and administration. It may be an outgrowth of the efforts of a districtwide public relations advisory committee and its building-level satellites, or it may come into existence as a distinct but parallel activity, initiated by the school's leadership. With the formation of a steering committee that is representative of the entire community and the subsequent designation of a campaign chair, campaign efforts begin to crystallize. Subcommittees are then created and their respective chairs named to handle a variety of tasks, among them campaign finances, strategy, publicity, and volunteer recruitment and training.

Actual campaign efforts may be organized on a precinct-by-precinct basis, as in political campaigns. Or they may center on the activities of individual schools, in which principal and parent share the leadership function (Rubin, 1979). Throughout the campaign the chair works closely with the school's leadership, particularly the school system's superintendent, to whom the ultimate leadership role is attributed. Even more important is the consensus and backing of the board on the need for the financial referendum and campaign. Important, too, is staff support and involvement.

The campaign timetable may encompass a year of planning and conclude with a publicity effort that lasts no more than a few weeks.

Considerations in the matter of choosing an election day typically exempt summer, when parents may be on vacation with their children; the period immediately preceding yuletide expenditures; and shortly before or after income tax time. Presumably, the period immediately following an extended teacher strike, during which time public resentment toward the schools has had an opportunity to build, would be quite inappropriate. Indeed, any activity that induces dubious or irate attitudes on the part of the school's citizenry is apt to interfere with the successful passage of a school referendum.

Personnel

On the assumption that every campaign volunteer is not only a worker, but a "yes" voter, it would behoove administrators to enlist the efforts of as many volunteers as they can. Aside from the numerous tasks they may be required to perform, volunteers have extensive spheres of personal influence—neighbors, close friends, acquaintances, and relatives—that are likely to act on their advice, particularly if they have come to see them as dependable sources of information about the schools. And these people, in turn, have similar contacts, as do those they contact. The result is an ever-widening circle of volunteer influence. Proselytizing the familiar before tackling the unknown and perhaps unreceptive, the campaign volunteer is in many respects like the neophyte, direct canvas salesperson who sells to relatives and friends first and strangers last.

Virtually anyone who is willing to carry the school banner should be inducted into campaign service. This includes members of both the immediate and the extended school family, all of whom can be given a role to play. Some of these roles will be small, especially in the case of students; others will be large—those played by leading citizens, parents, administrators, and teachers.

What is more, the cadre of volunteers selected should be trained for any special functions required of them and kept continuously informed. When questions arise about campaign issues, volunteers must be well-prepared to respond to them.

Methods

Methods of conducting campaigns may vary considerably from school system to school system; however, most share certain commonalities regardless of system. For example, campaign activity should be guided by the results of a survey designed to determine citizens' needs, interests, and aspirations for their children, along with their prevailing attitudes toward the services the schools currently offer. A well-planned survey sheds light on the direction a campaign should take. It reveals, as well, pockets of opposition that must be mitigated or overcome, but never overlooked.

Every campaign should have a theme, and this theme should be centered on the children the campaign is intended to serve. A raise in teacher salaries may be desperately needed to sustain or improve teacher quality; but when unrelated during a campaign to the educational needs of children, this raise probably will never materialize. Slogans and symbols are also appropriate. Symbolically, a little red schoolhouse is synonymous with grass-roots democracy. An open umbrella under which an assortment of people stand reflects the united and pervasive aspects of community education.

Too, letters of endorsement are important, particularly from community leaders, as are an almost infinite listing of names that represent support for the school system. Foremost among the community leaders whose help the school needs are the community's clergy. If they are supportive and are willing to proclaim their position, there is a good chance that their congregations will be just as supportive. Attaining the support of business and industry is no less important. Local clubs, organizations, and associations are also capable of making significant contributions to a campaign. And parent-teacher groups are indispensable.

To tell the school story and thereby amass additional support, a speakers bureau must be formed that penetrates every avenue of organized community activity. The more credible and influential the speaker, the greater the chance of a campaign message being well received. By involving select speakers in radio and television talk shows and forums, the widest possible coverage may be accomplished. While breakfasts, luncheons, and dinners may serve to launch a campaign, a speakers bureau will keep it moving at full steam.

Neighborhood school or districtwide information meetings that explain the purpose of the referendum should help to squelch rumors before they cloud or confuse the issue at hand. Hot lines will do much to alleviate confusion should it surface. In these instances the assistance of local parent-teacher groups should be sought. Keeping the media thoroughly informed, especially the press, at all stages of the campaign should further reduce the chances of being misinterpreted. A supportive press is a considerable asset in any campaign, but crucial in small towns in which no other media forms exist.

Once pro and con factions of a community have been identified, all efforts should be directed at getting potential "yes" voters to the polls while simultaneously creating sufficient cross-pressure, as indicated earlier, to keep "no" voters away from the polls. This may entail providing babysitting and transportation services to potential "yes" voters, as well as making sure they are registered to vote and then reminding them to go to the polls. As in a political election, getting out the vote for a school referendum also means a lot of telephone calling and direct canvassing for volunteers.

Overall campaign efforts, although primarily directed at meeting the educational needs of children, should not exclude the possibility of serving other groups. A strong community education program may be expected to meet the needs of young and old alike and garner additional support for the campaign.

Regardless of campaign success, great care should be taken to thank everyone who contributed to the effort. Properly thanked, preferably publicly and by letter, these same individuals may be willing to be of service in future campaigns. If not, they can surely be counted among the school's allies. On a positive note, being ready for the election outcome means having earlier prepared a victory speech.

Materials

Of the many materials that can be used to facilitate support, perhaps the most effective is a simple fact sheet that explains the purpose of the referendum, at the same time equating referendum cost to the purchase of some understandable commodity expenditure: the cost of a daily candy bar or cup of coffee or the price of a visit to the local cinema over a year's time. The language used in the fact sheet should be devoid of the jargon school people often bandy about in their professional lives. The message of the school must be comprehended with ease.

Posters, billboard and window displays, banners, yard signs, brochures, buttons, balloons, bumper stickers, T-shirts, bookmarks, and the like, along with media advertisements, all help to remind the citizenry of the importance of the referendum. The greater the variety, the broader will be the exposure. By being seen everywhere the message gains in force and clarity.

A brief slide presentation or a short film would be helpful to speakers in their attempts to muster referendum support. A preelection day parade, much like those put on by schools during homecoming, replete with floats, school band, cheerleaders, athletic teams, school clubs, and volunteers heralding the campaign theme, would also be helpful.

Photographs should be taken of children engaged in sundry classroom and school activities, together with teachers and volunteers; campaign workers immersed in their jobs; and influential and supportive individuals and groups backing the campaign. These photographs may be arranged in collages and publicly displayed, as well as selectively used to accompany press releases. In conveying the message that a civic-minded community cares about its schools and is actively involved in them, the photographs may produce a bandwagon effect.

There is probably no end to the materials that may be developed to keep the public thinking positively about its schools during an upcoming referendum. Limitations stem only from a lack of creativity.

Assessment

Successful or not, campaign efforts must be assessed. The assumption is that assessment will make the next campaign more effective than its predecessor. This means that each of the preceding four areas must be analyzed carefully in terms of its efficacy. For example, was the campaign organized and administered effectively? Was there ample leadership to ensure the appropriate actions of volunteers? How many community influentials were enlisted as leaders? Were enough volunteers available to carry out designated activities? Was volunteer training of a sufficient duration? Were enough subcommittees available to create a division of purpose and responsibility? Did the finance committee raise sufficient funds to carry out campaign goals? How could fundraising methods have been improved? What was the nature and extent of the publicity achieved by the committee charged with this responsibility? Was the survey accurate in depicting public receptivity to the proposed referendum? Did it measure what it was supposed to measure? Which of the methods used produced good results and which did not? Were materials ample and useful? Which had more appeal to the public than others? What was the level of response to salable materials? Was the campaign period too long or too short, and in what way might the campaign timetable be improved?

A meticulous assessment of the entire campaign may not ensure the passage of the next school financial referendum, but it most certainly will improve its chances of success. And school financial referenda need all the help they can get these days.

H-1 *Principle:* The flow of information up and down the school hierarchy and from school to community is always important, but during collective negotiations and strikes, communication becomes critical.

H-2 *Practice:* Delegating responsibility and devising information plans.

The importance of two-way communication in any school organization cannot be overemphasized. A free flow of information up and down the traditional school hierarchy between and among organizational members is essential to organizational health. Similarly, the flow of information from school to community and back again is the springboard to community support. When communication is impeded or breaks down, the school organization is characterized by dysfunctionalism. To educators and lay people alike, such dysfunctionalism has been made abundantly clear by the teacher strikes of recent years.

At the beginning of the 1975-1976 school year, for example, teacher strikes in 10 states prevented approximately 2 million children from attending school (*U.S. News & World Report,* 1975). That school year 203 teacher strikes occurred, with the following 2 school years, 1976-1977 and 1977-1978, reflecting a like number of 152 (Neal, 1978). During the 1979-1980 school year teacher strikes rose to 242 (Colton & Graber, 1982); then fell to 191 during 1980-1981 and to 106 during 1981-1982 (NSPRA, 1982).

But strikes, as already indicated, signify more than just numbers; translated, they mean not only children out of school, but also teachers out of jobs and lost work days. In 1980, 98,699 teachers were engaged in strikes lasting an average of 9 days (Phi Delta Kappan, 1982), numbers that when multiplied total up to an astounding loss of work days.

Although teacher strikes are prohibited in most states, several states with collective bargaining laws for teachers do permit them under certain limiting conditions (Barrett & Lobel, 1976). These states are Hawaii, Minnesota, Montana (court ruled), Oregon, Pennsylvania, Vermont, and Wyoming (Council of State Governments, 1982). But strikes have occurred not only in those states that have collective bargaining laws for teachers, but also in those that do not have them (Scott, 1982). While the Educational Commission of the States has identified 31 states with collective bargaining laws (Council of State Governments, 1982) and Wynn (1981) has characterized 33 states, regardless of such laws, as collective bargaining-intensive, Shannon (1981) has indicated that in all but 12 states some kind of collective bargaining occurs. Finally, although the end of public sector bargaining has been predicted by Lieberman (1981) by about the year 2000, a prediction that only the future can decide, collective bargaining in the public schools will, in the meantime, continue to pose a threat for internal and external educational public relations.

The trauma commonly associated with the onset of negotiations is usually most severe in school districts that have, for one reason or another, provided teachers with few opportunities to address their needs and even fewer to attain them. It is often difficult for teachers to appreciate the financial constraints imposed on boards of education when they seek higher salaries and increased fringe benefits; and it is just as difficult for boards to appreciate the clamor of teachers for more money when so little is generally available, particularly when the economy is depressed. Preoccupied with their own problems, both parties have trouble exchanging perspectives. Similar dilemmas are frequently engendered when teachers seek better working conditions or desire a more significant role in the educational decision-making process. Improved working conditions, unfortunately, often necessitate substantial tax increases, and educational decision making is generally construed as a strictly managerial prerogative. Change is, therefore, resisted by many boards and administrators for what appear to be quite logical reasons. The result is a series of communication impasses that may conceivably transform rather informal or pacific teacher groupings into highly organized and militant ones.

This kind of dysfunctionalism need not occur. Yet should it take place, it does not have to assume crisis proportions. If boards and administrators make every effort to provide teachers with a discretionary level of income, if they are both willing and eager to work with teachers toward the accomplishment of better learning environments, and if they maximize opportunities for teachers to participate in educational decisions that dramatically affect their everyday classroom performance, it is highly unlikely that the advent of formal negotiations will bring with it the dissension that often characterizes newly emerged bilateral relationships.

Despite the fact that most boards and administrators expend considerable energy in their efforts to satisfy the changing needs of their staffs, there is inevitably confronting them the grim realization that, like it or not, collective negotiation is essentially an adversarial process. This is especially true at the inception of collective negotiations, at which either or both sides, unaccustomed to bargaining, typically resort to crisis bargaining strategies (Perry & Wildman, 1975).

While it is true that administrators, as a general rule, are better prepared today than they were a decade ago to cope with the adversarial nature of collective negotiations, it is also true that teachers have not lagged behind in acquiring the skills to negotiate. Moreover, in districts in which collective bargaining is relatively new, teachers, who have much more to gain from it than administrators, are sometimes more formidably prepared than their superiors. And when it comes to securing assistance in negotiations, teachers, by virtue of their large numbers and association memberships, union or otherwise, are better able than administrators to obtain it.

According to Perry and Wildman (1975), there are two basic bargaining strategies: distributive and integrative. In their purest forms, the first leads to crisis bargaining and the early use of power tactics to attain even minor short-run gains, whereas the second leads to problem solving and a sharing of information. Although modifications of both do exist in the private sector, what is of primary importance is that distributive bargaining of any kind is incompatible with the sovereignty of school boards and the goals of the teaching profession, despite unionization. Nonetheless, problem-solving strategies, although difficult to develop, may be possible as bargaining relationships mature.

Through a systematic method of meeting employee needs, an extensive two-way communication network, and a fair and expeditious grievance machinery that resolves complaints at the lowest possible managerial level, much of the reasonableness that is indispensable to problem-solving bargaining may be gradually attained. As a prelude to initial or ongoing negotiations, these organizational practices pave the way for information sharing at the bargaining table, the setting of mutually developed short- and long-range goals, and the establishment of contracts that extend well beyond a single year, thereby ensuring the continued development of problem-solving strategies as well as new heights of cooperative relationships.

In conducting negotiations there are many leadership options available to schools. Boards may choose to do their own negotiating; and in the early stages of bargaining they frequently do. Here superintendents merely advise. Regardless of how well boards perform at the negotiating table, there is always the problem of time hovering over them. Negotiations demand a commitment that, when translated into hours, is often overwhelming. Furthermore, there are numerous legal implications. Boards may also elect to have their superintendents negotiate for them. In time the role of the chief negotiator may be assigned to other administrators, assistant superintendents, personnel directors, business managers, and principals. Outside negotiators have also been used. In large school districts a director of employee relations may perform this specialized role (AASA, 1974b).

As the specialized skills of the negotiator move to the fore of the bargaining arena, there emerges a distinct need for another kind of expertise. This expertise is provided by the educational public relations specialist, whose job in facilitating communication extends, not for a brief bargaining period, but throughout the school year. In the past the art and science of communicating may have received little more than token importance by administrators engulfed in the negotiating process. In the future the position of educational public relations specialist will attain importance in even the smallest school district, with this position going hand-in-hand with the negotiating process.

Collective negotiations, to be successful, call for a steady flow of communication; more importantly, community support and teacher and student morale demand it. Thus, the educational public relations specialist is admittedly not only a critical addition to the negotiating team, but an ongoing executor of organizational health. In other words, boards and top-level administrators who do not recognize the salient contribution of the educational public relations specialist to collective negotiations in its broadest sense are limiting their organizational effectiveness.

Unfortunately, a decision-making role for the educational public relations specialist in collective negotiations was not in keeping with a national sampling of the perceptions of school superintendents and educational public relations specialists, although the latter did see a stronger role for themselves in negotiations than did superintendents. Comments made by superintendents point to the lack of experience and training of educational public relations specialists in negotiations. Both groups, however, did see a communication role for the educational public relations specialist that might only indirectly affect the negotiation process (Traweek, 1980).

For example, superintendents and educational public relations specialists were in close agreement that establishing credibility with the media was the primary concern of the educational public relations specialist during negotiations. Indeed, the top six priorities of both groups targeted either the direct or indirect dealings of the educational public relations specialist with the media; indirectly, by giving advice to others, management team members as well as chief spokesperson, on how to deal with the media. During a strike, however, both groups identified as the first and second priorities of educational public relations specialists the operations of a communication center and the establishment of a volunteer-staffed hot line to handle inquiries of the local citizenry. After the strike the two top priorities of both groups pointed to the educational public relations specialist assisting the board in its communications with the community and in its preparation of data about the strike. Again, whereas the third priority of superintendents for public relations specialists was in helping principals to regain the support of their staffs through effective communications, the third priority that public relations specialists saw for themselves was in promoting contractual understanding among administrators (Traweek, 1981).

Some of the more obvious problems confronting administrators serving on negotiating teams and educational public relations specialists, regardless of team membership, are what the team's stance will be on the issuance of public statements; how management can keep the media on its side when no progress and, therefore, no new information is forthcoming from the bargaining table; how to prepare joint press releases; how to keep administrators and supervisors informed of proceedings without violating good faith bargaining; and what to do if information is somehow leaked that appears detrimental to the administration.

When a strike appears likely, new and more challenging problems beset administrators. Letters must be drafted to notify parents about the possibility of a strike and how normal services will be affected in the event that the schools remain open. News media lists must be prepared to identify media contact people who will expedite the transmission of strike news. Fact sheets about the district—depicting size of enrollment, size of staff, salaries of staff, current tax rate, school budget, and the like—should be compiled and readied for dissemination (Zambito, 1979). Efforts should be made to apprise potential strikers of the board's position, in the hope that this position may have been misunderstood. The board's position must also be presented to the media to relay to the community (NSPRA, 1978).

During a strike, provided school remains in session, substitute teachers must be recruited and nonstriking teachers, along with these substitute teachers, must be assured protection by police as they cross the picket line. A communication center must be established to maintain media contacts, to counteract rumors and allay citizen concern, and to channel information through citizen communication networks.

Printed reports should be prepared and distributed at public meetings to acquaint citizens with the facts (Richmond, 1976). School systems with strong volunteer programs and active parent-teacher groups would do well to take advantage of the resources both can provide instructionally in keeping the schools open. Administrators and supervisors should be prepared to assume classroom responsibilities.

At the building level principals assess their needs and draw up plans for superintendency approval that will assure the operations of their individual schools. Efforts to keep their neighborhoods informed about the nature and extent of school operations should be continuous. At the outset of the strike students should be assembled to receive information that will direct their altered instructional activities (Barkelew, 1979).

After the strike is over and everyone is notified that normal school operations have been resumed, instruction should become the focus of all communication between administrators and teachers. Unpleasantries experienced at the bargaining table or during strike activities by opposing sides are easy to recall, and tempers are quick to rekindle. The author can recall a conference session that brought together the superintendent, board president, and president of a local teachers association to discuss the events that led to a strike in their school district. The session was planned for the edification of those superintendents in attendance at the conference. As experiences were relived, the painfulness associated with the events became quite evident, even though the session was to be analytical in purpose. Recrimination and retribution have no place in an educational system.

True, principals need to become acquainted with the contract they must now administer, especially those who served neither on the district's negotiating team nor on its advisory committee. Parents and other community members must be informed about the nature of the settlement. People have to be thanked for their help, but beyond that everyone in the school family should promptly get back to the business of teaching, and work will suffice to blot out most unpleasantries. Thereafter, grievances should be expeditiously handled, and records of contractual misinterpretations, miscommunications, and violations compiled for review at the next bargaining session.

I-1   *Principle:* The school is an integral part of the community; a school closing is like a foreclosure on one's home.

I-2   *Practice:* Preparing for declining enrollments and school closings.

By 1979 there were 6 million fewer pupils of elementary school age in the nation than there were in 1970 (*Phi Delta Kappan,* 1980a). Between the fall of 1979 and the fall of 1980 elementary and secondary school enrollments declined, each by 400,000 (*Phi Delta Kappan,* 1980c). In 1980 700 public schools closed and enrollments declined by 600,000 (*Phi Delta Kappan,* 1981). Declines for the period 1970-1977 were much less prevalent in the South and West than in the North (*Phi Delta Kappan,* 1979). In 1979, while most of the nation's enrollments dipped, 10 states reflected an increase, with Arizona and Florida leading the group (*Phi Delta Kappan,* 1980b). The crux of the matter is that declining enrollments and school closings are now very much a part of the educational scene, a problem that continues to plague education officials and the communities they serve.

A school closing can be a difficult experience for almost everyone in the community: parents who have bought into a neighborhood to be near an elementary school; community groups that have used the neighborhood elementary school for sundry grass-roots activities, social, civic, and educational; students who must change schools, secondary as well as elementary, and be prematurely separated from their classmates and teachers, their clubs and teams, and, of course, their schools; teachers who may lose their jobs or be transferred to other schools within the district, some of them quite remote from their original schools; special services staff who suddenly may be without jobs; administrators who may have to resume full-time teaching assignments, accept transfers, or seek other jobs; and board members who have to make the generally unpleasant decision of closing a school. Because many lives are affected by a school closing, considerable planning must be done to prepare all to accept the shock.

Although there may be no ideal amount of time to set aside for the closing of a school, a four-year time line would seem to suffice, with three years reserved for planning and one year for the actual school closing (AASA, 1974a). Beginning with an intensive assessment of needs and costs, the three-year period culminates with a task force recommendation to the board and the board's decision to close a school. In between much time is spent on involving and keeping school personnel and the community informed and seeking media coverage. However, for closing a high school it has been recommended that planning take five years, during which a broad representation of school and community should be involved (NASSP, 1981).

The effort that goes into this planning should be much akin to that which goes into passing a referendum for a new building. Indeed, in some communities closing a school may be even more difficult than getting the money to build a new one. Thus, planning must be both early and comprehensive.

Planning worked well in Richmond, Virginia, where decreasing enrollments at the high school level resulted in combining seven high schools into three complexes. Through this consolidation expensive duplication of staff, facilities, instruction, and services was eliminated, while all of the district's high schools were retained. A 28-member task force, overseeing 3 committees of 100 members each, recommended the consolidation. Both task force and committees had broad community representation. To facilitate acceptance of the consolidation, staff members were kept constantly informed, and they, in turn, assisted in keeping the community informed. To acquaint staff with proposed instructional reorganization, special sessions were conducted. Parents received newsletters throughout the process and students were engaged in activities that would elicit their support for the change (Greene, Belsches, & Mladenoff, 1980).

Planning has taken other forms as well. Among the many actions taken by the Minnesota legislature to combat reduction in teacher force stemming from declining enrollments was to create laws and the funds to support them that would encourage teachers to take early retirement; give them an opportunity to teach only part time; allow them to take extended leaves of absences with the privilege of returning to their jobs; create portability among retirement systems within the public sector; extend teacher contractual dates to June 1; and help employing school districts with the financial support of experienced teachers compelled to take a leave of absence from their parent school district. The pairing of schools at the elementary school level across districts was to be used as a strategy for grade discontinuation and the shifting of students when specific grade enrollments declined (Mazzoni & Mueller, 1980).

Preventative measures, planning of still another kind, include the advising of prospective teachers at the outset of their teacher preparation, to major in areas in which shortages either already exist or are imminent. Prospective teachers should also be advised by state departments of education to become certified in more than one area, and development opportunities should be made available to teachers for career redirection (Gay, Dembowski, & McLennan, 1981).

But closing a school is one thing; what to do with it once it has been closed is another. The reuse of schools, although not a panacea for the ills associated with school closings, can help to allay much community concern, particularly if planning for closing and reusing are combined and if local involvement in reuse determination is expansive. Partial reuse activity, begun sometime before the actual school closing, can pave the way for a smooth transition. Although people may be averse to the closing of their neighborhood schools, schools with classrooms partially filled or empty can hardly be expected to continue, especially with the economic press on society and demands for increased board, administrator, and teacher accountability. Furthermore, should virtually empty schools not go under the economic ax, they can become community eyesores if not continually maintained; and maintenance costs can quickly outweigh the advantages of having these schools go unused. Reuse can generate new money within a community. Selling outright puts new tax money into the local coffers, from the sale and from the occupancy of the new landlord. Leasing can assure that a school is available at some future date. Meanwhile, the school can serve some valid community function (Fiala, 1983).

Surplus schools, even the oldest, can easily be converted into attractive, multiuse community education centers that provide instructional, recreational, and cultural opportunities for young and old simultaneously, provided communities are willing to take the time to plan accordingly (Brubaker, 1980). For example, declining enrollments in a junior high school in the Herrick Public Schools, New Hyde Park, New York resulted in the Herrick's Community Center. Administered by the school district and complemented by an advisory committee and a manager, the center was to offer a variety of programs, including centers for child care and the gifted; programs for youth and senior citizens; a museum; and university extension courses (National Community Education Association [NCEA], 1981).

Another step forward in public facility use was taken by the Council of Educational Facilities Planning (CEFP) at a conference that was cosponsored by 23 associations. There CEFP, along with representatives from a host of associations, directed the attention of conference participants to interagency facility use. Underscored by the conference were goals aimed at increasing agency awareness, cooperation, communication, and research to optimize public facility sharing. Legislation and funding related to public facility use were additional goals (Decker, 1982).

J-1 *Principle:* Effective school publications foster awareness, understanding, and support.

J-2 *Practice:* Planning and administering school publications.

Intent is fundamental in planning school publications. But the "why" of a publication is inseparable from the "for whom." Aim and audience go hand in hand, and specificity must be a strong consideration in determining both (Gelms, 1979). Once the aim and audience of a publication has been identified, content should naturally evolve. If a brochure is developed to recruit teachers, content that will help teachers decide whether to join a school district's staff would, by necessity, constitute the ingredients of that brochure.

The aim of a publication can be one-sided. An administration may perceive that the primary goal of an internal newsletter is to recognize staff achievements, whereas staff members may envision its aim as keeping them abreast of board and administrative decisions. To avoid such conflicts, staff should have a role in determining content. This can be done through initial and periodic surveys. The same is true of newsletters that are directed at the community. The successful newsletter targets the needs and interests of its intended audience.

The student newspaper is sometimes construed merely as a public relations vehicle. Students consequently have minimal input in content determination. Yet when input is sparse, needs may remain largely unmet. This does not lessen or obviate the importance of faculty advisement; direction becomes even more necessary when student newspapers are geared to address the needs and interests of a student body. Student newspapers, properly planned and executed, become valid learning experiences, particularly when responsibility for choice is intensified.

Likewise, the school district's annual report can be sheer puffery. Laden predominantly with photographs of majestic and confident-looking boards and administrators, and teachers and students happily involved in a variety of learning situations, it may create a false sense of security. If the aim of the annual report is to report on pupil progress and program effectiveness, it should be substantiated by an array of facts and viewed within a context of cost benefits. If new capital will be needed to further goal accomplishment, the annual report should address this need. Some of the annual reports issued by school districts would make corporate executives shudder. Yet the school is one of the biggest enterprises in a community.

All publications should be planned to get important messages across to their readership posthaste. Essentially, there are three kinds of readers. The first kind spends about 30 seconds reading a publication. If important messages are not up front and boldly stated, they are likely to be missed. The second kind of reader devotes about 3 minutes to the publication. Here scanning and skimming occur to extract important messages as quickly as possible. When captions do not provide cues, messages are again missed. The third kind of reader spends about 30 minutes on a publication, sifting through facts and ideas (Schoenfeld, 1977). Thus, great pains should be taken to design a format that will enable important messages to be spotted and digested quickly by readers.

Ordinarily, reader comprehension should be improved by increasing the readability of the contents of a publication. But certain factors sometimes alter this expectation. For example, a proper mix of available reading time and motivation may encourage readers to read beyond their normal reading levels to understand a topic, provided the reading gap between reader and material is not too wide. Similarly, oversimplification of a specialized topic may, to one familiar with it, detract from understanding by distorting accepted terminology. This oversimplification, while lauded by lay people, might also prove annoying to the specialist (Klare, 1963). Interest, then, should be a prime ingredient in a publication. In addition, publications should be tailored to target audiences.

Reading can be thwarted when the print on a page appears cluttered. However, if ample (but not extensive) white space is used to reduce this cluttering effect, the reader may be lured to read on. A dollar lain angularly across different parts of a page may serve to alleviate this problem. For if it should touch only text in these maneuvers and not captions or photos, it can be assumed that white space is lacking (Ondrasik, 1977). A second way to test cluttering is by reading up and down columns for a few minutes. The eyes will have the answer.

Photographs can do much to ensure the success of a publication; but each photo that goes into a publication must be selected to make its own statement and be devoid of artificiality (Weir, 1981). The adage that a picture is better than a thousand words has more than a simple ring of truth. Photos do in themselves tell a story. The author can recall an experience while serving as a school newspaper advisor that clearly illustrates this point.

In an attempt to admonish the student body at X high school for its lack of school spirit, the newspaper staff ran an editorial praising precisely what the students were, in fact, not displaying. The editorial's praise of the student body was extensive. But above the editorial was a photo of an empty bleacher stand, which indicated anything but school spirit. It took about half the day for the students to begin buzzing among themselves about the real meaning of the article. The photo had told the real story.

Publications must be attractive but not expensive. A format pleasing to the eye need not entail exorbitant costs. They must be concisely written and audience oriented. People desire recognition for work well done, staff and community included. They like to see this praise in print. Parents enjoy seeing photographs of their children in publications. Yesterday's school news is, for many, tomorrow's memorabilia. People also want to be kept informed about matters of concern to them. Parents want to learn about programs available to their children and how these programs will improve their instructional capabilities. Indeed, they are interested in learning about anything that affects their child's school life. Taxpayers want to know how wisely their taxes are being spent. Those involved in community education programs want to learn about new course availability. Publications must be planned to accommodate all these interests and needs, and more!

The question of who is to administer a school publication often arises. In school districts that have educational public relations specialists, the question answers itself. But individual schools may boast their own publications, and different people may be assigned to produce them. Still, if each building has its own public relations advisory committee, the problem of who does what may never have to be broached. Two exceptions might be the high school newspaper and yearbook, for which specific faculty serve as advisors.

Administering school publications also includes the matter of dissemination. Who gets what and when and, perhaps just as important, how do they get it are questions that loom in the minds of those charged with distribution. The best way to distribute publications is by mail or at meetings where designated audiences are inclined to gather. Sites where people tend to congregate, such as beauty salons, grocery stores, and banks, may serve as distribution points, provided someone is willing to oversee the dissemination process.

Hand carried by students with the best of intentions, school publications often never find their way into the hands of parents. They may be lost enroute or buried in a pile of books and paper, not to be rediscovered for weeks. Thus, the administration of publications must be a well-organized and coordinated effort. Otherwise what was once timely and important will simply be stale news.

SUMMARY

Educational public relations practices abound. But all stem from a small number of principles that exist in a well-developed public relations policy. This chapter draws upon some of these principles to examine practices in ten areas that have relevance for educational public relations. They are school surveys, educational consumerism, community education, leadership, communication, media, financial campaigns, collective negotiations, and school publications.

• 11 •

The Case Study

Didactically, the case study is as old as the Aesopian fable. Like the classical fable, its purpose is to instruct, to provide insights, and to redirect or affirm behavior. The case study can also be linked to the parable.

Aesthetically, the case study is deeply rooted in literature. Indeed, the typical case study often resembles a short story, replete with elements such as setting, character, plot, and dialogue. Provided its content is relevant, the short story can serve as a case study substitute, particularly if it is open-ended, or bereft of a denouement or conclusion.

The extended case study is somewhat akin to a novel. It is laden with detail, chronologically sequenced by events, and displays the complexities of plot. Unfortunately, it is generally found wanting in character development. An attempt to bridge the gap between novel and case study may be seen in *Providence High School: An Administrative Case Novel* (West, 1971), which adopted and applied techniques of fiction to impart to the case study method of teaching an emotive, as well as an authentic, dimension of administrative behavior. The entire effort, while centered on a single underlying organizational principle, illustrates an assortment of auxiliary principles. Since then, drama has been used to elucidate role theory (Lane & West, 1972); the novel to depict leadership styles (West & Lane, 1973) and charismatic communication (West & Armstrong, 1980); and poetry as a vehicle for effecting change in principals (West, 1975). In addition, the structural components of a novel have been viewed as a means of assessing character in the performance appraisal process (West, 1983).

The case study may also appear as a vignette, with a task or issue-oriented narrative of paragraph size serving as the basis for problem resolution. Clinically, the case study is a laboratory in which behavior can be observed, analyzed, evaluated, and explained. In many respects a case study investigator is like a sleuth searching for clues to solve a riddle. A case study capsulizes and contains life. It may be a rendering of a single experience or a composite of several experiences, drawn from a particular setting or several settings. While many of these experiences are firsthand, others result from inquiries, observations, conversations, and literature searches.

The purpose of a case study is to simulate a problem that can be experienced and resolved in classroom or inservice settings rather than on the spot. By amassing a multitude of vicarious experiences, potential or practicing administrators alleviate the trauma associated with surprise and unpreparedness. The case study provides a decision-making structure that spurs the creation and rejection, or refinement, of an array of problem-solving alternatives, or decision options. It also affords a testing ground for theoretical concepts that might otherwise never be translated into practice. Administrative success may not be a direct derivative of the case study method, but early exposure to simulated administrative problems undoubtedly works toward the reduction of possible failure.

Used to prepare students for a variety of fields, the case study method of teaching has been around for over a century. Its debut dates back to about 1870, when Langdell began using it at the Harvard Law School. By 1915 most of the nation's widely-known law schools were using the method. Continuing to prosper, the method was soon to become popular at both the Harvard Medical and Business schools. Some 30 years after its appearance in the Harvard Business School, the method was, in fact, cited by Harvard's President Conant in his 1950-1951 annual report as playing a crucial role in the school's success. Although the case method was used in public administration preparatory programs in the 1930s and in educational administration preparatory programs about a decade later, the first case study textbook in educational administration did not appear until 1955. That year Cyril Sargent and Eugene Belisle published *Educational Administration: Cases and Concepts* (Culbertson, Jacobson, & Reller, 1960). The book was an outgrowth of a career program for educational administrators that began in the Graduate School of Education at Harvard University in 1952 (Sargent & Belisle, 1955).

Thereafter, an increasing number of case study efforts surfaced in educational administration and related fields. Most of these efforts are contained in outdated anthologies; some have appeared in journals as single cases; others have helped form a series of individually authored cases of varying lengths for the University Council for Educational Administration (UCEA). Currently, the UCEA is updating its series. Today the case study approach is as formidable as it ever was.

CASE STUDY ANALYSIS

Through case study simulations an investigator is exposed to a wide range of problems without ever being touched by them personally. Mistakes can be made in a controlled environment that might prove disastrous if made in the field. While it is unlikely that every problem in the field can be captured in a case study simulation, involvement in any simulation has transference value. By honing his or her decision-making skills, the investigator is in a better position to cope with the unexpected. Figure 6 depicts a Decision-Making Skills Hierarchy that engenders and facilitates case study problem resolution. The hierarchy also has relevance for the resolution of problems cropping up in the field, provided time is taken to think through its seven levels.

Locate the Problem

On the first level several problems may be evident. Whether these problems are tantamount to one another or interrelated is not important to determine at this point of the analysis. The purpose here is to identify all of the problems that exist in a case.

Sort Out Contributing Factors and Clues

At the second level it is necessary to match contributing factors and clues with problems identified at the preceding level. Contributing factors are more tangible than clues. They constitute the history, geography, and demography of a community; increases or decreases in number of administrators, staff, and students; the nature of curricular thrusts; the number and kinds of parent-teacher groups and citizen advisory committees; dialogues between and among individuals; specific events; and so forth. Clues, on the other hand, include, among other things, nuances and contradictions in behavior and speech, or what is implied rather spoken; employee performance patterns, or what

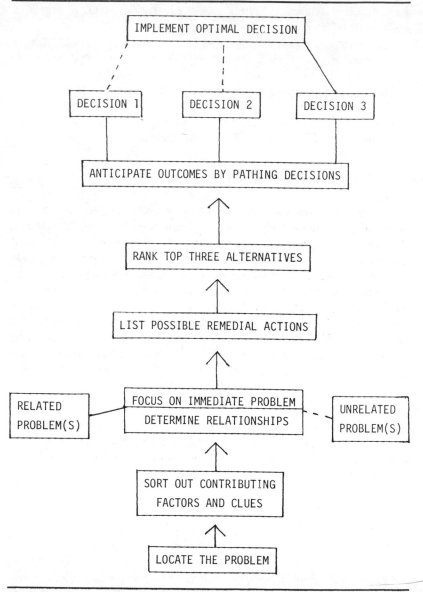

Figure 6   A Decision-Making Skills Hierarchy

may be anticipated as a result of past and present work contributions; community trends that contributing factors, when taken as a group, may portend; and intuitive insights that are suggested by arraying information in different ways.

Focus on the Immediate Problem

As factors and clues are manipulated and massaged, problem formations occur. Some of the problems that emerge from these formations are so closely linked that it is difficult to distinguish whether they are directly or indirectly related to the resolution of the problem at hand. Although the resolution of a related problem may eventually eradicate a school district's most pressing problem, the actions necessitated by this resolution attempt may be so extensive that it takes years to eliminate the immediate problem. Meanwhile, some of the consequences wrought by this delay may produce administrative and staff resignations; lowered school and community morale; an influx of crowded schools; inhibited student learning; and a denial of community support.

Problem formation, in revealing a lack of community support, can point to a need for greater community support, which, in turn, requires a variety of programs to induce this involvement. But the more immediate problem may be to pass a badly needed building referenda, and a carefully planned and executed information campaign could be all that is necessary to accomplish that goal. Furthermore, it is possible that time, money, and human and material resources spent on clearing up one problem will do nothing to resolve another. Meanwhile, students and staff have to endure split shifts or overcrowdedness. Therefore, it is important to deal with the immediate problem first, related problems second, and unrelated problems last, despite the possibility that an immediate problem may owe its origin to a much broader related problem.

List Possible Remedial Actions

Once the immediate problem is targeted, actions that hasten its elimination should be determined. By listing all the possible remedial actions that may be taken, the investigator prepares the stage for decision refinement. While the list may vary from case to case, it is recommended that about ten possible courses of action be identified.

Rank Top Three Decision Options

Once courses of action are identified and listed, they should be ranked from most to least preferred. Then the top three decision options should be extracted and carried forward to the next level for testing to occur.

Anticipate Outcomes by Pathing Decisions

Each of the three decision options should be extrapolated to determine the consequences of selection. Decision paths should be constructed to reveal opportunities, impediments, detours, and likely dead ends. Costs to pursue one path over another should be carefully assessed in terms of requisite resource allocation before implementation is allowed to occur.

Implementation of Optimal Decision

No decision is fail-safe. Facts can always be overlooked or distorted; conditions can be under- or overestimated; people may change their minds; societal interests and concerns may suddenly shift; and technological innovations can rapidly usher in obsolescence. Nevertheless, decisions must be made and consequences accepted. Anticipatory decision making brings with it no assurance of absolutes. Grounded in fact and catapulted by intuition, this kind of decision making borders on reality and illusion. Despite this fallibility, it is absolutely vital in contemporary education.

CASES

Picking a PR Director

H. Payne Roberts twirled from side to side in a black vinyl upholstered office chair while his eyes wearily traveled over the piles of paper that cluttered the desk. He had reduced the 33 applications for the position of director of educational public relations to 5, and now he was trying to prioritize his selections on a scale of 1 to 5, with 1 signifying the most desirable candidate and 5 the least.

To establish a reasonable basis for comparison, it was his intention to interview the top 2 candidates. If one proved more ideally suited than the other for the position, the interviewing process would cease and a recommendation to the superintendent would be made. However, if neither showed promise during the interview, or if he had any lingering doubts about the merits of the candidates after interviewing them, the succeeding candidate would be called in for an interview, with the interviewing process coming to a halt only when the 5 candidates had all been interviewed. It was, of course, possible that all of the candidates might prove unsuitable and that he might have to dip back into the pile of 33 applications to choose another 5 candidates. But Roberts gave little thought to that possibility. Buttressed by his 15 years as personnel director for the Brand Public Schools, he felt confident that he would make the right choice.

Serving a population of approximately 50,000 people, Brand had about 13,000 students enrolled in its schools. It was a thriving suburban community that was situated 43 miles from Stonewall, the largest city in the state with a population of 1.5 million. It was a city destined to grow as the distance between it and Stonewall was seemingly shortened by a four-lane highway, already dotted by fast food restaurants and filling stations. But most of the roads that led into Brand were still relatively rural in flavor and farms of various sizes lay at the city's outskirts.

Brand's chief growth was originally precipitated by its proximity to the big city. Then largely a bedroom community, it later became the site of several small electronic firms and attracted a sizeable work force of its own. Thus, when other communities were experiencing an appreciable decline in student enrollments, Brand was reflecting marked expansion of schools and administrative and teaching personnel.

Currently Brand had a central administration staff of 16, principals and assistant principals numbering 28, and a teaching faculty of 548. What Brand did not have, however, was a director of educational public relations, and it was Roberts's task to hire one.

The need for a public relations director had recently become apparent. Morale at Brand was at ebb tide. Communication between the central administration and the teachers was vastly in need of improvement. Information, complained teachers, was at a premium in Brand. With this complaint the community was often in agreement. Also, nobody seemed to give much attention to public relations either in or outside the classroom, except the superintendent, who had once been an educational public relations director himself. Therefore, a good deal of administrative and staff inservice was needed, and the PR director would be expected to assume that responsibility too.

Roberts reexamined the credentials of the 5 candidates of his choice, carefully scrutinizing, as before, letters of application and recommendation, completed application forms, vitaes, and placement papers. In the process he jotted down notes that he would use to order his choices and guide the employment interviews. In preparing these blurbs, Roberts frequently referred to the job description he had devised. (This description is contained in Figure 7.)

MARY KNOWLES

Just graduated with a master's degree in English from an Ivy League college in the East; earlier received a bachelor's degree in political science from same college; undergraduate minor was communications; both degrees received with honors; worked 3 years in Washington, D. C. as a senatorial aide after receiving bachelor's degree. While in undergraduate school, worked as editor of the college paper; writes prolifically; has free-lanced in writing with considerable success, her articles appearing in several major magazines; hobby is photography; very active in community; staunch supporter of women's rights; has superior recommendations; lives in adjoining state; is apparently unmarried; photo on vita shows candidate to be exceptionally attractive.

JACK FLOUR

Holder of bachelor's degree in secondary education with a specialization in English. Master's degree is in educational administration; graduated from state teachers' college; taught English in grades 10 through 12 for 7 years and served as a department head of secondary English for 3 in same school system; supervised 20 teachers of English; also served as newspaper and yearbook advisor; prior to teaching, worked as department head in retail chain for 3 years; also worked in retail while attending college; is active in a variety of professional and community associations; served in the U. S. Army for 3 years; married and has 5 children; has average recommendations; lives at other end of the state.

MYRNA SLOANE

A recipient of bachelor's and master's degrees in journalism from an exclusive Southern university; received less than average grades, but extremely active in school affairs and won state beauty contest; has worked as a reporter on a local newspaper for 5 years; 4 years on the society column and 1 year as education editor; as native of Brand, knows community well; parents prominent figures in community; has traveled extensively throughout the United States and abroad; is active

```
                            JOB DESCRIPTION
Job Code:  0170

Brand Public Schools

Title:  Director of Educational Public Relations

Primary Responsibility:  To organize and administer an educational public
relations program that facilitates communication between the Brand schools
and their internal and external publics.

Related Duties:  To direct the preparation of all school district publi-
cations; to communicate board policy to staff and community; to develop
and provide PR inservice for administrators and staff; to establish and
maintain a systematic plan for communicating with the media; to assist
in the planning of all financial campaigns and special school events;
and to devise and apply methods for evaluating the PR program.

To Whom Responsible:  The director of educational public relations
reports directly to the superintendent of schools and serves as a voting
member of the administrative team.

Qualifications:  A master's degree in educational administration, educa-
tional communications, journalism, or English.

Experience:  Administrative and/or journalistic experience preferred.

Skills:  Ability to write and speak effectively; ability to provide
programmatic leadership; ability to relate well to diverse individuals
and groups; and ability to design and conduct an opinion poll or school
survey.

Understandings:  Recognition of the importance of public opinion in a
democratic society; at least rudimentary knowledge of computer technology
and its implications for educational public relations.

Salary:  $20,000 to $30,000, depending on academic training and job
experience.
```

Figure 7   Job Description

in community; has glowing recommendations; Brand *Bugle* recently announced her engagement to an upstate physician; her uncle is on the school board.

RICHARD DOUGLAS

Has a bachelor's degree in secondary education with a specialization in chemistry; master's degree was in journalism with a minor in management; both degrees taken in far West at private denominational college; had average grades; taught chemistry for 2 years and served as an assistant principal for 1 year in adjoining state; later, after receiving a master's degree, worked as an educational public relations director in two other states for a period of 8 years; claims to have organized and administered programs in both school systems; served 4 years in U. S. Navy; has two superior recommendations and one average; is evidently unmarried; reflects little community involvement.

DELORES GOLD

Is graduate of state teacher's college with a bachelor's degree in elementary education; upon graduation, served in U. S. Army 3 years as a public information officer; has a master's degree in educational administration with a specialization in educational public relations; was editor of high school and undergraduate college newspapers; taught elementary school for 3 years and served as an elementary school principal in the same school system for 2; husband has just been employed as a junior high principal in the Brand school system; has above average recommendations.

When he finished putting his thoughts down on paper, Roberts spread the five sheets of paper across his desk. Glancing from one to another, he began to number his choices. In a matter of a few minutes he was on the phone calling his first choice. "___," he began. . . .

DECISION AIDS

1. Describe the Brand school system and the community in which it is situated.

2. What were some of the reasons influencing the decision of the Brand Public Schools to employ an educational public relations director?

3. Discuss the suitability of Roberts's method of selecting an educational public relations director.

4. To what extent did the blurbs of Roberts target the requirements outlined in the job description? Did any of the 5 blurbs contain clues that might cause him to accept or reject a candidate? Give examples.

5. List in preferential order, from 1 through 5, your choices for the position of public relations director. Then provide reasons for your rankings.

DECISION ACTIVITIES

1. Using the text, make a list of the attributes, responsibilities, qualifications, and the like that educational public relations directors

should possess, and compare them with Brand's job description. If differences are notable, write a new job description.

2. There is no job description that neatly fits the needs of every school district. With this thought in mind, design a job description for an educational public relations director that meets your school district's needs.

3. Role play the interview that takes place between Roberts and whomever you think should be his first choice. Assume that Roberts is uncertain about whether his first choice is the right choice, and role play a meeting between him and a possible second candidate. Then, on the basis of the two interviews, decide who is more qualified for the job.

4. Set up a group interview, allowing members of the class an opportunity to question all of the 5 candidates. Then have the class vote on the best candidate for the position.

5. Change the singular selection process to a committee chaired by Roberts and consisting of two principals, two teachers, one student, and two community members. Then have the committee review Roberts's blurbs and make its selection.

A Giver of Gifts

He had a hangdog look. So doleful was he at times that it seemed as if he had only seconds before lost his best friend. But a gentle nudge, an arm curled around his shoulder in an amicable embrace, or a simple squeeze of a handshake would have him radiating the innocence and excitement of a 2-year-old just beginning to discover the delights around him. Generally he resembled that same child caught with his hand in a cookie jar.

Everybody liked him; few people took him seriously. Joshua Raddiger, who directed English throughout the Lacyville Independent School District, hired him because they were both from the same town, though 20 years apart. Had he carefully examined his qualifications, he might have chosen 100 others, perhaps more, before employing him.

Mayhew Colly had never really distinguished himself, but he did get by, and very well at that. Part of the reason for the smattering of success he enjoyed was that he was a giver of gifts. Another part was that he professed absolute loyalty to his superiors, often making it appear as if he would brave a firing squad before revealing the smallest of confidences. Actually, he was a fount of rumors, but his claim to faithfulness usually obscured this fact. The final part was that nobody ever expected him to stay very long in his or her employ, so they never bothered to get rid of him. For at 29 he had spent over a decade working at various jobs, the longest of which had been a 3-year stint in the army, the only job he never sought.

Still, the army had not been bad for him; for soon after basic training he was promoted to corporal and a plush desk job in the transportation division, where he tried hard to do nothing all day. Later, while his closest friends were feverishly in contention for their sergeant's stripes, he, not they, had surfaced as the victor. Strangely enough, they could not even remember his having taken the test, so easily did he slip in and out of places.

Later it was rumored that Colly had bragged about having the connections to pass any exam. All it took was the right price, he was reputed to say. But nobody paid any attention to him, having concluded long ago that he lived in a dream world. Even with rank they had thought him harmless, and so he was in his perpetual idleness, which seemed to motivate others to do what he would not. The next time anyone knew of his presence was at the time of his discharge.

Raddiger considered him one of the laziest, most irresponsible persons he had ever met. When Colly was supposed to be correcting compositions during a period allotted for that purpose, he was reading either a newspaper or a magazine. If students were waiting to see him for extra help, he was in the faculty lounge playing bridge. When faculty meetings were taking place, he always managed to be running an errand for the principal. When evaluation time came around and his teaching performance was to be observed by Raddiger, he was typically administering an examination. Indeed, whenever he was supposed to be doing one thing, he was doing another.

Raddiger could never quite figure out whether Colly was brilliant or stupid, whether he was being used by Colly or whether he was using Colly to gratify his own ego. Although Colly's behavior exasperated Raddiger, he liked him, nevertheless. It was difficult for him to do otherwise. Colly was repeatedly telling him how much he admired him and giving him gifts.

Once Raddiger had casually complimented him on the fine pen with which he was correcting his compositions and the pen had instantly become his. Although he had politely refused the gift, Colly's childlike persistence had won out and he had acquired a pen and a guilt he really did not want.

On another occasion he found two tickets in his faculty mailbox to a play that he had wanted to see but could not get tickets for. The tickets were enclosed in an envelope along with a short note.

Dear Josh:

Thought you might enjoy these tickets. I am leaving town on business over the weekend and won't be able to use them. Pleasant watching!

Your friend,

Colly

The tickets had been placed in his mailbox late on a Friday afternoon, and Colly was nowhere to be found to return them to. Not wanting to see the tickets wasted, Raddiger decided to accept them and pay Colly for them on the following Monday. But when Monday came, Colly adamantly refused payment and Raddiger was further in his debt, much to his discomfiture.

The next time Raddiger came into Colly's debt was on his birthday. No one had remembered the date, neither his wife nor his children. But Colly had known, and Raddiger was amazed to find a birthday cake on his desk in the English office with "Happy Birthday, Josh" written on it. His amazement had turned to a gush of sentiment when, soon after his discovery, Colly led a group of teachers into the office to sing "happy birthday" to him.

Aside from the many gifts Raddiger had received from Colly, there was also the matter of Colly mimicking Raddiger in so many different ways, which both flattered and frightened him. Colly tried to ape his writing style, his clothes, his manner of speaking. In fact, whenever Raddiger spoke to him, he produced a notebook to write down words that he would thereafter incorporate into his own vocabulary.

He also sent him a card for almost any occasion: get well cards when Raddiger was out sick for a day or two; anniversary cards; Thanksgiving cards; yuletide cards; and postcards when Colly was on summer vacation.

Raddiger loved and hated the attention Colly gave him, and while the struggle ensued within him, the years passed. Raddiger had assumed that Colly would never stay beyond a year. Colly was perennially at the typewriter preparing letters and filling out applications for teaching jobs all over the country. Unfortunately, he received few interviews; and when they did occur and Colly had a chance to leave, he always turned the job down.

It was in his third year that Colly seemed to take an interest in his work. There was an opening for an advisor on the high school newspaper and Colly wanted the assignment, which meant much extra work, but an additional free period to do it in. Raddiger, by then, had long given up the notion of motivating Colly and was thrilled to see Colly genuinely enthused about something.

In consultation with the principal, Raddiger turned over the advisorship of the paper to Colly. It did not take him long to convince the principal of Colly's merits, for he had been doing precisely that over the years. As a matter of fact, when Colly's performance was at its lowest ebb, Raddiger's laudatory remarks about him to the principal were at their zenith.

Colly began his newspaper advisorship with a zest that impressed Raddiger, but the effort needed to sustain it was beyond his temperament. The assignment had lost its glitter. Meanwhile, Raddiger, fearful that Colly's failure would be perceived as his own, was soon doing all the work. The result was a prizewinning paper, an exhausted Raddiger, and a boastful Colly who (his energy level having suddenly risen) dashed around the building taking bows.

By the close of the year Raddiger despised Colly for abusing his friendship. But Raddiger's feelings were unnoticed by Colly, whose allegiance had shifted to the principal. Colly had become the principal's shadow and also his press agent. Despite Colly's desultory nature, he managed to focus his attention on a single task, which was to get the principal's picture in the local weeklies as often as he could. And, with the help of his newspaper staff, he was able to make the principal feel like a celebrity. Having been trained well by Raddiger, the students produced second and third newspapers almost equal to their first. Initially, every minute of Colly's free time was spent loitering in the main office, waiting for the principal to emerge from his office. Later the principal sought Colly out. In time they seemed inseparable, and many wondered who was running the school.

When the superintendent called the principal to notify him that he was looking for a public relations director to replace the one who was leaving, the principal automatically recommended Colly for the job. Ecstatic about the opportunity, Colly begged the principal to press his superior for a favorable response.

The superintendent knew Raddiger well, both having served in the system for about two decades, and wanted his recommendation before proceeding with the appointment.

Raddiger was stunned when he received a call from the superintendent about Colly. But the stun turned to shock when he learned the reason for the call. The superintendent wanted him to recommend Colly for a public relations position that he might or might not be able to fill, with the latter more likely than the former. If Raddiger recommended Colly, he would be getting rid of him, something that would make him extremely happy. Even if he spoke against him, he probably would not be believed, particularly in view of how he had previously evaluated the man's performance. Then, too, the man was a born press agent for himself, so why not for the school district? After all, he reasoned, what was public relations anyway but a glossy exterior and a vacuous center.

On the other hand, was it not time for him to reveal the truth for the sake of the system and in spite of his own credibility? The funny part about the situation, thought Raddiger, was that he still really liked Colly. Thus, should he be the one who jeopardized the man's career? Perhaps the superintendent should make his own decision.

DECISION AIDS

1. On what criteria did Raddiger base his decision to hire Colly?

2. When it became evident to Raddiger that Colly was lazy and irresponsible, why did he not recommend that Colly be fired?

3. Why did Colly shift his allegiance to the principal after Raddiger had been so kind to him?

4. Why was the principal attracted to Colly?

5. In responding to the superintendent's inquiry about Colly, what should Raddiger say? What will he say?

6. What are the chances of Colly succeeding as an educational public relations director?

7. Whose behavior is more indefensible? Colly's or Raddiger's?

8. To what extent can Colly be called brilliant or stupid?

DECISION ACTIVITIES

1. Role play an early meeting between Raddiger and Colly to improve Colly's performance.

2. List the options available to Raddiger at the close of the case study. Then produce a solution that will allow Raddiger to maintain his credibility while preventing Colly from assuming the public relations directorship.

3. Assume the roles of Raddiger, principal, and superintendent at a special meeting called to determine whether Colly is the right person for the public relations position.

4. Extend the case study to depict Colly's relationship with the superintendent after 6 months of service in the central office.

5. Prepare a letter of application that Colly might write to obtain another position.

6. Draft a letter of recommendation that Raddiger might write for Colly.

What the Traffic Will Bear

It was 9:30 a.m., about 20 minutes after the beginning of the first period class, when the motorized golf cart turned the corner of the empty rear, left-wing corridor. Driving the cart was Alfie Donaldson, one of the four assistant principals who worked at Devonshire High School. Donaldson stopped the cart at the entrance of room 140, disembarked, opened the door, and marched over to where Alice Worster stood teaching her tenth grade biology class. As he handed her an invoice pad to sign, some of the students began to giggle.

When Worster refused to sign, claiming that she was not late for school this morning, Donaldson reminded her that she could contest the ticket later, but that she must sign now. Not wanting to prolong either the disturbance that had already occurred or her embarrassment, Worster quickly capitulated, grabbing the pad and scratching her signature on it in what might have been Sanskrit. In a few moments the cart was gone, and Worster was bracing herself to endure the balance of the period, which seemed to her to pass in slow motion. As her anxiety to see the principal mounted, minutes stretched into hours. She had been unfairly treated and she ached to tell the world about it.

Arthur Lancer, principal of a staff of 130 (including the four assistant principals) and a student body of 2,423, greeted Worster like an icy gale, matching in intensity the blustery weather that the Northeastern city had been experiencing for the past month.

"Mr. Lancer, I do not deserve this ticket," said Worster indignantly, her hand opening to produce a crumpled piece of paper. "I was not late this morning." The ticket fell to the floor, but Worster made no effort to retrieve it.

Lancer smiled, the smile freezing on his face. Stooping over to pick up the ticket, he queried acidly, "What proof do you have?" Before she could answer, he added, "I believe you have been late three other times."

"That's true, but I was not late this morning." The mention of her previous tardiness deprived her of some of her confidence. "Ask Mrs. Mineagaroon; she knows." Worster sank in a nearby chair, suddenly feeling tired. She was doubting the righteousness of her cause. It took five tickets to necessitate a trip to the principal's office, and she had managed it on four.

Lancer, buzzing his secretary, asked her to bring in her teacher attendance sheets. When the two women confronted each other in Lancer's office, it took little prompting from Worster to get Mineagaroon to recall her arrival and admit that she had made a mistake.

"Yes, I remember now." Mineagaroon was flustered. "You did not want to wait in line. You had a test to run off." Mineagaroon quaked apologetically. "I am quite sorry. There were so many waiting to be checked in that I forgot all about you."

"You needn't be apologetic," said Lancer firmly. "It is Mrs. Worster's responsibility to make sure that she is checked in, not yours." His smile had turned into a scowl. "The ticket stands," he snapped.

Worster left Lancer's office with leaden feet. She still had 20 minutes of her preparation period as she moved toward the faculty lounge. In a trance she invoked the past.

Two years ago tickets in Haley Heights were strictly within the province of the local traffic cop. Then a handful of teachers had complained to the principal about the inequities of faculty discipline at the high school. Some teachers, they claimed, could get away with anything, whereas others were admonished for the smallest infraction. Rankled, but sympathetic to their protest, Lancer had instituted the ticket system. If you broke a rule, you got a ticket. Five tickets and you had to see the principal. Four visits and you were advised to seek employment elsewhere. Since the ticket system began, four teachers had been dismissed.

All day long two golf carts patrolled the corridors, the four assistant principals taking turns to ride them. And the ticket business flourished.

There was a ticket for arriving late and one for leaving early, both of which, if applicable, were extremely difficult to avoid unless, of course, the teacher parked in the student lot. The faculty lot was locked at 8:40 a.m. and unlocked at 4:10 p.m.; and to get in or out one needed a key that the principal and his assistants carried.

Tickets were also given for not standing outside the doorway of your classroom while students changed classes; for leaving your classroom at any time students were present; for arriving late to your class; for absenting a duty station; for not punctually submitting a copy of your lesson plan to the principal's office; for allowing your students to carry around their school textbooks without paper covers; for leaving school textbooks on classroom shelves when class was not in session; for marked up student desks in the classroom in which you taught; and so ran the list, long enough to fill a student notebook.

Worster found sympathetic ears in the faculty lounge. One person, however, seemed oblivious to the chatter that surrounded him. He wore a pained expression. Occasionally he leaned over to massage the lower part of his legs. But most of the time he sat erect, gulping hot coffee.

Harry Hayworth whispered to Worster, who was still nursing her own wounds, "You think you got it bad. George, over there, has got over 25 years at the high school and almost as many tickets to match them." Hayworth winked slyly. "But he's not going to stand for any harassment. Already, he's been talking to friends of his on the school board and now, I think, they are beginning to listen."

"How on earth did he get all those tickets?" blurted Worster, agog by the vision of a paper heap. "And how come he's still here?"

"Because, my dear," interrupted George Tucker, with about as much bravado as he could muster, "I am a veritable monument here at Devonshire, don't you know. And old monuments never die; they just get ticketed." Tucker forced a laugh, limped to the door, and left.

"He seems pretty sure of himself, doesn't he?" Worster perked. "I'd be in the lower depths forever with all those tickets. I feel better already."

"I would say that he has good reason for feeling the way he does," said Hayworth, frowning. "Last year he developed a case of arthritis and they have been after him ever since. He gets all his tickets for not standing outside his classroom in between classes. Usually, he's sitting behind his desk resting his legs when they catch him or, I guess, taking medication somewhere." Hayworth glanced at his watch. The bell would be ringing shortly, and he wanted to be outside his classroom when it did.

"He's got two more years before he can retire with full teacher benefits, and he wants to stick it out to age 65, no matter what," continued Hayworth. "He doesn't complain much, though, not to the teachers anyway. But George knows a lot of people in this community. He's got more tenure than anyone else in the district and twice as much as our superintendent. Two of his students were elected to the board this year."

Hayworth took another look at his watch and rose. Worster, made nervous by his repeated glances at his watch, was already on her feet.

"I guess we should go." Worster smiled weakly.

"How would you feel about signing a petition against the present administration?" Hayworth dropped the bait. "Some of the board members might take it very seriously." But Worster was not ready to be hooked.

"I really don't like to sign anything," she said with downcast eyes. "Besides, I need this job."

"So do we all!" said Hayworth kindly. "Think about it. We can talk again later."

During the next three weeks two significant but opposing events occurred. The first took place about a week after Worster got her fourth ticket. When the Haley Heights Independent School District administrative team met, the superintendent heartily endorsed a recommendation by one of the principals that the entire district adopt and implement the ticketing system. As the system had worked so well at Devonshire in helping to due process out of the district teachers who should have been encouraged to leave years ago, the team unanimously decided that all schools should employ it without further ado.

Two weeks later a petition was submitted to the Haley Heights school board, bearing the signatures of about 800 teachers. The petition also bore the signatures of a considerable number of Haley Heights' most influential citizens, plus countless signatures of parents. The petition had the backing of the state teachers' association.

The petition claimed that the ticket system unduly harassed teachers, inflicted a militaristic regime on an academic environment, encouraged talented teachers to leave the district, created low morale, and spawned an unresponsive student body because of low teacher status. The petition also alluded to a walkout by teachers should their grievance be unmet.

That same evening the superintendent had planned to inform the board of the administrative team's decision to implement the ticketing system throughout the district. He had even brought the principal of Devonshire with him to explain how well the system was working there. Now he was not so sure of the appropriateness or timeliness of the team action. Indeed, he was already beginning to regret Lancer's presence at the board meeting.

Board members, on the other hand, all of whom were by now aware of the team decision, were reluctant to admit their knowledge and even more ambivalent about their stand on the issue. All except one board member had originally favored the system. Now there were two other members who were against it. Thus, the board was weakening in its resolve.

Principal Lancer was hurting too, despite his avowed preference for the system. That day he had received a letter from Tucker's lawyer claiming that the harassment of his client was contributing to his poor health. After the board meeting, he planned to show the letter to his superintendent.

Adding to the confusion was a recent editorial in the Haley Heights *Star* about how a ticketing system had turned an average high school into a model educational institution by making its faculty more accountable to taxpayers. An independent citizen's committee shared this feeling and its spokesperson, accompanied by several committee members, was prepared to support the issue. They were seated amid a throng of teachers who were there to deal with the opposition.

DECISION AIDS

1. Why did Worster believe that she did not deserve the ticket she received, and why did Lancer disagree with her? To what extent could either be considered right or wrong?

2. What prompted the institution of the ticket system at Devonshire High School?

3. What were some of the reasons for getting a ticket?

4. Why was Tucker the recipient of so many tickets, and did he deserve them?

5. What prompted Haley Heights' teachers to sign Hayworth's petition? Who, besides teachers, signed the petition? Why was Worster reluctant to sign?

6. Why was the superintendent sorry he had brought Lancer to the board meeting?

7. What did an editorial in the Haley Heights *Star* say about the Devonshire ticketing system? Who added fuel to the editorial?

8. What decision was the Haley Heights board of education likely to reach on the ticketing issue?

DECISION ACTIVITIES

1. Role play the Haley Heights board meeting, with representatives from each of the groups in attendance called to address the issue of the Devonshire ticketing system.

2. List the options available to teachers if the board opts to extend the ticketing system throughout the entire school district.

3. Select a panel to discuss the implications of such a ticketing system for a school district's public relations program.

4. Devise a system of appeals for teachers to contest an unfair ticket.

5. Write a paper that challenges the use of a ticketing system in an educational environment.

6. Write a response to the editorial that appeared in the Haley Heights *Star*.

Raspberries

The Berries had been planning on a July vacation in New Hampshire, but May was all they could get. Computertechnics, the corporation by which Alex Berry was employed as an assistant vice president, would be undergoing some serious changes in its line of products in July, and his superior wanted him on hand when the overhaul began.

The last time Berry had been to New Hampshire was three years before, just before he joined Computertechnics. He and his wife Susan and their daughter Martha had spent two weeks there, visiting with his parents, both of whom were now in their early 70s.

Berry did not like to take his vacation in May; it meant taking his daughter out of school and perhaps jeopardizing her grades. She was already experiencing some difficulty in her tenth grade algebra class, and he did not want to exacerbate the situation. Still, his mother had been of poor health lately and it was always possible that next year she might not be around to visit. And, of course, his father was not getting any younger either. Equally important was that they were expecting him and particularly excited about seeing their granddaughter again.

In his dilemma Berry turned to his daughter for relief. Mainly he wanted reassurance that a week away from school would not cause her to fail algebra. To his surprise, Martha explained that her recent D in algebra did not accurately reflect her classroom achievement. Although she readily admitted that she was no A student in algebra, neither had she deserved the D she had received on her last card. The reason she gave for her less-than-satisfactory performance was that she was being penalized for her conduct in class. The assessment, however, she considered unfair; for it was guilt more by association than by actual misbehavior. True, she had not been a perfect lady in class. At times she talked when she should have been listening and laughed when she should have kept a straight face. But she could not be labeled all that bad either. Her main flaw was her friendship with Irene Casey, whose company she very much enjoyed and with whom she could be seen spending most of her time in and out of school.

Irene, claimed Martha, was constantly feuding with Mrs. Hellena, their algebra teacher. Sometimes they boisterously exchanged insults; sometimes they merely ignored each other, Irene staring out the window while Hellena tried to teach the rest of the students in the class who, much to her chagrin, were following Irene's lead and also beginning to look out the window. Actually, explained Martha, they were simply bored by the constant bickering of the two and sought the window as a source of diversion.

Infuriated by Irene's misbehavior, Mrs. Hellena usually marched Irene to the assistant principal's office twice weekly. Then there were times when Mrs. Hellena's anger gave way to tears. When this happened, Irene generally assumed her best behavior.

It was unclear to Martha, and to everyone else in the class, why the two were continually arguing. They should have been good friends. Irene looked and acted a lot like Mrs. Hellena. They were both small, had similar features and coloring, were normally soft spoken but had quick tempers, and Irene was "a regular whiz" in math. But Irene had fared no better than Martha on her last report card, having also received a D.

Their conversation concluded with Martha's assurance that she would do better in algebra next card marking and that she would keep up with all of her studies while she was in New Hampshire. Alex Berry gave his daughter equal assurance that, in the future, she could count on him for help with her homework, regardless of how busy he was.

Seated at his office desk the following day, Berry inwardly chastised himself for not being a better father. He was the one who was supposed to be the mathematician in the family, yet he could not recollect taking an interest in his daughter's mathematics homework since she was in elementary school. He always left it up to his wife to help her with her homework. And his daughter, who was obstinately independent, typically did not seek the assistance of either her mother or her father until she had exhausted all other resources. Promising himself he would turn over a new leaf, he picked up the phone and made an appointment to see his daughter's algebra teacher.

A guidance counselor by the name of Loretta Shelby ushered him into a small conference room where they were shortly joined by Mrs. Hellena. As Shelby introduced Hellena, Berry was struck by their contrasting appearances. Shelby was a tall middle-aged brunette, bursting at the seams in a navy blazer and matching skirt. Hellena was a petite, frail blond, hidden in a white flowery dress that had lace around the collar and three-quarter length sleeves.

Although Berry's attention was focused on Hellena when he spoke, his eyes periodically glanced at Shelby to include her in the conversation. But Shelby remained aloof to the proceedings, assuming the role of monitor rather than participant. After explaining to Hellena why he wanted to take his daughter out of school for a week, Berry shifted his thoughts to the most important purpose of his visit. Shelby had already made the necessary arrangements with Martha's other teachers to provide her with the study assignments she would need while she was away.

"How much effect do you think my daughter's absence will have on her classroom performance?" he asked Hellena as pleasantly as he could, while fearing what she might say.

"I don't think it will make any difference," Hellena remarked matter-of-factly.

"Are you implying that my daughter is beyond help in your class?" Berry almost choked on his words. He thought that he was prepared for anything, but now he knew that he was not.

"I wouldn't say that!" said Hellena quickly. "But I must point out that algebra is largely a mental exercise."

"So?" quizzed Berry, his eyebrows drawing together as his forehead furrowed.

"Well, some students are better gymnasts than others, and it is much easier for them to conceptualize." Hellena paused to smile sweetly. "Your daughter, I'm afraid, just isn't one of those students."

"I thought educators had denounced the mind-as-a-muscle routine several decades ago. And here you are spouting off that my daughter can't do algebra because she has a flabby muscle in her head." Berry could feel his heart thumping in his throat. "I can't believe this!" Shelby was shaken out of her trance by the rising pitch in Berry's voice. Her eyes bulged in their sockets in sheer amazement. She was aghast at the sudden turn of events. Berry continued, making every effort to subdue his mounting anger.

"Aren't we confusing a discipline problem with a mathematics problem?" It had not been Berry's intention to interject Hellena's classroom discipline problems into their conversation. He wanted to help his daughter, not make trouble for her. But once mentioned, he pursued the topic tenaciously.

"My daughter tells me that you are having a lot of discipline problems lately, and that she is evidently being classified as one of them, all because of her friendship with a student you keep sending to the principal's office. I truly hope that these difficulties are not clouding your judgment of her mathematical capabilities. Up to now, she has always done well in math."

Hellena's eyes were directed downward on a small gouge in the conference table. When she looked up, Berry could see tears trickling down her cheeks.

"You don't understand how hard it is to teach students when they misbehave, students who would rather be anywhere but in your class, students who hate algebra," blubbered Hellena. "I do my best. I try. What more can I do?" Sobbing, she leaned over and buried her face in her hands.

Berry was at once apologetic, and Hellena raised her head. Although he and Shelby tried to soothe her by changing the subject, tears continued to roll down her cheeks. Finally, Shelby was able to quiet her down and Berry departed, feeling like a monster.

That night at his home, he received a phone call from Mr. Hellena.

"Just who do you think you are, Berry?" the voice shouted. "You must be proud of yourself, a big grown-up man like you, pushing around a defenseless woman probably less than half your size. Is that the way you treat your wife?" Berry's ears were ringing from the shouting when he broke the connection.

About a minute later the phone rang again, and the voice, even louder than before, began a second litany. Trembling, Berry hung up the phone once more; then ignored it for the rest of the evening as it periodically broke the stillness of his home. His wife and daughter wore pale, grim faces.

The next day at work Berry received a call from Shelby. Sounding extremely upset, she wanted to know if he had gotten a call from Mr.

Hellena the night before. When he said yes, they proceeded to share their disconcerting experiences. Shelby seemed terrified about losing her job and was continually rebuking herself for allowing the conference to get out of hand. According to her, Mr. Hellena had called up everyone of any importance in the entire school system, the presidents of the board of education and the teachers association, the superintendent of schools, the director of personnel, the principal and assistant principal at Mrs. Hellena's high school, her own superior, and heaven knows who else, maybe even the mayor. Berry was shocked and sorry—for his daughter and himself and for Mrs. Shelby who kept groaning throughout their conversation.

It immediately became obvious to Berry that he would have to request that his daughter be transferred to another algebra class. It would be terribly embarrassing for his daughter to remain in Hellena's class after all that had happened. Moreover, she was just a short step away from failure now, and it would not take much to put her over the edge. It took another visit to the high school and a very unpleasant session with the assistant principal to effect the transfer.

The Berries left for New Hampshire the following week, and in a few days had all but managed to erase from their minds the trouble Alex had stirred up. But their troubles were not to be easily set aside. For soon after they returned, Martha informed her parents that her new algebra teacher was even worse than her last. He would make extra help appointments with her and then rarely keep them. When she did corner him, he usually sent her away in a matter of minutes. On a couple of occasions she was able to get him to discuss two or three of the problems she had failed to solve correctly on a previous week's quiz, but his answers were vague and equivocal and of little assistance to her.

Her history teacher, too, was giving her trouble. Although he had said she would not be penalized for her week of absence from school, provided she submitted her homework to him when she returned, he was now unwilling to count her homework on her sixth card marking grade. He claimed that because her absence was illegal, the work could not be legitimately applied to her grade point average. The result was a C instead of B. One of her other teachers was contemplating a similar action but changed her mind at the last moment, after Alex Berry had pleaded with her on the phone.

Despite his good intentions Berry spent little time helping his daughter with her homework. By the end of May he was deeply immersed in work at the plant. When Martha received a failing grade in algebra at the end of the year, Berry did, however, pay a visit to the superintendent of schools to present his case. But the superintendent, having been fully informed about the troublemaker that Berry was, quickly but politely dispatched him after a few minutes of conversation.

In summer school Martha retook and passed algebra with an A in an adjoining school district. In the fall she entered a parochial school, where she was to remain until she graduated and went on to college.

Eventually Berry joined an independent citizen's committee and sallied forth on a brilliant crusade to right all wrongs. The committee was dedicated to making teachers and administrators more accountable to parents. In time Berry ran for a seat on the school board and was elected. The superintendent had no recollection of Berry by then and could not understand the unreasonableness of the new board member. The way the man was leading the board against him, he might soon be looking for another superintendency.

DECISION AIDS

1. What explanation did Martha Berry give to her father for getting a D on her last report card?

2. Who was Irene Casey, and how did she contribute to Martha Berry's problem?

3. What caused the sudden rift between Berry and Hellena, his daughter's algebra teacher, during the parent-teacher conference Shelby had arranged?

4. Why did Berry receive a call from Hellena's husband? Who else received a call from him?

5. What action had Hellena taken, and how did Berry respond to it?

6. What happened to Berry's daughter when she returned from her trip?

7. When Berry paid a visit to the superintendent of schools, what kind of reaction did he get from him? What subsequent action did Berry take?

8. What might the superintendent expect from Berry as a member of his board of education? To what extent would Berry's behavior be justified?

DECISION ACTIVITIES

1. Assume the roles of Berry, Hellena, and Shelby in the meeting that took place in a small conference room of the guidance department, but this time have Shelby prevent the trouble that ensued.

2. Describe in a paragraph the meeting between Berry and the superintendent of schools.

3. Prepare a list of the actions taken by Berry in the case study. Then determine to what extent he was responsible for his own dilemma.

4. Describe in a paragraph what kind of changes in the school system Berry might seek as a board member.

5. Rewrite the case study to produce a positive ending.

No Bridge to Cross

With the arrival of Metro's new superintendent, the long wait of Jenny Cross seemed over. Unfortunately, another was just beginning. The perfunctory inspection he had given her public relations department during his first week on the job told her little about her future. The fact that she was, in many instances, the last to know about a lot of changes that were now occurring in the Metro Public Schools did, however, appear ominous to her.

The former superintendent had included her in virtually all that went on in the sprawling Western school system. She knew of events almost as soon as they happened. When the media called, she was always prepared with a story to give them. She was a frequent contributor at administrative team meetings and sometimes the only one when school public relations became the central issue. But no longer!

One of Cross's major contributions to the system's educational public relations program was the establishment of building-level public relations advisory committees, operated under the auspices of the school's principal but generally chaired by a public relations representative designated by the principal. This committee was comprised of a cross-strata of the neighborhood in which the school was located. Similarly, Cross had instituted and chaired a districtwide committee that coordinated the efforts of the building-level committees. And until recently the committee structure had enjoyed a large measure of success.

The communication breakdown had occurred when the previous superintendent had been prompted by a majority of the board to start a magnet school program in the district. The program was intended to alleviate some of the district's lagging problems with desegregation. Forced busing had not worked well, but busing by choice to an array of specialized schools was thought to have considerable promise. Other large cities across the country had successfully used the magnet concept to facilitate integration, so why not Metro, the board had surmised.

But Metro, despite its glistening new buildings and boasted sophistication, was quite traditional in focus. Metro did not necessarily like what it had, but it was reluctant to admit that there was anything better. Moreover, Metro had always prided itself on its grass-roots approach to education and was unwilling to allow its schools, particularly its revered neighborhood schools, to become a cafeteria of choice, or so the editorials claimed in the Metro *Pioneer,* a daily that was invited into the homes of most of Metro's 300,000 inhabitants.

As rumored, Metro's tried and tested "3-R approach" (reading, writing, and arithmetic) was to be replaced by a horde of specialized schools, elementary and secondary, and little would remain the same. It was said that there would be the career, gifted, Montessori, classical, and futures elementary schools, on the one hand, and secondary schools for the performing arts, computer technology, business, and trades, on the other, with fearful gaps in between. Actually, the list changed daily, with rumor rampant.

In the thick of the battle, superintendent Willard Hasp tossed in his resignation and moved on to tranquil pastures, having given 10 years of his life to what he used to refer to as "good ol' Metro." The man who always kept his door open to everyone, especially his public relations director, had finally closed it and left.

More determined than ever to have a magnet school program, the Metro Board of Education had launched a national search for Hasp's replacement. And after three months of painstaking labor, the board had hired Dr. David Smith, a tall, youthful, middle-aged man, whose reputation lay claim to the slaying of a number of community dragons in school districts for which he had provided leadership during the past 12 years.

Cross could understand why Smith did not have much time for her, busy as he was warding off the fiery attacks of the media, which seemed dead set in their opposition to the magnet school program. But she doubted the wisdom of his not involving her in these media matters. After all, that was her job. It was embarrassing for her to respond to some of the inquiries of the media; for what once was an informative reply was now very often a surreptitious "no comment." Unable to tolerate the situation any longer, Cross decided to bring the matter out in the open with the new superintendent.

The meeting took place on a rainy October afternoon, with the gloom of the weather hovering over her head like a black cloud.

"Come in, Ms. Cross," said the superintendent, rising from his chair. "I apologize for being a little delinquent in having this chat with you."

The room seemed to brighten with his pleasant smile. "Please have a seat." He left his desk to sit next to her.

When he shook her hand, Cross felt some of the tenseness she had stored up leave her body. Then, in a rush of words, she said, "I just want to help. It's difficult for me to do my job when the media seems to know more than I do about what's going on in my own school system." The anger she felt had managed to creep into her voice.

"I appreciate your being up front with me," Smith said soothingly. "I enjoy honesty with a dash of assertiveness." Laughing softly, Smith added, "Henceforth, I plan to immerse you in my information problems." He leaned forward, hands clasped and elbows resting on his knees. "How do you like that?"

"I am, to say the least, delighted." Cross smiled and relaxed.

"The first thing I'm going to do for you is increase your PR staff," Smith said magnanimously, palms up and arms outstretched.

"Oh!" Cross stammered, unable to hide her surprise and seriously at a loss for words.

"Starting tomorrow, I am giving you my secretary, Helen Mayberry, to serve as your assistant."

"But Mrs. Mayberry is not trained to do PR work, and I don't need another secretary." Cross looked puzzled.

"She's a fast learner. And she did request the change."

Cross did not pursue the matter, having quickly concluded that now that the drawbridge had been lowered and access made possible, anything less than her full cooperation might jeopardize any future passage.

"Another thing," Smith said in a hushed voice, as if sharing a confidence with a close friend, "It is my plan to centralize our PR operation. I know you've done some fine work with your advisory committees, but you must admit they haven't been of much help with this magnet issue. I am also cancelling, for the next few weeks, our administrative team meetings. My idea is to set up a select committee of administrators to work on the magnet program and to keep the proceedings on a 'need to know' basis until we have worked out the snags in our plan of action." Staring directly into her eyes, Smith concluded, "Rest assured, I'll keep you informed and busy."

When Cross returned to her office, she called a meeting of her staff. This staff consisted of a secretary, a graphic artist, and a coordinator of community programs such as PTAs, volunteer instructional aides, and a speakers bureau. Her first announcement was that the department was getting a new staff member. This announcement, until clarified, alarmed the departmental secretary, but brightened the hopes of the coordinator who, for some time, had been searching for a sign that she was getting the elementary principalship she had long desired. The next announcement was the flow of work that could be expected as a result of efforts to get the magnet school program accepted by the community.

For the next few weeks Cross was doubly busy from the involvement Smith had promised and from her labors in trying to find something for Mrs. Mayberry to do. Cross found it interesting to learn by way of the grapevine that Mrs. Mayberry not only hated her new assignment, but also had been completely averse to her transfer. But the thought was entertained for only a moment and then stored away for future contemplation. Mayberry was, after all, legend for her complaints. For now, Cross was deeply engrossed in responding to media inquiries and in preparing copy for press releases, brochures, fliers, the district newspaper, and public service announcements for radio and television. She also spent a good deal of time assisting and peering over the shoulder of her graphics artist, Tim Delaney, who was besieged by deadlines and, at times, losing the battle.

For a while everything seemed to be going fine. Cross did miss her involvement in administrative team activities, but these activities, she consoled herself, would be reinstated once the magnet program was accepted by the Metro citizenry. Too, she missed getting out to the schools to do a little public relations inservice at the building level. But her wistful longings were lost in the fast shuffle of activity that kept everyone working, including Mayberry, who spend an inordinate amount of time trying to figure out what she wanted to do. Then Rhoda Barnes was suddenly whisked out of the public relations department to begin training as a building-level principal in one of the proposed magnet elementary schools, and no replacement was forthcoming.

Now Cross was really overwhelmed, doing the work of Barnes, keeping Mayberry happy, and running the department. For about a month Cross continued to carry her burden without complaint. Then she decided to share her problem with Superintendent Smith.

When the two met again for a protracted discussion, Smith was as jovial as ever, perhaps more so, as the magnet program was now being better received by the community. Even the Metro *Pioneer*'s editorials were becoming favorable to the school system's educational plan, and a number of talk shows had clearly allayed some of the community's misgivings about the gradually evolving program.

"Dr. Smith," Cross said calmly but firmly, "I really am having a problem trying keep abreast of my work, with Barnes out of the department and Mayberry still searching for something she can comfortably handle. At times, I feel it is about as time consuming for me to keep Mayberry busy and satisfied as it is to do Barnes's work."

"Ms. Cross," the superintendent said with a trace of irritation in his voice and an almost imperceptible curl of his upper lip, "would you not *agree* that it is not our job to keep Mrs. Mayberry happy, but only productive?"

"Of course, I believe she should be productive, but it would help if she were the least bit happy, too." Cross hesitated, her assessment of the situation now clearly in question; then she burst out, "And she's not! She needs a work setting more in keeping with her skills."

"I quite agree with you." The superintendent left the chair beside her and moved slowly behind his desk. He looked awesome in his full height, towering over her at his desk, a seeming contradiction to the pleasant tone of his voice. "Please trust me to handle the matter to your satisfaction. I truly appreciate all the work you are doing."

Two weeks later, after a lot of hammering and moving of furniture, a new office was partitioned adjacent to the superintendent's office, and a person hired to occupy it. To Cross's surprise, the nameplate on the door read "Administrative Assistant to the Superintendent." Wondering how this new position would affect her own, Cross paid another visit to her superintendent, but was denied access by the superintendent's recently hired secretary.

"Any future dealings with Dr. Smith will have to be cleared by his administrative assistant," said the secretary with a sneer on her face. "Her name, in case you haven't heard, is Dr. Debra Ellison."

Cross did not exchange amenities with Dr. Ellison until about a week after she had stormed out of the superintendent's outer office. Ellison was too busy familiarizing herself with the operations of the school district to see anybody except those she chose to see, and Cross was evidently not one of those people, not yet anyway.

Meanwhile, Cross was having a problem getting her information straight and her assignments clarified. Denied access to the superintendent, she was forced to depend on information from secondhand sources. Then, when Ellison began relaying orders to her from Dr. Smith, they were not always clear, the neophyte still unsure of what was going on. After a few botch-ups that caused a bit of embarrassment to her and to some of the other administrators in the school system, notwithstanding the superintendent, Cross again found herself in Smith's office.

Smith rose to meet her and welcomed her into the office like a long-lost friend, restoring immediately some of Cross's trust in him.

"Once again, I apologize for making it so difficult for you to see me. You won't have any problems in the future." In a warming gesture Smith boyishly swept a wisp of long, dark brown hair from his eyes. "I have been so busy, so very busy, and Dr. Ellison does have a tendency to shelter me from the madding crowd." Smith stifled a budding snicker.

"It's just that my not having direct access to you has reduced my effectiveness. Dr. Ellison, in her newness on the job, sometimes doesn't recognize my problems." Ready to shout one moment and now apologetic the next, Cross wondered how she could ever have doubted the intentions of so fine a person. "I also asked again and again about a reassignment for Mayberry and a replacement for Barnes, and I have yet to receive an encouraging reply."

"I'll look into the matter at once," Smith said, with determination creeping into his face.

"Thank you." Cross left happily, her future looking rosy again.

But the happiness of Cross was to be short-lived. True, the next day Mayberry was reassigned, but no replacement seemed imminent for Barnes, especially as days turned into weeks. Cross also noticed Ellison lingering in the public relations department for undue periods of time, asking many questions, but giving few answers.

Lately, Superintendent Smith seemed to be more out of the administration building than in. Rumor had it (and that's all Cross had to go on) that the superintendent was doing a lot of public relations work in the community. At the same time, Ellison, now a member of the superintendent's special magnet committee, was providing Cross with not only a paucity of information, but also information that was inaccurate. Too, some of the assignments Cross was given one day were cancelled the next, and Cross, along with her staff, was regretably innundated with work. Eventually the remaining two members of her department began looking directly to Ellison for their orders, and Cross took to locking herself in her office for long periods of time.

In January the magnet school program was in full operation, with substantial community support. On the other hand, the Metro Public Schools' public relations department was on the verge of being defunct.

That same month Cross strongly considered giving her resignation to Superintendent Smith.

Walking into Smith's office with a letter of resignation, in one of her recent dejected moods, Cross was almost swept off her feet by her superintendent's ecstatic greeting. Excitedly, Smith began to tell Cross about his plans for the district and how she might fit into them. Ellison, he said, was to be assigned to a magnet high school, and she, Cross, was to become his administrative assistant for community relations. A new PR director would be hired to take her place, but she would still be in charge of the public relations department. Also, Barnes's replacement would soon be on board. Cross left Smith's office, taking with her at least half of his enthusiasm.

In February nothing yet had happened to change Cross's situation. And Ellison was spending most of her time in the public relations department, ordering Cross and her staff around. No replacement had yet appeared for Barnes and almost all of the principals for the magnet high schools had been officially named.

In this dilemma Cross daily eyed the drawer that contained the letter of resignation she had intuitively decided to save. Then one day, while still uncertain about what actions she should take, she discovered that the letter had disappeared. How long it had been gone she did not know. Worse yet, was what to do about her new predicament. She had to do something quickly. Time was not on her side.

DECISION AIDS

1. Describe Cross's position in the organizational structure prior to the arrival of the new superintendent.

2. Why did the former superintendent resign, and on what basis did the Metro Board of Education choose his replacement?

3. What was the community's reaction to the implementation of a magnet concept?

4. Why was Cross unhappy with the assistant the superintendent assigned to her?

5. What fundamental educational public relations principle did the superintendent violate when he excluded Cross from the information process?

6. When the superintendent denied Cross access to him, what other educational public relations principle did he violate?

7. What role is Ellison likely to play in the superintendent's cabinet?

8. How much truth and how much fiction seem to be present in Smith's dealings with Cross?

9. What kind of future is in store for Cross in the Metro system?

10. Should Cross resign? If so, why?

DECISION ACTIVITIES

1. Discuss the traits and actions of the new superintendent and determine if there is a leadership style that adequately encompasses them.

2. Describe what is meant by an administrative team and discuss whether Cross should be included in its membership.

3. Prepare an organizational chart that depicts the relation of the educational public relations director to other administrators in a school system.

4. Briefly enumerate the role and responsibilities of an educational public relations director and compare them with what is expected of Cross in her job.

5. Role play a final scene in which Cross submits her resignation to Smith.

The Image Maker

Paul Dickerson passed the door marked "Superintendent of Schools" twice before he decided to stop. As he raised his hand to knock, the door opened and Superintendent Crowley stuck his head out. Dickerson's hand remained suspended in midair as Crowley and he briefly faced each other. Then Crowley looked beyond him, his eyes darting from right to left. The superintendent scowled when he saw that Mrs. Dawson, his secretary, was not in the outer office.

"Everytime I need her for something, she's not around," grumbled Crowley. "One of these days I'm going to send her packing." Crowley paused. "You want to see me?"

"Yes, if you can spare a minute," replied Dickerson sheepishly.

"That's about all I can spare," said Crowley glancing at his watch and moving toward his desk.

"Well," said Dickerson, trailing Crowley into his office, "I just want to apologize for not having better organized, for the board last night, all the costs on the inservice package you wanted them to consider."

Easing himself into the chair directly across from the superintendent, Dickerson innocently added, "It was such short notice."

"Trouble with you, Paul, is you're always trying to come up with some kind of masterpiece." Crowley picked up some papers and began studying them. "Next time," he admonished, "don't try to be fancy—stick to the basics! Granted, your report looked arty enough, but it would have taken a French impressionist to figure out what you were trying to say. Anyway, you heard what old what's-his-name said about it last night!"

"You mean Dr. Sanducloy?"

"Yeah, the eye doctor," said Crowley resentfully.

"I didn't think he was just talking about my report," said Dickerson defensively. "He seemed upset about everything."

Crowley's eyes peered over the rims of his glasses. "He can be belligerent at times," said Crowley, more to himself than to the personnel director.

"If I didn't have to spend so much time compiling data for negotiations and then sitting at the bargaining table until all hours of the night, I'd have no difficulty in keeping up with all my paperwork." Dickerson suddenly seemed tired. "I do the best I can."

"It could be worse, Paul," said Crowley, raising his head and staring down the other man. "You could be chief negotiator." Dickerson shuddered. "No, on second thought, you're definitely not the chief negotiator type," teased Crowley. "You'd want the contract to be a masterpiece."

"That might not be a bad idea," said Dickerson peevishly, "considering all the grievances we've gotten this year."

Warming up to the conversation, Crowley volunteered, "I guess we could use a little PR, couldn't we?"

Dickerson nodded. "Things are likely to get worse, too." Frowning, he said, "I heard some of our principals and supervisors also want to negotiate with the board."

Alarmed, Crowley's voice fell to a whisper. "Who told you?" he asked.

"Lawrence Daly asked me if I would be interested in joining the group," responded Dickerson in a whisper that matched his superior's.

The two men talked for about 30 minutes. At the close of their discussion, Dickerson left with the feeling that he was once again in the good graces of his superintendent. This was important to him because he was certain that any day now the post of assistant superintendent of personnel was going to be created, and he badly wanted that position. Crowley, on the other hand, was convinced that he was going to have to do something about improving his image in the district. With the principals and supervisors wanting to negotiate, he was liable to find himself without a job.

Beginning the following Monday, he would make what he called his "PR rounds" throughout the district. Lately, he had seldom left the administration building. It was far easier to conduct group meetings with his 12 principals there than it was to visit them individually at their schools. In the future, however, he would visit the principals at their schools and seek their friendship and support. He would keep a running log of his PR rounds and assess the results of his efforts at the close of each week. The more he thought about his plan, the more excited he became. He was anxious for Monday to come.

His first stop on Monday was at the Wright Elementary School. Dave Jackson, the school's principal for the past seven years, met him at the entrance to the building and ushered him to the office.

"I'm real pleased you came down to pay us a visit here," said Jackson happily. "There are times when I get the feeling that I'm really out in the boonies."

"Dave, you're lucky being at the other side of the city," said Crowley patronizingly. "If you were principal of one of our newer, more modern facilities, you'd really have your hands full. The parents in those new housing developments are pretty demanding." Jackson winced.

"I'm inclined to think my school community is just as demanding as any other, maybe more so, since my youngsters have greater needs, social and academic, coming as they do from low-income homes. And it's my policy to give my clientele more than they expect as often as I can." Jackson rambled on enthusiastically as Crowley's eyes darted around the room. When he noticed that Crowley was staring out the window, Jackson stopped talking and looked out the window, too.

Startled by the sudden silence, Crowley remarked offhandedly, "Your custodian didn't do a very neat job of cleaning up that walk out there. He seems to be resting more than he's working. He's new, isn't he?"

"He's a good man," defended Jackson. "And his children, who attend school here, are model students."

"Interesting, but not necessarily pertinent." Crowley flashed a broad grin that vanished almost as quickly as it had appeared. Jackson was not very astute, he concluded.

Crowley toured the building with the principal for about an hour and a half, stopping off in a number of classrooms where he spent more time looking at his watch and worrying about his luncheon appointment at another elementary school than he did listening to the innovations of the teachers.

At 11:30 Crowley bade farewell to Jackson, feeling that he had made considerable progress during his first public relations visit. In a parting gesture of friendliness, Crowley shook Jackson's hand warmly. "I really appreciated the tour of the classrooms. Overall, I'd say that your teachers are doing some fine work. But they could do better if they exercised a little more control over their students. Some of those kids were pretty unruly. But do keep up the good work, Dave," said Crowley, leaning up against the building.

On his way to the Quentor Elementary School, Crowley stopped at a small grocery store to buy some tobacco. The store was owned by one of his board members. Ordinarily, Crowley did not patronize the store; in fact, he had only been there about a half dozen times during the past four years. But as he was in the neighborhood and definitely out of tobacco, he decided to include the store among his PR rounds.

Eliot Smith was waiting on a customer when Crowley entered the store and waved to him. By the time he had selected his favorite brand of tobacco, four people were ahead of him at the register, all waiting to have several purchases rung up. Still in a hurry, Crowley did not want to wait out his turn. Had he the correct change, he would have dumped it on the counter, bid adieu to Smith with one of his best smiles, and left the store. Unfortunately, he had only a couple of $10 bills in his wallet. He thought of putting the tobacco back on the shelf and easing himself out of the store as unobstrusively as possible, but figured he would create more harm than good when Smith realized what he had done. He could tell Smith that he would be back later, but he did not want to feel obligated to return.

In view of his busy schedule, there was, for him, only one course of action, and he took it with embarrassment creeping up his cheeks.

"Eliot, would you please ring up this purchase?" asked Crowley, moving up to the front of the counter. "I'm in a terrible rush."

Smith's eyes darted from Crowley to his regular customers and back again. He could see that they were annoyed that someone was trying to get ahead of them and also curious about who this someone was. Reaching out his hand for the $10 bill Crowley was dangling, Smith said, "Busy day, eh, Superintendent Crowley?"

"Very busy." Crowley laughed nervously. All eyes were upon him. Crowley grabbed his change and dashed out of the store smiling. "Thanks, Eliot; you too, folks," he shouted.

Outside Quentor Elementary School, Crowley made two entries in his public relations log. It took him about two minutes. At 12:30 Crowley walked into the office of Ernestine Mays, Quentor's principal.

"Good to see you, Mrs. Mays," said Crowley with a blank expression on his face. He was already thinking about his next appointment.

"It's good to have you visit us. We don't see you as often as we'd like," said Mays cordially. "I'll have our lunches delivered to my office."

"I wouldn't think of it," said Crowley majestically. "I want to eat with the little people. I came to Quentor to visit the school, not to sit in your office. As much as I may enjoy your company," he added.

On his way to the cafeteria Crowley stooped down to pick up a couple pieces of paper and crumpled them into a tight ball.

"Every litter bit helps," he joked. "I never could stand a dirtied up hallway," he continued, suddenly becoming very serious. Mays stiffened. "It makes for poor discipline and bad PR."

While the two lunched, Crowley went to great lengths to pass on to Mays some of the experience he had gained from being a principal of both an elementary and a secondary school. Because Mays was so attentive, Crowley lingered over lunch longer than he had planned.

Crowley's visit came to an abrupt end when he and Mays returned to her office. No sooner than they had sat down, when Mays's secretary was knocking at the door.

"Dr. Mays," she said when the door opened, "Mrs. Graham, your 2 o'clock appointment, is here."

"It was time I was leaving, anyway," said Crowley, rising from his chair. And in a moment he was out on the road again.

Crowley arrived at the Raney Senior High School about 2:45. It was his last stop for the day before getting back to the administration building. Ray Tanner was with a parent when he arrived, so Crowley toured the building by himself. Hunched over, with his forehead furrowed in deep thought and his hands tightly clenched in his coat pockets, Crowley failed to attract many hello's from those who recognized him. Instead, they appeared to avoid him whenever possible.

Not more than ten minutes after the superintendent and his principal exchanged social amenities, Crowley was interrogating Tanner about the reasons for the large number of teacher grievances that had occurred in his school. Dissatisfied with Tanner's explanations, but feeling it pointless to press the matter further, Crowley began criticizing unions in general and teacher unions in particular. Eventually, he got around to asking Tanner how he felt about middle-management unions. Tanner was slow to reply.

"Principals don't like being on the sidelines when important decisions are made," he said, shifting about in his chair. "They like it even less when they have to administer a negotiated contract they've had no part in shaping. In the final analysis, principals just want to be heard occasionally," Tanner sighed.

"I think your criticism is unwarranted," said Crowley heatedly. "I give you people all kinds of opportunities to make suggestions, and I get very few. Furthermore, what I do get is generally impractical. But I didn't come here to argue with you. I came over to tell you that the board and I think you're doing a great job here at Raney. Keep on producing and you might have my job one day." Crowley's arms were covered with goose pimples. "In the meantime, there's always the possibility of an assistant superintendency spot opening up."

Tanner brightened and relaxed. A glimmer of ambition shone in his eyes.

"Thank you for your confidence in me," he said happily. "I'd like very much to work with you at the administration building. In fact, I can't think of anything I'd like to do more."

Moving toward the door, Crowley extended his hand, which Tanner clasped firmly. "Just keep your distance from Lawrence Daly and you'll go places in this district," confided the superintendent. Tanner's hand went limp and he stood frozen in his tracks. Crowley left the building assured that he had just enlisted a strong ally in his cause against midmanagement unions.

Crowley was tired when he entered his office, but not too tired to examine the day's activities. The entries in his log showed four trips, all of which were devoted to improving his public relations image in the district. But how much had he really accomplished? To make this determination, he must assess in careful detail the entries he had made. Too keyed up to wait until the end of the week to make the assessment, he began his analysis. Before he went home tonight, he would know all he needed to know about the public relations image he had projected.

While he scrutinized his log, the buzzer on his phone sounded. He removed the receiver from its cradle and brought it up to his ear.

9:00 AM	Visited Wright Elementary School Discussed Dave Jackson's educational philosophy with him. Toured the school building with Jackson. Complimented Jackson on how well his teachers were performing. Complimented Jackson on his good work.
11:45 AM	Dropped in on Eliot Smith at his grocery store Patronized his store, and am sure he appreciated the visit, since he was so very helpful. Made it obvious that I was very busy working. Thanked him for his kindness.
12:30 PM	Visited the Quentor Elementary School Met with Mrs. Mays and had lunch with her in the cafeteria. Good exposure to students. Explained how important clean buildings are in promoting PR. Gave Mays the benefit of my many years of administrative experience; noted her extreme interest.

2:45 PM	Visited the Raney Senior High School
	Toured the school building making myself available to faculty
	  and students.
	Met Ray Tanner; had a nice long talk with him about teacher and
	  mid-management unions; Tanner was very responsive.
	Complimented Tanner on his work; feel certain that Tanner will
	  be a strong ally against proposed mid-management union.

4:00 PM	Returned to administration building

Figure 8 Superintendent Crowley's Log

"What is it, Mrs. Dawson?" he snapped. "Don't you know I'm busy?"

"It's Mr. McDaniels, the president of the Cumberland Junior High PTA," whined Dawson.

"What's that fussbudget want now?" shouted Crowley into the phone. "Tell him I'll call him back later."

"He's here, Mr. Crowley, standing right next to me," squeaked Dawson, pushing the phone away from her ear.

"Tell him I'll be right out."

He threw his pen down on the desk in disgust. His public relations image would have to wait a little longer.

DECISION AIDS

1. What is Crowley's general attitude toward people? Describe his temperament.

2. What evidence is there that Dickerson fears Crowley? Why is it important to Dickerson that he stay in the good graces of Crowley? How is Dickerson treated by Crowley?

3. Why does Crowley want to improve his public relations image, and how does he intend to do it?

4. In making the first round of his public relations odyssey, how does Crowley immediately upset his host? How much good will has Crowley gained from his visit?

5. What is Crowley's logic for moving ahead of a long line of customers in Smith's store, and how does Smith react to this breach of etiquette? Why does Crowley decide to stop at Smith's store in the first place?

6. What propriety does Crowley overlook with Mays? Who becomes the conversational topic when he lunches with Mays?

7. During Crowley's visit with Tanner, what does he say that momentarily makes him an ally? How does he shatter this budding relationship?

8. What is wrong with Crowley's log?

DECISION ACTIVITIES

1. Design a series of public relations strategies that will improve Crowley's school and community image.

2. Review Crowley's conversations with each of his three principals to list the number of times he complimented and insulted them.

3. Prepare a list of personal qualifications (attributes and people skills) that a superintendent should possess and evaluate Crowley's behavior using this list.

4. Rewrite Crowley's log to show what actually happened during his public relations odyssey.

5. Extend the case study to show what happened to Crowley.

The Beginning or the End

Taylor Montgomery had one more year to serve on the Latimer Board of Education and he was going to make it a memorable one. Montgomery, a civic-minded and prosperous business person, was completing his second stint of board service, only this time as president. Montgomery, himself a product of the Latimer school system and still beaming handsomely in the high school yearbook as the one "most likely to

succeed," had confirmed beyond belief all expectations of his classmates. From the proverbial shoestring and a wildcat oil well, he had
built a lavish Latimer empire—a bank, a shopping mall, a construction
company, and a real estate corporation. And he attributed all of his
success to the rigorous athletic training he had received in high school
where, as a four letter bearer, he had served as captain of the football,
basketball, baseball, and track team. Athletics built stamina, steadfast-
ness, a keen mind, and a healthy body, according to Montgomery.

But Latimer was not doing very well in athletics these days and had
not really done anything of consequence since Montgomery was a high
school student. The trouble seemed to be a lack of enthusiasm among
board members to have a winning team, a feeling generally shared by
Latimer's new superintendent, Morris Street, who was an ardent propo-
nent of the basics. Montgomery did not dispute the notion of teaching
Latimer's students the basics; he merely argued that physical fitness was
predominant among them.

Of all the sports that endeared themselves to Montgomery, football
ranked highest in his sentiments. He loved football with a passion,
hearing often in the reminiscing of his youth the thunderous roar of the
crowd when he scored a touchdown and led his team to victory. And
before he quit the board, he wanted Latimer to savor a football cham-
pionship once again.

Winning championships, however, was not the goal of head football
coach Roger Quimberly, who prized sportsmanship first and winning
second. Quimberly had been losing with regularity for the past ten
years, and it seemed not to bother him at all. But it did begin to bother
some of the newer board members, who, like Montgomery, thought
that winning in school athletics had a lot to do with preparing one for
winning in life. After all, reasoned one of the board members, anybody
could lose.

Under ordinary circumstances, Montgomery, a generous alumni
contributor, could have rid Latimer of Quimberly long ago. But there
was nothing ordinary about Quimberly, whose primary influence extended beyond the gridiron. He was active in almost every phase of
school and community life, counseling students, chairing clothing and
paper drives for worthy causes, and serving as president of at least two
civic groups. Because of his tireless efforts, he was respected and liked
by both students and the Latimer citizenry. There were those, of course,
who complained that his energies would be better spent doing the job
he was paid to do, but until recently these clamors had been in the

minority. So, amid a rippling in an endless tranquil stream, on went the uneventful career of Coach Quimberly.

Then, with the sudden departure of Latimer's athletic director and the board's initiation of a search committee, rumors relevant to Quimberly's future began spreading like wildfire. One of the rumors was that a winning head football coach from a neighboring school system had been offered the job as athletic director, but had turned it down. Another was that the same head coach had taken the job as both director and head football coach and that Quimberly had been given notice. Still another was that Quimberly was being promoted and a new football coach had been hired.

When Montgomery was contacted by a reporter from the Latimer *Press*, he refused to comment on the proceedings.

"When a decision is made, you will be the first to know," he said briskly and somewhat irately to the young reporter.

A similar but lengthier reply was received by the same reporter when he contacted Coach Quimberly.

"I know nothing about any replacement. I have served the district well and prefer to spend the rest of my years here in Latimer, working with the people, particularly the kids, whom I have come to know and cherish. When I learn anything definite, I will be pleased to inform the *Press*."

Superintendent Street was quick to deny to the *Press* any firsthand knowledge about the issue. When deluged by a camera crew from Latimer's only television station, he did say, however, that if Coach Quimberly was replaced, he would resign.

"Sports," he added, "are not fundamental to an academic learning situation. We need cooperation, not competition, in the classroom. Coaches are teachers first and athletes second in this school system."

Meanwhile, the Latimer *Press* had interviewed the neighboring coach about the alleged offer.

"Yes," admitted the coach, "I was offered the position of athletic director and head coach, but I did not accept it. I am happy right where I am."

The reporter continued, with excitement in his voice, "Is it true that you were offered a salary equivalent to the salary of Latimer's superintendent of schools?"

The coach smiled coyly, obviously relishing all the attention he was getting. "Frankly, I don't know what he makes. Nor do I care."

"The superintendent makes $50,000 a year," prodded the reporter.

"Do you mind telling me what you were offered?"

"I would prefer not to answer that question. I suggest you ask the Latimer school board." His smile widened as he turned and made his way through the cluster of onlookers encircling him.

Shortly after the interview appeared in the Latimer *Press,* another rumor began circulating. Someone, it was said, had accepted the position of athletic director and head coach, and the salary paid him was to be even higher than that of Latimer's superintendent.

When the media, newspaper, radio, and television next interviewed the superintendent of Latimer's schools, they were soon joined by a small crowd that had gathered outside the administration building to protest the alleged firing of Coach Quimberly. As the day wore on, different people appeared on the scene, as if trading places with those departing, and voiced the same objection. Later that evening meetings took place all over the city to discuss the Quimberly issue.

Tension continued to build in the community throughout the remainder of the week, unabated by a subsequent *Press* interview with Montgomery negating the current rumor and indicating that negotiations were still pending and that no firm offer had yet been made to the second candidate.

At the next board meeting, which occurred just three days after Montgomery's *Press* statement, the board conference room was jammed to capacity. Standing and sitting were about 200 people demanding, individually or through their chief spokesperson, answers from the board. Latimer's general citizenry wanted to know how the board could justify paying a coach such an exorbitant salary just to win high school football games. Ordinarily, this would be bad enough, one of them had remarked, but when 17% of Latimer's work force were either collecting unemployment benefits or on relief, it was disastrous. The friends of Quimberly, who were impressive in number, wanted an explanation of why a fine man such as he should be fired because he chose children over winning. A third group of protesters was Latimer's teachers, who were abashed by the incredible sum the new coach would receive while they were paid only slightly above the state base salary. There was also some concern expressed by one of Latimer's coaches, who felt that the high salary of the new director would vastly aggravate existing salary inequities among the present coaching staff.

There were, nevertheless, those in attendance who welcomed the board's proposed action. It was their contention that a new and accomplished director would stimulate championships in the other athletic areas as well, and that it was about time Latimer did something to improve its archaic athletic program. In the rear of the conference room a few students could be seen waving placards, on which was printed in big black letters, "Coach Quimberly Must Stay."

At the close of the board meeting, Superintendent Street submitted his resignation to Montgomery, who refused to accept it. While the latter glossed over the incident with some of the board members, openly excusing the overwrought superintendent but silently ruing his action, a harried Street hastened to his car and drove home. A vexed president of the Latimer Teachers Association collided into Montgomery as she stormed out the door without saying a word, and some of the Latimer citizenry made it clear to him on their way out of the building that the issue was far from dead.

As Montgomery left the board room that night, he tried to line up in his mind the pros and cons of the impending board action.

CONS

(1) The superintendent would insist on resigning if Quimberly was fired, if only to save face on the salary issue.
(2) The friends of Quimberly, who were evidently numerous, would cause him no end of the grief during the rest of his term.
(3) It would be difficult to pass a bond or budget referendum for some time.
(4) The student body would definitely miss Quimberly if he was discharged and think of him, Montgomery, as some kind of ogre instead of the Latimer benefactor that he was. He loved Latimer, that, nobody could deny.
(5) It would be difficult to get along with the teachers for a while. They would be crying union again.
(6) The coaches would be tempted to give less than a 100% effort to their new boss because of the disparity between his and their salaries.
(7) Some of the board members now on his side might begin to oppose him because of his disfavor with much of the public and their guilt by association.

PROS

(1) He would offer the superintendent more money than the coach, thereby reinstating his credibility and worth in the community.

(2) The friends of Quimberly would forget him when Latimer began winning athletic championships. Caught up in their own problems, they would shortly forget him anyway.

(3) The economic situation would soon improve, and prosperity would reign once again in Latimer. He, in fact, would make a significant effort to create some jobs. He had several projects in the works now that could ease the situation.

(4) The students would love winning more than they liked Quimberly, and the school spirit of Latimer would soon soar.

(5) The teachers were in line for a raise anyway, and the raise would dissipate their anger.

(6) The coaches, now disgruntled by salary differences, would be inspired by an accomplished director, whose training and contacts would vastly improve their careers and, consequently, their salaries.

(7) He was confident that the board would be pleased with its decision once Quimberly had departed and the issue was put to rest.

(8) He would fulfill a personal dream.

Or, he finally concluded, he would create a nightmare that would make him one of the most disliked people in the community he called home—for a long, long time; perhaps forever.

What should he do? Or worse, was there anything he really could do at this time to rectify the situation while still saving face?

DECISION AIDS

1. To what did Montgomery attribute his success in life?

2. How did Montgomery and Street differ in their educational philosophies?

3. What did Quimberly see as the primary purpose of an athletic program?

4. When Latimer's athletic director suddenly departed, what was rumored about Quimberly's future?

5. Who wanted to get rid of Latimer's head football coach, and why? If the Latimer coach were replaced, what did Street say he would do?

6. What did the coach in the neighboring school district tell the Latimer *Press* during an interview? By not responding to a question asked by a Latimer reporter, what did the coach imply?

7. Why was the Latimer citizenry upset? Who else was upset for similar reasons?

8. On the basis of what he viewed as the pros and cons of the situation at hand, how was Montgomery likely to act?

DECISION ACTIVITIES

1. Write a paper on the function of athletics in a total educational program.

2. Set up a panel to discuss the importance of winning in school athletics.

3. Role play Montgomery and Quimberly in a debate about the function of athletics in a total educational program.

4. Write a paper describing what would happen if Quimberly were replaced.

5. Trace the history of athletics in the public school system.

6. Compare the function of athletics in classical (Hellenic) and contemporary society.

7. Define what is meant by the "basics," and discuss their applicability to education in the future.

8. Prepare a press release reporting the board's decision to hire a new athletic director and head football coach.

When Old Friends Meet

Dierdre O'Connor considered herself one of the luckiest people on earth when they made her principal of the Theodore R. Bright Elementary School. Now she acted like one of the unhappiest.

O'Connor's unhappiness began shortly after Penelope Drew, her predecessor and superior for eight years, returned to Bright to teach third grade. Drew and her husband Mark, a senior high chemistry teacher, had left Maybody and New England to pursue their doctorates at one of the Big Ten universities in the Midwest, Mark in chemistry and she in educational administration.

Although the Drews had no intention of returning to Maybody when they left, money problems during their second year of doctoral study prompted them to reverse their decision. The expense of supporting a family of four, three of whom were now attending college (themselves and, as of the fall, their son Murray), had virtually depleted their savings. Thus, in December Penelope and Mark, with almost all of their coursework done and with their dissertations yet to write, decided to contact the superintendent of Maybody to see if he had any midyear teaching jobs available.

When Superintendent Ian Flaherty received the phone call from Penelope, he was overjoyed to hear from her. Drew had been one of his best principals, and he had been extremely sorry to see her go. Fortunately, there was an opening that Penelope could fill, recently made available by a maternity leave. It was at the third grade level in the school where she had served as principal. Furthermore, although he did not have a chemistry teaching assignment available for her husband, he could use him as a permanent substitute, if Mark was willing to give it a try. On the other hand, he could check out some of the adjoining districts to see if they had any chemistry jobs open. In any case, he suggested that the Drews return as quickly as possible to get settled before the holidays were over. The remainder of their conversation centered on Penelope's doctoral work in educational administration.

After Drew hung up the phone, Flaherty reviewed the highlights of her career at Maybody. Drew had spent 15 years in the Maybody School District, 5 years longer than he had. In her third year, and once again in her seventh, she had been named best teacher of the year by the Maybody Teachers Association. In her eighth he had persuaded her to accept the principalship at Bright.

Drew had also twice received a citation from the PTA presidents of 10 elementary schools in the district for being an outstanding principal. And throughout the state she had gained considerable recognition for her work. It was considered somewhat of an honor by the teachers of Maybody to be assigned to Bright when Drew was principal. Under her supervision Bright had come to symbolize education at its best.

Yes, Flaherty mused, it would be good to have Drew back. Too bad she couldn't have her old job back. Still, O'Connor had been her protegee, a fact that could not easily be dismissed.

O'Connor was startled when Flaherty informed her of Drew's impending return. At first she was almost certain that the new development meant that she was going back to the classroom. If Flaherty had not continued talking, she might even have volunteered to make the switch. But the lack of a pause after his jarring news, strung out by the explanation that followed, gave her sufficient opportunity to steel up her determination to stay on as principal of Bright.

She had nothing to fear, she assured herself; for had she not been a model principal during Drew's hiatus? For over a year she had been administering, with a large degree of success, a teaching faculty of 25 and a student body of 650. She had chaired a dozen committees, placated parents from all walks of life, and earned the respect of her peers at administrative team meetings. Indeed, the more she thought about her tenure as principal, the more assured she was of herself, until she actually welcomed the challenge implicit in her mentor's arrival.

But the challenge she received was much more than she had anticipated. It was not the old Drew whom she encountered when school resumed, but someone who appeared to have just stepped out of a fashion magazine, looking at least a decade younger than her 42 years. Always so absorbed in her work in the past that she seldom worried about whether what she wore was in or out of style or what or how much she ate, the new Drew was, at first glance, almost unrecognizable to O'Connor. The change seemed ominous to her.

Having Drew, their ex-principal, as a member of their peer group seemed to delight most of the teachers at Bright, and it was not long before many of them began turning to her for advice. Once simply respected and admired, Drew now found genuine friendship among the faculty, and the pleasure this new relationship gave her was reflected in a widening circle of friends.

The strength of this friendship was made vividly clear to O'Connor one afternoon a few weeks after Drew's arrival. While O'Connor was in her office, with her door to the corridor partially open, she overheard part of a conversation that caused her considerable discomfort.

"I just wish you were our principal instead of Mrs. O'Connor," said a first-year fourth grade teacher. The sincerity in her tone of voice sent a shiver down O'Connor's spine. "Then we could do some really fine things in the classroom."

On another occasion, when O'Connor was having a private meeting with the president of the Bright PTA, Drew entered her office unannounced.

"Forgive me, Dierdre, for barging in," said Drew sweetly, "but I saw Mrs. Fredericks go into your office and I just had to say hello. It's so good to see you again, Eileen." Drew leaned over sideways and gave Fredericks a big hug. "How is our boy Bobby these days?"

"Fine," said Fredericks beaming. "He loves junior high." Rising from her chair to face Drew, Fredericks turned her back to O'Connor. "You're looking simply marvelous, Penelope." Her eyes carefully absorbed the change in Drew's appearance. "That Midwestern climate must have agreed with you." Glancing back at O'Connor, she said abruptly, "We're through here, aren't we?" O'Connor wanted to say no, would have said no; but before she could respond, Fredericks was talking to Drew again.

"Penelope, you must tell me all about your stay at the university. Why don't we go the faculty lounge and have coffee." O'Connor was left with the feeling that she had just been dismissed.

On the way down the hall, O'Connor could hear Fredericks saying, "It's so wonderful to have you back, dear. I'm surprised you weren't able to resume your principalship."

"That's easier said than done," said Drew pleasantly.

"I must speak to Ian about this." She giggled. "He and Sarah will take potluck the next time they dine with us."

"Speaking of dinner," interjected Drew, "why don't you and George come over Friday evening. I'll fix something light, and we can view the slides I took while I was in the Midwest."

"That sounds like a great idea," responded Fredericks enthusiastically. "I'm sure George would love to see them. You know how infatuated he is with photography," laughed Fredericks. O'Connor listened until the two were out of hearing range, then stepped back into her office to sulk.

On subsequent occasions Drew was responsible for disciplining both the principal's secretary and the custodian, the former for the way she had responded to a parent on the phone and the latter for not properly attending to the school grounds. When they lodged complaints with O'Connor, she promised to look into the matters. Secretly, however, she was pleased that they had been admonished. Mildred Tykes, her secretary, was always giving somebody a difficult time on the phone, perhaps hoping that if she was miserable enough, people would stop calling and her job would be that much easier. Flaherty had even complained about Mildred's rudeness on the phone. Cal, on the other hand, was acting as if he was on vacation these days, compelling the faculty, by his lack of effort, to attend to an increasing number of household chores.

Yet while they undoubtedly deserved the reprimand they had received, concluded O'Connor, the reproof should have come from her, not Drew, who was definitely overstepping her bounds. In any event, she ultimately said nothing to Drew about her dissatisfaction with her behavior.

The most blatant attack on her authority occurred during a faculty meeting when Drew vehemently disagreed with her on a curricular matter. The result was that the faculty took sides on the issue, with about half supporting her and the other half Drew. Although it was she in her capacity as principal who made the decision, the quarrel that erupted during the meeting was to grow until the split became permanent.

Feeling terribly alone and unable, at least for the moment, to bear the animosity that now permeated her school, O'Connor drove to the administration building to share her problem with Superintendent Flaherty. She spoke uninterrupted for about 15 minutes while Flaherty listened sympathetically to her story.

"I can appreciate the pressure you are under," said Flaherty consolingly. He liked O'Connor. She had been doing a good job until Drew returned; and when Drew finally finished her coursework and dissertation and left again, which she was very likely to do, O'Connor would still be there doing a good job. "And I am willing to step in anytime you want me to." O'Connor thought she noted a trace of equivocation in his voice.

"No, I really want to handle the situation myself," said O'Connor resolutely, her hands curling into fists. "It's just that I thought you should know about what has been going on at Bright."

"Well, do what you have to do, but don't make any unnecessary waves doing it." Flaherty looked worried. "Remember, Drew has quite a following both in the school district and in the community. I admit I wanted her back, and I would like to keep her in Maybody, if at all possible. But right now you, not Drew, are the principal, and she should know better than most the importance of protocol." Flaherty shook O'Connor's hand while he maneuvered her to the door. Wearing a faint smile, she departed.

The showdown between O'Connor and Drew took place shortly after O'Connor had chastised a faculty member for repeatedly not turning in his lesson plan on time. With the aggrieved faculty member trailing behind her, Drew had stormed into O'Connor's office to defend the young man. In her hand she held a lesson plan which, she loudly pointed out, had been misfiled by O'Connor's secretary. While Drew ranted on, a number of faculty buzzed around O'Connor's open door.

"Mrs. Drew, I consider your attitude insubordinate." The principal slammed her door. Her voice trembled and her body shook. "And I will not tolerate insubordination. If you persist in this attitude, believe me, it won't be at Bright." Taking deep breaths, she said vehemently, "If, instead of barging in here, you had taken the time to study all the facts, you would have discovered that I was not addressing a single instance of neglect, but a whole series of lapses in carrying out school policy."

Drew was on the verge of arguing that the other charges were probably just as trumped up as this one, but wisdom becoming the better part of valor prompted her to retreat. As she did, she glared at the young man who seemed to cower beside her.

Still seething, Drew picked up the phone in the outer office and dialed Superintendent Flaherty's number. Carrying the receiver to the far corner of the room, she discussed the incident with Flaherty, with considerable emphasis on her point of view. He listened patiently, but his answer was not the one she had expected.

Flaherty insisted that he must side with O'Connor, just as he once had sided with her. After all, O'Connor was the principal at Bright, and she was serving in that capacity largely because of Drew's recommendation.

"Think back, Penelope," prodded the superintendent gently, "and you'll remember that it was you who extolled the virtues of O'Connor. Then, you thought she could do no wrong."

"Perhaps I made a mistake." The receiver was moist.

"Perhaps we both did," said Flaherty, slowly putting the receiver back on its cradle.

As the incident spread throughout the district, distorted and magnified, Drew took on heroic proportions. Now viewed as a defender of the underdog, a great but unappreciated teacher, and a once highly effective and applauded principal by the administration, Drew was cajoled by a contingency of teachers to run for the presidency of the teachers association. In the meantime, they also wanted her to sit in at the bargaining table. They were convinced that the stalwart Drew could help them forge out a contract that would make previous contracts insignificant in comparison. Overcome by the urging of peers and feeling betrayed by Flaherty and her own protegee, Drew accepted both offers.

After a month of negotiating, Drew had the entire administration unnerved. She was brilliant in her insights and fierce in her demands. Nobody would ever get the opportunity again to say that she had not done her homework. Her motto now was to be prepared for any event. At Bright she stayed clear of O'Connor; the principal, in turn, avoided her. But the tyrannical influence of Drew still pervaded Bright, and if O'Connor's life had been miserable before, it was absolutely deplorable now. Behind the scenes Drew was taking over the entire faculty. Although O'Connor knew what was happening, she did nothing to prevent Drew's coup.

Every administrator in the district was aware of O'Connor's plight, but few sympathized with her.

"If she can't stand the heat," said one of her counterparts, "let her get out of the frying pan."

Flaherty finally began to have doubts about O'Connor's leadership capability. Morale was never worse at Bright, and the antagonism being generated there was spreading throughout the district.

It was a bright spring day when Flaherty phoned O'Connor. While the sun glared through the window, O'Connor pushed the receiver tightly against her ear.

"Dierdre, we've discussed the Drew matter several times now, and to no avail." His voice was firm and his words carefully calculated. "Your inaction has made her a hero in the district. It is no longer appropriate for me to deal amicably with Drew about her conduct at Bright. She is deeply immersed in negotiations, and anything I say might be construed by the teachers association as a reaction to her performance at the bargaining table, rather than because of our long-standing friendship. You, however, are principal at Bright and have every reason to talk to her about her flagrant disregard for the policies she helped to develop." Flaherty paused, as if contemplating his next words. "It is my preference that you and Drew resolve the predicament as quickly and as peacefully as possible. Her high standing in the community does not seem to dictate otherwise. If that cannot be accomplished, you will be faced with another decision. At the moment that decision is yours. Later it might well be mine. I'm sure Drew would have no trouble making a similar decision, were she once again principal."

The receiver clicked and O'Connor felt more alone and friendless than she had ever been in her life. But the decision was hers, and come what may she was going to make it. With a flick of a button she announced, "Mrs. Tykes, please have Mrs. Drew report to me at once."

"But she's in class," piped Tykes, "and I'm busy filling out a report."

"Mildred," yelled O'Connor, "if you have no plans of working anywhere else this year, I suggest you get Drew in her at once. And you can stay there with her class until she returns."

Mildred was hurrying down the hallway before O'Connor finished her last sentence.

O'Connor sat back and waited, wondering if Drew would even show up, and what she would do if she did not.

DECISION AIDS

1. Why was O'Connor unhappy?

2. Why did Drew return to Maybody, and who was anxious to have her return?

3. Who had been the protegee of Drew?

4. What surprised O'Connor and made her less confident of her leadership role?

5. Identify two incidents that unnerved O'Connor in her determination.

6. What actions of Drew both pleased and disturbed O'Connor?

7. Why did O'Connor pay a visit to Flaherty, and what was his reaction to her visit?

8. When did the showdown take place between O'Connor and Drew, and what transpired at that time?

9. How did O'Connor's peers feel about her dilemma?

10. What was the decision O'Connor was compelled to make, and did she make it?

DECISION ACTIVITIES

1. Role play O'Connor in a final confrontation with Drew.

2. Consider the aforementioned confrontation a stalemate, and have the superintendent resolve the problem in a meeting with O'Connor and Drew.

3. Extend the case study to describe the final confrontation between O'Connor and Drew.

4. Discuss the leadership styles of O'Connor, Drew, and Flaherty as they manifest themselves in their communications with one another.

5. Write a paper arguing in behalf of either O'Connor or Drew as principal of Bright. Draw from the literature on the principalship to support this argument.

WHAT TO DO "VIGNETTES"

COLLECTIVE NEGOTIATIONS

After spending an enormous number of hours at the negotiating table, Principal Bernice Hazelbee concluded that a teacher strike was inevitable. When she reported her observations to her superintendent, he asked her to prepare a contingency plan that would ensure, throughout the conjectured strike, not only a meaningful degree of instructional continuity, but also a steady flow of information from school to community. He gave her a week to prepare the plan.

TEACHER COMPETENCY

When 40% of the Dovertown Public Schools teaching faculty failed a teacher competency test, Superintendent Noah Barticky was barraged by the media. When he refused to comment, the media became more aggressive in their demands. Finally, he called a media conference to deliver a prepared statement that he hoped would serve to appease both media and what was rapidly becoming an insurgent community. The statement read: ____.

CLASSROOM MANAGEMENT

Billy Burger was a brilliant and enigmatic first-year chemistry teacher who had a burgeoning problem with maintaining discipline in his laboratory. He was also the board president's son and the grandson of the town's former superintendent of some 30 years. Principal Emily Ames could have helped him with his problem were he not oblivious to it. He had the rowdiest class in the school, and his students were constantly complaining to her about him. Ames was being considered for the soon-to-be-created post of assistant superintendent of curriculum and was uneasy about jeopardizing her chances. Yet she felt it her duty to take some kind of remediating action without further delay, as Burger had paid little heed to her suggestions. How stringent this action should be, she was yet uncertain.

ADVISORY COMMITTEES

Superintendent Harry Tiber applauded community activity in the schools, but he disdained citizen advisory committees. It was his feeling that schools were meant to be run by professionals and not by a bunch of lay people, who, because of their lack of training, tended to slow down the decision-making process. Thus, he used advisory committees sparingly and then only to rubber stamp his ideas. Eventually, advisory committee members began to complain about the passive roles they were expected to play. In an effort to placate the complaining members, who were gradually increasing in number, he responded by saying that he would construct a plan that would be mutually advantageous. Unfortunately, he was not sure how or where to begin.

FINANCIAL REFERENDA

A building referendum had failed twice at the polls in recent months. In the past 20 years the school district had never failed to pass either a budget or a building referendum. The district desperately needed a new high school, but the superintendent did not know what action to take to ensure the referendum's passage at the polls. At an administrative team meeting, a motion was made and seconded that a building campaign be conducted. Although the group unanimously favored the motion, no one knew exactly who should do what and how they should do it. One of the principals suggested that a public relations director be hired to do the job, but instead she was saddled with the leadership responsibility. When the meeting ended, she briefly remained to mull over her assignment. Streaming across her mind were a number of ideas: the involvement of the PTAs and citizen advisory committees; the development of brochures and other informational items; the conducting of surveys; and the use of the media. However, until her ideas were linked in the right way and fully developed, they would do nothing for the proposed referendum.

CONDUCTING A SURVEY

Ellie Sandar, the school district's new public relations director, considered person-to-person contact the primary ingredient of an effective public relations program. So when her superintendent, Julie Haycox, asked her to conduct a survey to determine whether a substantially increased budget referendum could be passed, it was no surprise that Sandar opted for a door-to-door approach rather than a telephone or mail-out approach. Sandar enlisted the aid of dozens of the local citizenry and set them to work interviewing the random sample she had chosen. The response to the referendum was extremely positive, as was the enthusiasm of the people who led in the interviewing process. Nevertheless, the referendum failed at the polls. Haycox called for an explanation and Sandar tried to come up with the answers as quickly as she could. But the answers were not immediately forthcoming.

MORALE

Nicholas Groman, English department head, initiated a policy that required (much to the chagrin of his faculty) a weekly submission of detailed lesson plans. Due on Friday of each week, the lesson plans would be read and approved by Groman prior to the subsequent Monday. The new policy was designed to serve four purposes: (1) to make sure faculty members were always prepared; (2) to give direction to substitutes when teachers suddenly became ill; (3) to provide Groman with a better opportunity to coordinate and articulate all instructional efforts in grades 10 through 12; and (4) to allow Groman to call to the attention of the faculty instructional techniques and activities that might be of special interest to them. For a while the policy worked well, and faculty morale was high. Then a tenured and long-time teacher in the department began to make it a practice of turning in his lesson plans late or not at all, while his peers continued to turn in their plans on time. When approached, he had a dozen reasons for his noncompliance. With morale now at ebb tide, Groman was obliged to take some kind of disciplinary action. Somewhat inhibiting him was the fact that the policy offender was not only his administrative predecessor, but also the teacher whose popularity had earned him the district's best teacher award only two years before.

DECLINING ENROLLMENTS

Most of the school districts surrounding Basilberg were experiencing appreciable declines in secondary school enrollments. Reduction in force (RIF) plans had already been put into effect by these districts, putting large numbers of teachers out of work and forcing them to move to other parts of the state to find employment. Basilberg, however, seemed for the moment to exist in a vacuum, unscathed by the problems cropping up around it. But Superintendent Lloyd Van Tyre saw the writing on the wall spelling trouble for the Basilberg schools in about two years. Argosville, Basilberg's immediate neighbor, had only recently erected a second junior high school to accommodate the children of a growing number of Brexol Steel employees. When the plant suddenly closed, Argosville sought to negotiate an agreement with Basilberg to pick up some of its junior high school enrollments; the board wanted to lease the newest of its two junior high schools to an insurance company. A couple of other districts were willing to accept Argosville's students, but Argosville preferred an arrangement with Basilberg because of the nearby location of its junior high school. Superintendent Van Tyre, who thought Basilberg could, with some overcrowding, handle its neighbor's students, met with his board to convince it that such an action could stave off future RIF problems. Half the board favored the notion, while the remainder did not. The opinions of the parents of the Basilberg junior high school students were mixed, as were the opinions of parents with elementary school children. Teachers, too, had mixed opinions; many of them were averse to an increase in class size. Van Tyre, himself, was finally uncertain about what to do, yet he knew that something had to be done soon. A massive information program might be his best bet, but information alone would not do the trick.

SUMMARY

Over 100 years old, the case method of teaching has only been used in educational administration for about 30 years. Within a case context students can translate theory into practice. A useful strategy for this transition is a Decision-Making Skills Hierarchy. The 8 case studies and 8 vignettes included in this chapter deal with a broad range of problems that administrators encounter in their work. Accompanying each case is a set of Decision Aids and Decision Activities that enhance analysis. In at least four of the cases, imagery is a problem—the image of a superintendent, a teacher, a school's athletic program, and a school as a friendly, caring place. In others, communication becomes the focus. In all, organizational principles and practices are interwoven. Among the specific problems addressed by the vignettes are classroom management, teacher competency, advisory committees, and declining enrollments.

Notes

1. From "The Basics of a Written PR Policy" by P. T. West, 1981, *Journal of Educational Communication*, 4, pp. 24–25. Copyright 1981 by the Educational Communicational Center, Camp Hill, PA. Reprinted by permission.

2. From *Criteria for Evaluating a Public School System Public Relations Program as Perceived by Public School Public Relations Directors* (Table 21, pp. 118–119 and Table 38, pp. 154–155) by T. J. Oberg, 1983, unpublished doctoral dissertation, Texas A&M University, College Station, TX. Adapted by permission.

References

CHAPTER 1

Alexander, C., & Theisen, W. W. (1921). *Publicity campaigns for better school support.* New York: World Book.

American Association of School Administrators. (1950). *Public relations for America's schools.* Arlington, VA: Author.

Banach, W. J. (1981). The Macomb intermediate school district marketing plan. *Journal of Educational Communication, 5*(2), 4–18.

Bernays, E. L. (1952). *Public relations.* Norman: University of Oklahoma Press.

Bortner, D. M. (1972). *Public relations for public schools.* Cambridge, MA: Schenkman.

Brownell, C. L., Gans, L., & Maroon, T. Z. (1955). *Public relations in education: A textbook for teachers.* New York: McGraw-Hill.

Campbell, R. F., & Ramseyer, J. A. (1955). *The dynamics of school-community relationships.* New York: Allyn & Bacon.

Cutlip, S. M., & Center, A. H. (1971). *Effective public relations* (4th ed.). Englewood Cliffs, NJ: Prentice-Hall.

Ellison, B. (1980). It pays to advertise. *Journal of Educational Communication, 4*(2), 10–15.

Griswold, G., & Griswold, D. (1948). Public relations—Its responsibilities and potentialities. In G. Griswold & D. Griswold (Eds.), *Your public relations: The standard public relations handbook* (pp. 3–19). New York: Funk & Wagnalls in association with *Modern Industry Magazine.*

Harlow, R. F., & Black, M. M. (1952). *Practical public relations* (rev. ed.). New York: Harper & Row.

Hallal, J. (1952). *Tested public relations for schools.* Norman: University of Oklahoma Press.

Hiebert, R. E. (1966). Myths about Ivy Lee. In R. Simon (Ed.), *Perspectives in public relations* (pp. 4–12). Norman: University of Oklahoma Press.

Kindred, L. W., Bagin, D., & Gallagher, D. R. (1976). *The school and community relations.* Englewood Cliffs, NJ: Prentice-Hall.

Miller, C. R., & Charles, F. (1924). *Publicity and the public schools.* Boston: Houghton Mifflin.

275

Moehlman, A. B. (1927). *Public school relations.* Chicago: Rand McNally.

Moehlman, A. B. (1938a). Social interpretation: A study in conceptual evolution. *Education, 58,* 577–580.

Moehlman, A. B. (1938b). *Social interpretation: Principles and practices of community and public-school interpretation.* New York: Appleton-Century-Crofts.

Moehlman, A. B., & van Zwoll, J. A. (1957). *School public relations.* New York: Appleton-Century-Crofts.

Ostrow, B. J. (1980). Marketing—A necessary addition to a school system's communication program. *Journal of Educational Communication, 4*(2), 4–9.

Saxe, R. W. (1975). *School-community interaction.* Berkeley, CA: McCutchan.

Stearns, H. L. (1955). *Community relations and the public schools.* Englewood Cliffs, NJ: Prentice-Hall.

Steinberg, C. S. (1958). *The mass communicators: Public relations, public opinion, and mass media.* New York: Harper & Row.

West, P. T. (1982, September). School PR: Building credibility. *Community Education Today,* pp. 4–5.

Wherry, J. H. (1982). Educational public relations: An historical perspective. *Educational Considerations, 9*(1), 6–9.

CHAPTER 3

Andrews, M. (1983). A computer in every home. *Video Test Annual and Buyers Guide, 6,* 114–115, 138.

Bireen, F. (1945). *Selling with color.* New York: McGraw-Hill.

Cheskin, L. (1947). *Colors: What they can do for you.* New York: Liveright.

Edwards, K. (1982). Broadcast teletext: The next mass medium? *Futurist, 16*(5), 21–24.

Jackson, C. (1981). *Color me beautiful.* New York: Ballantine.

Luscher, M. (1971). *The Luscher color test.* New York: Pocket Books.

National Association of Secondary School Principals. (1981, January). The big picture: A look into the future of projection television. *New Technology,* pp. 6–7.

National Association of Secondary School Principals. (1982, May). Free computer centers—With a congressional contingency. *New Technology,* pp. 6–8.

Piele, P. K. (1983). People and politics in an electronic age. *Community Education Journal, 10*(4), 7–8.

West, P. T. (1974). Wild in the schools. *Thrust, 4*(1), 3–7.

West, P. T. (1981). Imagery and change in the twenty-first century. *Theory Into Practice, 20,* 229–236.

West, P. T. (1983). The techno-basics. *The School Administrator, 40*(3), 23–24.

Zettl, H. (1976). *Television production handbook* (3rd ed.). Belmont, CA: Wadsworth.

CHAPTER 4

American Association of School Administrators. (1983). *The excellence report: Using it to improve your schools.* Arlington, VA: Author.

Brannen, D. E. (1980). Comparison of role perceptions for male and female public school public relations directors (Doctoral dissertation, Texas A&M University, 1979). *Dissertation Abstracts International, 40,* 6081A.

Brannen, D. E. (1981). Men paid higher salaries than women in educational public relations. *Journal of Educational Communication, 5*(1), 37.

Burke, M. A. (1981). Video technology and education: Genie in a bottle or Pandora's box? *T.H.E. Journal, 8*(5), 54, 66.

Dierksen, J.C.N. (1982). The role of the public school public relations director on the administrative team (Doctoral dissertation, Texas A&M University, 1982). *Dissertation Abstracts International, 43,* 1764A.

Dysinger, G. M. (1979). A comparison of critical tasks of educational information specialists (Doctoral dissertation, Texas A&M University, 1979). *Dissertation Abstracts International, 40,* 1173A.

Flatt, J. L. (1982). The role of the educational public relations director. *Educational Considerations, 9*(1), 10–12.

Gallup, G. H. (1983). The 15th annual Gallup poll of the public's attitudes toward the public schools. *Phi Delta Kappan, 65,* 33–47.

Kazemzadeh, L. D. (1983). *Public school superintendents' perceptions of the role of the public school public relations director on the administrative team.* Unpublished doctoral dissertation, Texas A&M University, College Station.

Lester, P. G. (1979). A forecast of critical tasks for educational information specialists (Doctoral dissertation, Texas A&M University, 1978). *Dissertation Abstracts International, 39,* 6437A.

Lester, P. G., & West, P. T. (1979). How fares the future of the educational information specialist? *Kappa Delta Pi Record, 16*(2), 60–62.

National Association of Secondary School Principals. (1983, September). Principals say computers boost learning. *School Tech News,* p. 1.

National School Public Relations Association. (1982-1983). *NSPRA membership directory.* Arlington, VA: Author.

National School Public Relations Association. (1984, February). 1983 survey profiles of NSPRA members. *Paragraphs,* p. 1.

Oberg, T. J. (1983). *Criteria for evaluating a public school system public relations program as perceived by public school public relations directors.* Unpublished doctoral dissertation, Texas A&M University, College Station.

West, P. T. (1974). Wild in the schools. *Thrust, 4*(1), 3–7.

West, P. T. (1980). The making of a school PR director. *Journal of Educational Communication, 4*(1), 28–29.

West, P. T. (1982). The PR director and the future. *Educational Considerations, 9*(1), 23–26.

West, P. T. (1983). Learning to live with technology. *Community Education Journal, 10*(4), 17–18.

CHAPTER 5

American Association of School Administrators. (1979a). The president's message: Building public confidence. *The School Administrator, 36*(5), 3.

American Association of School Administrators. (1979b). The president's message: Improving public confidence. *The School Administrator, 36*(2), 3.

Gallup, G. H. (1981). The 13th annual Gallup poll of the public's attitudes toward the public schools. *Phi Delta Kappan, 63,* 33–47.

Gallup, G. H. (1983). The 15th annual Gallup poll of the public's attitudes toward the public schools. *Phi Delta Kappan, 65,* 33–47.

National School Public Relations Association. (1978). *Building public confidence in your schools.* Arlington, VA: Author.

CHAPTER 6

American Association of School Administrators. (1950). *Public relations for America's schools.* Arlington, VA: Author.

Banach, W. J. (1982). How healthy is your communication? *Educational Considerations, 9*(1), 27–29.

Barber, P. E. (1982). Perceptions of public school superintendents and school board presidents regarding selected public relations policy descriptors (Doctoral dissertation, Texas A&M University, 1982). *Dissertation Abstracts International, 43,* 598A.

Bortner, D. M. (1972). *Public relations for public schools.* Cambridge, MA: Schenkman.

Bortner, D. M. (1979). Benchmarks for school public relations. *Journal of Educational Communication, 3*(2), 8–19.

Brannen, D. E. (1980). Comparisons of role perceptions for male and female public school relations directors (Doctoral dissertation, Texas A&M University, 1979). *Dissertation Abstracts International, 40,* 6081A.

Caress, C. W. (1979). A poll on PR policy. *School and Community, 66*(4), 13.

Colgate, T. P. (1970). How good is your district's public relations program? Take this test. *American School Board Journal, 157*(10), 8–10.

Dierksen, J.C.N. (1982). The role of the public school public relations director on the administrative team (Doctoral dissertation, Texas A&M University, 1982). *Dissertation Abstracts International, 43,* 1764A.

Dysinger, G. M. (1979). A comparison of critical tasks of educational information specialists (Doctoral dissertation, Texas A&M University, 1979). *Dissertation Abstracts International, 40,* 1173A.

Fine, B. (1955). Planning. In E. L. Bernays (Ed.), *The engineering of consent* (pp. 185–213). Norman: University of Oklahoma Press.

Hatley, R. V., & Ritter, J. R. (1981). Voting behavior can be influenced by school districts. *Journal of Educational Communication, 5*(2), 32.

Kindred, L. W., Bagin, D., & Gallagher, D. R. (1976). *The school and community relations.* Englewood Cliffs, NJ: Prentice-Hall.

Mayer, F. (1974). *Public relations for school personnel.* Midland, MI: Pendell.

McCloskey, G. (1967). *Education and public understanding* (2nd ed.). New York: Harper & Row.

Moehlman, A. B. (1927). *Public school relations.* Chicago: Rand McNally.

National School Public Relations Association. (1983, October). How to evaluate your PR program. *Paragraphs,* p. 4.

Oberg, T. J. (1983). *Criteria for evaluating a public school system public relations program as perceived by public school public relations directors.* Unpublished doctoral dissertation, Texas A&M University, College Station.

Oberg, T., & West, P. T. (1983). *PROWESS.* Unpublished evaluation instrument.

Parker, B. (1978). Eight basics for good school PR. *American School Board Journal, 165*(8), 27–28.

Samstag, N. (1955). Strategies. In E. L. Bernays (Ed.), *The engineering of consent* (pp. 94–137). Norman: University of Oklahoma Press.

Tolson, R. B. (1982). Utilization of regional services in the development of school-community relations programs in small school districts of Texas (Professional report, Texas A&M University, 1982). *Dissertation Abstracts International, 43,* 1786A.

West, P. T. (1980a). An analysis of public relations policy development in selected public school districts. Paper presented at the 34th annual conference of the National Conference of Professors of Educational Administration, Norfolk, VA, August 11. (ERIC Document Reproduction Service No. ED 207 245.)

West, P. T. (1980b). The effect of administrative certification on the policy development perceptions of school PR directors. *Planning & Changing, 11*(2), 59–62.

West, P. T. (1980c). The making of a school PR director. *Journal of Educational Communication, 4*(1), 28–29.

West, P. T. (1981). The basics of a written PR policy. *Journal of Educational Communication, 4*(4), 23–24.

West, P. T. (1983). School district size has little effect on policy opinions of PR directors. *Journal of Educational Communication, 6*(4), 36.

Whisler, N. L. (1983). PR activities no panacea for changing opinion. *Journal of Educational Communication, 6*(3), 39.

CHAPTER 7

Allen, H. C. (1982). PR training needed by community educators. *Journal of Educational Communication, 5*(4), 9.

American Association of School Administrators. (1950). *Public relations for America's schools.* Arlington, VA: Author.

American Association of School Administrators. (1980). *Roles and relationships: School boards and superintendents.* Arlington, VA: Author.

Anderson, R. E. (1983). Board members emphasize communication factors when selecting a superintendent of schools. *Journal of Educational Communication, 6*(3), 36–37.

Bortner, D. M. (1972). *Public relations for public schools.* Cambridge, MA: Schenkman.

Byrne, R., & Powell, E. (1976). *Strengthening school-community relations.* Reston, VA: National Association of Secondary School Principals.

Carr, D. S., & Lows, R. L. (1982). Principals and school-community relations: A status report. *Journal of Educational Communication, 6*(1), 4–7.

Carruthers, R. J., Jr. (1980). Importance of communication affirmed by school superintendents. *Journal of Educational Communication, 4*(2), 36.

Dennis, J. B. (1980). School community relations ranked high as job priority. *Journal of Educational Communication, 4*(1), 30.

Dierksen, C. N., & Oberg, T. (1981). Students are the best source of school information for parents. *Journal of Educational Communication, 5*(1), 36–37.

Dubia, D. (1979). Students are your best PR. *NASSP Bulletin, 63*(423), 65–66.

Etzioni, A. (1964). *Modern organizations.* Englewood Cliffs, NJ: Prentice-Hall.

Gorton, D., & Strobel, P. (1981). Principals' actions fall short of stated attitudes toward community relations. *Journal of Educational Communication, 5*(1), 35–36.

Hinojosa, D. (1983). Participation improves student-school retention. *Journal of Educational Communication, 6*(3), 37.

Kilgore, A. M. (1980). Teachers say school-community relations are important. *Journal of Educational Communication, 4*(2), 36.

Kindred, L. W., Bagin, D., & Gallagher, D. R. (1976). *The school and community relations.* Englewood Cliffs, NJ: Prentice-Hall.

Kline, C. E., & Tweedy, T. J. (1981). Elementary school principals favor community involvement. *Journal of Educational Communication, 4*(4), 32–33.

Lane, W. R., Corwin, R. G., & Monahan, W. G. (1967). *Foundations of educational administration: A behavioral analysis.* New York: Macmillan.

Mayer, F. (1974). *Public relations for school personnel.* Midland, MI: Pendell.

Nasstrom, R. R. (1981). Principals view parents as enemies. *Journal of Educational Communication, 5*(1), 35.

Rafky, D. M. (1972). Blue-collar power: The social impact of urban school custodians. *Urban Education, 6*, 349–372.

Rainey, M. F. (1982). School leaders rate communications skills tops. *Journal of Educational Communication, 6*(1), 37.

Schuur, E., & Houden, D. H. (1977). School nurses' public relations. *Journal of School Health, 47*, 613–614.

Vaupel, C. F., Jr., & Sweat, J. P. (1982). Internal relations have the highest priority of secondary principals. *Journal of Educational Communication, 5*(3), 36–37.

Wells, J. C. (1980). School community relations ranked fourth as needed internship experience. *Journal of Educational Communication, 4*(3), 34–35.

West, P. T. (1977). The PR prospects of community education. *Planning & Changing, 8*, 212–217.

CHAPTER 8

Grand Prairie School District. *Senior citizens handbook.* Grand Prairie, TX: Author.

Larkin, F. P. (1982). Communicating with senior citizens. *Journal of Educational Communication, 5*(3), 4–7.

Mastors, C. (1975). *School volunteers: Who needs them?* Bloomington, IN: Phi Delta Kappa Educational Foundation.

National Association of Secondary School Principals. (1981, January). Volunteers in the secondary school: A valuable resource. *The Practitioner,* p. 1.

Texas Education Agency. *Volunteers in Texas schools (VITS)* (GE3 243 01). Austin: Author.

Tierce, J. W. (1982). Volunteers strengthen school community relations. *Journal of Educational Communication, 5*(4), 8–9.

Tierce, J. W. (1983). The role of the secondary school volunteer as perceived by school volunteer coordinators (Doctoral dissertation, Texas A&M University, 1982). *Dissertation Abstracts International, 43*, 620A.

CHAPTER 9

Anderson, J. E., Murray, R. W., & Farley, E. E. (1975). *Texas politics: An introduction* (2nd ed.). New York: Harper & Row.

Arnstein, S. R. (1971). Eight rungs on the ladder of citizen participation. In E. S. Cahn & B. A. Passett (Eds.), *Citizen participation: Effecting community change* (pp. 69–91). New York: Praeger.

Azarnoff, R. (1974). A new model for working with school community councils. *NASSP Bulletin, 58*(378), 58–62.

Campbell, T. W. (1983). Identifying the issues. *Public Relations Journal, 39*(8), 19–20.

Dillehay, J. A., & Medcalf, R. L. (1983). Gaining access to the power structure. *The School Administrator, 40*(4), cover, 10–11.

Ewing, R. P. (1980). Evaluating issues management. *Public Relations Journal, 36*(6), 14–16.

Ferguson, D. L. (1983a, February). Issues management: An emerging PR function. *Paragraphs,* pp. 4–5.

Ferguson, D. L. (1983b). Issues management. *The School Administrator, 40*(2), 18–20.

Goble, N., & Holliday, A. (1980). Guidelines for productive advisory committees. *Journal of Educational Communication, 4*(2), 32–33.

Golding, W. (1954). *Lord of the flies.* New York: Perigee Books.

Kaplan, G. R. (1982). Pushing and shoving in lobbyland U.S.A. *Phi Delta Kappan, 64,* 108–112.

Lazar, I. (1971). Which citizens to participate on what? In E. S. Cahn & B. A. Passett (Eds.), *Citizen participation: Effecting community change* (pp. 92–109). New York: Praeger.

Lewis, G. D. (1983). Communication with your legislators. *Texas Lone Star, 1*(2), 1, 25.

Lutz, F. W., & Garnon, F. (1979). Citizen participation in educational decisions. *Planning & Changing, 10,* 108–117.

National School Public Relations Association. (1973). *Citizens advisory committees: Public participation increases; Guides change in American education.* Arlington, VA: Author.

National School Public Relations Association. (1983, October). Issues management: New opportunities for PR pro. *Scanner,* pp. 1–2.

Pettus, B. E., & Bland, R. W. (1976). *Texas government today: Structures, functions, political processes.* Homewood, IL: Dorsey Press.

Renfro, W. L., & Morrison, J. L. (1982). Merging two futures concepts: Issues management and policy impact analysis. *The Futurist, 16*(5), 54–56.

Riedel, J. A. (1972). Citizen participation: Myths and realities. *Public Administration Review, 32,* 211–220.

Robert, H. M. (1978). *Robert's rules of order: The classic manual of parliamentary procedure.* New York: Bell.

Yonally, J. L. (1980). Lobby for results. *Journal of Educational Communication, 4*(3), 39–41.

CHAPTER 10

American Association of Schools Administrators. (1974a). *Declining enrollment: What to do.* Arlington, VA: Author.

American Association of School Administrators. (1974b). *Helping administrators negotiate.* Arlington, VA: Author.

American Association of School Administrators. (1981). In Washington, D.C.: Tuition tax credit referendum provides textbook example. *The School Administrator, 38*(11), 24–25.

American Association of School Administrators. (1982). Eroding public trust: National groups mobilize attack on public education. *The School Administrator, 39*(1), 24–25.

American Association of School Administrators. (1983a). Proposed 1984 AASA platforms and resolutions. *The School Administrator, 40*(11), 34–38.

American Association of School Administrators. (1983b). Tuition tax credits fact sheet. *The School Administrator, 40*(5), 18.

Argyris, C. (1960). Individual actualization in complex organizations. *Mental Hygiene, 44,* 226–237.

Barett, J. T., & Lobel, I. B. (1976). Public sector strikes—Legislative and court treatment. In R. C. Rowan (Ed.), *Readings in labor economics and labor relations* (3rd ed.) (pp. 333-336). Homewood, IL: Irwin.

Barkelew, A. (1979). Communications during negotiations, strikes, impasse, mediation. *NASSP Bulletin, 63*(423), 51-53.

Bird, L. A. (1978). Development and evaluation of a model public relations department for a non-metropolitan community college (Doctoral dissertation, Texas A&M University, 1978). *Dissertation Abstracts International, 39,* 5890A.

Brubaker, C. W. (1980). Surplus school space—An opportunity for community education. *Community Education Journal, 7*(2), 14–15.

Carr, L. (1980). Listen, nothing is getting through. *Vocational Education, 55*(6), 24.

Clutterbuck, D. (1981). How Sperry made people listen. *Interpersonal Management, 36*(2), 20–21.

Colton, D. L., & Graber, E. E. (1982). *Teacher strikes and the courts.* Lexington, MA: Lexington Books.

Cooperman, S., & Clement, S. M. (1980). A practical guide to a successful financial levy. *Journal of Educational Communication, 4*(3), 5–11.

Council of State Governments. (1982). *The book of the states, 1982-1983.* Lexington, KY: Author.

Decker, V. A. (1982, June). CEFP conference looks at interagency facility use. *Community Education Today,* p. 3.

Doan, R., & West, P. T. (1976). The transactional child. *Educational Forum, 41,* 75–79.

ERIC Clearinghouse on Educational Management. (1977). *School financial elections* (Research Action Brief 1). Eugene: University of Oregon.

Fege, A. (1982). Funny money revisited. *The School Administrator, 39*(1), 12–13.

Fiala, H. H. (1983). Recycling surplus schools. *The School Administrator, 40*(7), cover, 6–9.

Flesch, R. (1977). *Look it up: A deskbook of American spelling and style.* New York: Harper & Row.

French, C. W., Powell, E. A., & Angione, H. (Eds.). (1983). *The Associated Press stylebook and libel manual.* Reading, MA: Addison-Wesley.

Gay, G., Dembowski, F. L., & McLennan, R. L. (1981). Preserving quality of education during enrollment declines. *Phi Delta Kappan, 62,* 655–657.

Gelms, K. T. (1979). The overlooked communications tool: Building-level publications. *NASSP Bulletin, 63*(423), 39–45.

Getzels, J. W., & Guba, E. G. (1957). Social behavior and the administrative process. *School Review, 65,* 423–441.

Gifford, B. (1982). Community needs: School finance campaigns. *Educational Considerations, 9*(1), 3–5.

Greene, R. T., Belsches, C., & Mladenoff, M. (1980). Richmond's progressive solution to declining high school enrollments. *Phi Delta Kappan, 61,* 616–617.

Harris, T. E. (1980). Enhancing listening effectiveness. *Supervision, 42*(10), 3–4.

Harrison, C. H. (1972). Take six steps to pass a bond issue. *Nation's Schools, 89*(6), 56.

Hayes, J. L. (1981). Are you listening? *American School & University, 53*(9), 32–33.

Henry, W. E. (1979). Working with the media. *NASSP Bulletin, 63*(423), 10–16.

Herzberg, F. (1966). *Work and the nature of man.* Cleveland, OH: World Publishing.

Herzberg, F. (1976). *The managerial choice: To be efficient and to be human.* Homewood, IL: Dow Jones-Irwin.

Hodgkinson, H. (1979). What's right with education. *Phi Delta Kappan, 61,* 159–162.

Hyder, L. R., & Achilles, C. M. (1982). Direct contact is preferred means of communicating to and with the public. *Journal of Educational Communication, 6*(1), 38–39.

Ishaq, Y. (1984). PR plays a minor role in desegregation efforts. *Journal of Educational Public Relations, 7*(1), 30.

Jordan, L. (Ed.). (1976). *The New York Times manual of style and usage: A desk book of guidelines for writers and editors.* New York: New York Times.

Klare, G. R. (1963). *The measurement of readability.* Ames: Iowa State University Press.

Lane, W. R., & West, P. T. (1972). If you can't pretend, you can't be king. *Phi Delta Kappan, 53,* 659–661.

Lieberman, M. (1981). Teacher bargaining: An autopsy. *Phi Delta Kappan, 63,* 231–234.

Lutz, F. (1980). For referendum success: Convince your friends and confound your foes. *American School Board Journal, 167*(2), 21–23.

Maslow, A. H. (1970). *Motivation and personality* (2nd ed.). New York: Harper & Row.

Mazzoni, T. L., & Mueller, V. D. (1980). School district planning for enrollment decline: The Minnesota approach. *Phi Delta Kappan, 61,* 406–410.

McCain, T. A., & Wall, V. D., Jr. (1976). A communication perspective of a school bond failure. *Educational Administration Quarterly, 12*(2), 1–17.

McGregor, D. M. (1957). The human side of enterprise. *Management Review, 46*(11), 22–28, 88–92.

McMullen, S., & Oberg, T. (1982). Changes needed for increased TV coverage. *Journal of Educational Communication, 5*(3), 37.

Mendenhall, W., Ott, L., & Scheaffer, R. L. (1971). *Elementary survey sampling.* Belmont, CA: Duxbury Press.

National Association of School Principals. (1981, March). Declining enrollment and school closing—A principal concern. *The Practitioner,* pp. 1–12.

National Community Education Association. (1981, January). Closed junior high school becomes community center. *Community Education Today,* p. 5.

National School Public Relations Association. (1978). *Building public confidence for your schools.* Arlington, VA: Author.

National School Public Relations Association. (1980a, November). Good news about the schools spreads. *Paragraphs,* p. 7.

National School Public Relations Association. (1980b, November). NSPRA takes a stand. *Paragraphs,* p. 6.

National School Public Relations Association. (1982). *School labor strife: Rebuilding the team.* Arlington, VA: Author.

Neal, R. G. (1978). The U.S. teacher strike scene, 1978-1979. *Phi Delta Kappan, 60,* 327–328.

Ondrasik, B. P. (1977). Get good vibes from a versatile house organ. *Journal of Educational Communication, 2*(2), 12–21.

Ouchi, W. G. (1982). *Theory Z.* New York: Avon.

Palmer, E. J. (1982). Assertive listening—Breaking out of the cocoon. *Data Management, 20*(6), 6.

Pauk, W. (1981). Some nonsense about listening. *Reading World, 21,* 134–135.

Perry, C. R., & Wildman, W. A. (1975). *The impact of negotiations in public education: The evidence from the schools.* Worthington, OH: Charles A. Jones.

Phi Delta Kappa. (1979). Beginning of the decline: School population drops. *Phi Delta Kappan, 60,* 544.

Phi Delta Kappa. (1980a). Census figures confirm declining enrollments. *Phi Delta Kappan, 61,* 516.

Phi Delta Kappa. (1980b). Enrollment fell 7.2% in seventies: NCES. *Phi Delta Kappan, 61,* 668.

Phi Delta Kappa. (1980c). Enrollments still trend downward: 1.3% in 1980. *Phi Delta Kappan, 62,* 166.

Phi Delta Kappa. (1981). Enrollments down; Expenses up. *Phi Delta Kappan, 63,* 4.

Phi Delta Kappa. (1982). Unionization and work stoppages characterize educators; Census bureau. *Phi Delta Kappan, 63,* 571.

Powell, J. T. (1981). Listening to help the hostile employee. *Supervisory Management, 25*(11), 2–5.

Premazon, J., & West, P. T. (1977). Requiem or rebirth? From voucher to magnet. *Clearing House, 51*(1), 34–38.

Raudsepp, E. (1982). The art of listening. *Computer Decisions, 14,* 206, 208, 210.

Richmond, J. B. (1976). School communication during a strike. *Journal of Educational Communication, 2*(1), 22.

Rubin, A. (1979). Election strategy that works. *NASSP Bulletin, 63*(423), 54–57.

Samaras, J. T. (1980). Two-way communication practices for managers. *Personnel Journal, 59,* 645–648.

Schoenfeld, C. (1977, February). Thirty seconds to live. *Writer's Digest,* p. 29.

Scott, K. (1982). The case against collective bargaining in public education. *Government Union Review, 3*(2), 16–25.

Sergiovanni, T. J., & Carver, F. D. (1980). *The new school executive: A theory of administrators* (2nd ed.). New York: Harper & Row.

Shannon, T. A. (1981). Guidelines for dismantling collective bargaining. *Phi Delta Kappan, 63,* 235.

Traweek, E. (1980). PR director has limited role in collective negotiations. *Journal of Educational Communication, 4*(3), 34.

Traweek, E. L. (1981). The role of the school public relations director in collective negotiations as perceived by school public relations directors and superintendents of schools (Doctoral dissertation, Texas A&M University, 1980). *Dissertation Abstracts International, 41,* 3259A.

Trouble in schools: Will it get worse? (1975, September). *U.S. News & World Report,* pp. 15–18.

Vining, J. W., & Yrle, A. C. (1980). How do you rate as a listener? *Supervisory Management, 25*(1), 22–25.

Webb, R. A. (Ed.). (1978). *The Washington Post deskbook on style*. New York: McGraw-Hill.

Weir, K. L. (1981). How to improve your publications. *Community Education Journal, 8*(3), 16–17.

Weisberg, H. F., & Bowen, B. D. (1977). *An introduction to survey research and data analysis*. San Francisco: W. H. Freeman.

West, P. T. (1974). Wild in the schools. *Thrust, 4*(1), 3–7.

West, P. T. (1976). Participation and responsibility in educational decision-making. *Kappa Delta Pi Record, 13*(2), 50–52.

West, P. T. (1977a). The leadership prerogative in community education. *Planning & Changing, 8,* 67–74.

West, P. T. (1977b). The PR prospects of community education. *Planning & Changing, 8,* 212–217.

West, P. T. (1981a). Big bucks and funny money. *The School Administrator, 38*(11), 14–15.

West, P. T. (1981b). Community education as persuasion. *Community Education Journal, 8*(3), 2–4.

West, P. T., & West, J. E. (1978). The perimeters of process. *Planning & Changing, 9,* 218–223.

Wynn, R. (1981). The relationship of collective bargaining and teacher salaries. *Phi Delta Kappan, 63,* 237–242.

Zambito, S. A. (1979). A new PR person can handle a teachers' strike without being bowled over. *Journal of Educational Communication, 3*(2), 27–29.

CHAPTER 11

Culbertson, J. A., Jacobson, P. B., & Reller, T. D. (1960). *Administrative relationships: A case book*. Englewood Cliffs, NJ: Prentice-Hall.

Lane, W. R., & West, P. T. (1972). If you can't pretend, you can't be king. *Phi Delta Kappan, 53,* 659–661.

Sargent, C. G., & Belisle, E. L. (1955). *Educational administration: Cases and concepts*. Boston: Houghton Mifflin.

West, P. T. (1971). Providence High School: An administrative case-novel (Doctoral dissertation, University of Iowa, 1971). *Dissertation Abstracts International, 32,* 1248A.

West, P. T. (1975). Excelsior: Poetics of the principalship. *Clearing House, 49*(1), 16–20.

West, P. T. (1983, Summer). More on leadership in literature: Caricature or character. *AASA Professor,* pp. 9–11.

West, P. T., & Armstrong, J. (1980). Follow the gleam: Charisma—Studying its elusive nature. *NASSP Bulletin, 64*(438), 70–77.

West, P. T., & Lane, W. R. (1973). P. S. Caine. *NASSP Bulletin, 57*(376), 8–18.

About the Author

Philip T. West is a professor of educational administration in the Department of Educational Administration at Texas A&M University. For a decade he has coordinated a graduate specialization in educational public relations there. He also teaches courses in educational public relations and personnel administration.

The Department of Educational Administration at Texas A&M University was recently designated by the University Council for Educational Administration (a consortium of universities and partnership school districts) as the site for a center for Educational Public Relations. Dr. West will be directing this center.

Currently, West is Research editor and School PR Case Study Workshop editor for the *Journal of Educational Public Relations;* the Case Corner editor for the *Community Education Journal;* the Case Studies editor for the University Council for Educational Administration; and the editor of *The AASA Professor.* He is past editor-in-chief of *Educational Administration Abstracts.*

West has served twice as a guest editor for the *Community Education Journal.* One of these theme issues was devoted to educational public relations. In *Educational Considerations* he served as a coguest editor for this same theme. An author and/or coauthor of a variety of journal articles, he is also coauthor of *Training the Community Educator: A Case-Study Approach.*

Prior to his arrival at Texas A&M University, West served as a department head at both the secondary school and the university levels. His earlier experiences include sales and managerial roles in business and industry.

West received his baccalaureate from Boston University, his master's degree from Hofstra University, and his doctorate from the University of Iowa.